We *surrender* to love. We *win* another's heart, or call a *truce* in a lover's quarrel . . . there is a warrior's code to winning the battle of the sexes!

Revered in China, Sun Tzu's *The Art of War* was first introduced to the West shortly before the French Revolution. Legend has it that Napoleon used the essays as a blueprint for his conquest of Western Europe. In this century, Mao Tse-tung's strategic theories were drawn from the ancient credo. But *The Art of War*—and Sun Tzu's astounding observations on human nature—hold meaning far beyond the world of men at war.

As on the battlefield, victory in love requires thoughtful planning, time-tested tactics, and careful execution. In THE ART OF WAR FOR LOVERS, Sun Tzu's wisdom is the basis for a step-by-step program for taking charge, gaining a commitment, sustaining love, strengthening intimacy, and enlivening passion in a partnership—not by force, but by inner strategizing.

This revolutionary approach to relationships provides a systematic plan for the development of enduring love—a charted course for a woman's internal journey to becoming a strong, confident warrior with the knowledge to win at love, without a battle or a wounded heart.

Books by Dr. Connell Cowan

Smart Women/Foolish Choices
Women Men Love/Women Men Leave
Husbands and Wives

Books by Gail Parent

Sheila Levine Is Dead and Living in New York
David Meyer Is a Mother
The Best-Laid Plans
A Little Bit Married
A Sign of the Eighties

THE
ART *of* WAR *for* LOVERS

DR. CONNELL COWAN
and
GAIL PARENT

POCKET BOOKS
New York   London   Toronto   Sydney   Tokyo   Singapore

An *Original* Publication of POCKET BOOKS

 POCKET BOOKS, a division of Simon & Schuster Inc.
1230 Avenue of the Americas, New York, NY 10020

ISBN: 978-0-671-00063-9

First Pocket Books trade paperback printing February 1998

10 9 8 7 6 5 4 3 2 1

POCKET and colophon are registered trademarks of
Simon & Schuster Inc.

Cover design and illustration by Franco Accornero

Printed in the U.S.A.

CONTENTS

CONTENTS

PART 2
GAIL PARENT'S TAKE ON THE
BATTLE OF THE SEXES *195*

FOREWORD: ON SUN TZU'S *THE ART OF WAR*

In China, twenty-five centuries ago, a little known warrior-philosopher named Sun Tzu wrote his now classic essays for *The Art of War.* This unique and perceptive book is much more than simply an interesting tale; it is arguably the world's most widely read work on how to form strategies that will resolve conflict. What makes the book so powerful is its uncanny grasp of what it is to be human and how our humanity works either for or against us in the pursuit of our goals. Although *The Art of War* is still consulted today, by everyone from military leaders to corporate executives, it is unfortunate that Sun Tzu's central message — to win without fighting — is rarely heeded.

Introduction: On The Art of War for Lovers

What drew us to *The Art of War* and made us want to apply its wisdom to issues of love was that Sun Tzu's thoughts are a veritable blueprint of the human strengths and weaknesses that lead to success or failure. His book provides timeless insights into motivation, the need for a spiritual and moral center, hidden weaknesses that can become dangerous flaws, and untapped strengths that with a little effort can be realized.

In that women and men approach and see love in different ways, we thought it best to have both a male and female point of view. We've each taken a section of Sun Tzu's thoughts and interpreted his words as they apply to the art of love.

Part One is written from a male perspective by clinical psychologist and self-help author Dr. Connell Cowan. "In my practice I see the value of using strategy in our love relationships on a daily basis. And nowhere is strategy more intelligently described than in Sun Tzu's work."

Part Two, the female slant, is written by novelist and screenwriter Ms. Gail Parent: "Mostly all of my writing comes from a female perspective. As a woman and an author, I have lived in the trenches and shared my experiences through my novels and screenplays. Sun Tzu has taught me that women need to be prepared for love in order not to be defeated by it."

By combining our experiences and expertise, we hope to give you a deeper understanding of the emotional roots of the battle of the sexes. We've also tried to gather together some specific tools that, if put to use, will allow you to not only make your relationships work, but make them work in a better and more loving and reciprocal way.

THE BACK STORY

Why doesn't love seem to work for so many women? Most certainly, women want to find love and fulfillment with the men in their lives. Why then do so many seem to find only frustration and disappointment instead? Are men so trying or complicated? Is being in a relationship so difficult?

Answers, as usual, are more elusive than questions, but there do seem to be a number of factors at play. We all have one foot stuck in romance and idealism and the other submerged in the sticky goo of tradition, social conditioning, and genetic coding. In the most simplified terms, women have historically traded elements of submission for protection, respect for adoration, and autonomy for security. Whether they were ever content with these choices is obviously questionable, but trade they did. Men, in turn, also made their trades: intimacy for independence, partnership for control, and love for respect. The upside of these unconscious decisions, if there was one, was that women and men felt some sense of comfort in the familiarity of these roles. But there were sacrifices as well. The key to maintaining this delicate balance was an underlying inequality. Regardless of what men may have given up emotionally to support the status quo, they were more than willing to do so. Women were not. They became itchy, feeling cheated of their share of the power base.

Despite the vast changes we've seen in the last few decades, remnants of this cultural gender conflict remain. And, available information doesn't give women many options. One, she surrenders to tradition, relinquishing equality, which makes the man happy and herself miserable. Or two, she fights for her rights, which often creates an adversarial relationship, and lives with the ongoing pitched battles that leave both women and men at odds and disillusioned. Are the only choices then internal conflict or strife? We think not.

The very differences between men and women are what ensure mutual fascination. In love, we try to give without losing ourselves; we try to get what we need without being selfish. Conflict is the normal dynamic, the natural interplay between the real and the ideal, between us and our partners. Conflict isn't some terrible cosmic joke, it is the necessary energy system that keeps all of us on our toes.

The most consistent and fundamental error many women make with men is in assuming they are really like them. Despite all that's been written in the area of relationship, some women continue to be baffled by men's thoughts, emotional reactions, and behavior. This painful and frustrating mystery is related to a common, underlying calculus: women see men as being driven by goals, motives, and image systems similar to their own. The truth is that men and women are governed by very different comfort zones, notions of security, and underlying motivations.

During the past twenty years, there have been count-less attempts to homogenize the genders guided by the belief that the most constructive male/female union is an androgynous amalgam of the two. This attempt to reduce differences has led to one of the most confusing and dissatisfying eras in relationship history.

We would like to reverse this trend not by ignoring differences but rather by highlighting, understanding, and celebrating contrasts between the sexes. For some, this book may seem reactionary, for it is not fettered by constraints of fairness or thoughts about how things should be. Our thoughts are bound by only one guiding principle: a description of the way things are minus any misguided idealism. It is written to help women have more successful and satisfying experiences with men by understanding and enjoying the intrinsic differences between the sexes. It is not for the faint of heart, the egalitarian purist, or the myth-laden, why-can't-men-be-more-like-us, kind of woman. It is for the "warrior woman."

WHO IS THE WARRIOR WOMAN?

The warrior woman understands from her first meet-ings with men that the battle of the sexes is an age-old turf war. Having the knowledge that she is entering a conflict zone is her finest weapon, for men are the last to acknowledge that they are under siege. The warrior woman sees men the way they are, not shrouded behind the rosy glow of how she would like them to be. She is guided by overall goals and not blinded by temporary roadblocks. Her knowledge allows her to get what she wants. She knows how a man falls in love with a woman as well as what holds his continued interest in her. She understands her own needs clearly and moves into a man's heart without his defensive awareness. Her confidence is such that she has no need to call attention to the struggle that is under way. She wins the war without a battle.

An impediment for many women is their tendency to settle for "getting along" by concentrating on meeting the needs of men and neglecting their own. Warrior women don't simply get along, they also get what they want. And not by increasing their "marketability," but by making themselves smarter and more powerful in their relations with men.

Is biology destiny, as Freud suggested? Are women more dominated by their quest for romance than they are by their need for equality? Are, as some advice books suggest, women unrealistic in their wish for respect and equal treatment in their love relations? Must women be quiet, frail, and dependent to be loved? To all these questions our answer is a resounding NO!

Warrior women don't look to a man for completion. They bring wholeness to the relationship and expect no less from their partners. They know how to create romantic moments but never make romance the centerpiece of the relationship. Warrior women are not drama queens. Love, friendship, and peace are their goals, and they know how to accomplish them. Warrior women know successful relationships require leadership and willingly accept that role.

YES . . . LOVE *DOES* REQUIRE WORK

Many of us have been led to believe that the key to a romantic connection is finding someone who likes us "just the way we are." The problem is that we've become so self-centered that anything that sounds as if it requires thought and effort feels vaguely manipulative, or just plain work—something we shouldn't have to do. The truth is that every complex process involves "art" or technique, and love is no exception. Nowhere is "art" any more important than in the conduct of love. To develop "art" one must be reflective, able to get out of your shoes at times and into those of your partner, and willing to experience times of discomfort—which are all elements of love's work. Healthy relationships survive only when both people win. But winning is not something that happens by chance; it's shaped by knowing what works for you and by being able to get that without diminishing your partner's ability to do the same.

The Art of War for Lovers' goals are to be psychologically accurate, not politically correct; to show what a woman can do to be smarter, more powerful and effective, and to examine love in the context of the enduring values of generosity of spirit, clarity of purpose, and personal honesty.

PART 1

CONNELL COWAN'S TAKE ON THE BATTLE OF THE SEXES

From a Psychologist Who's Talked
to the Women in the Trenches

CHAPTER 1

TACTICS . . .
TAKING THE
INTERNAL JOURNEY

In ancient times, capable warriors worked first upon making themselves invincible and only then watched for the enemy's points of vulnerability. Invincibility deals with oneself. And vulnerability in the enemy depends only upon him. For this reason, skilled warriors can become invincible but cannot make an enemy vulnerable.

— Sun Tzu

LOOKING FIRST TO YOURSELF FOR STRENGTH

Entering the domain of love can be dangerous. It can bring the sweet balm of comfort and safety we all need and want, or it can rob us of our belief in ourselves, which is the anchor of our existence. For this reason, it is essential that we learn to make ourselves invincible. Invincibility of love is the only protection anyone can count upon. It is an internal process requiring no one else's cooperation or even participation other than our own.

Invincibility is the belief in being able to survive with

9

dignity with or without a man. It is supported by a spiritual core of contentedness. It is creating a wholeness of self where the love of a man is only the frosting not the cake. Unfortunately, some women like the frosting best. They can end up with temporary sweetness but then find themselves at risk if the man changes his feelings.

Invincibility Is a Personal Thing

Invincibility, or self-love, is very different from self-involvement. Self-love is internally nurturing, affirming, accepting. Self-involvement is just the opposite: affirmation and acceptance are sought through some external agent (most often a lover). Invincibility is instinctively protective. However, it is protective of your integrity and core values rather than of your personal comfort or insecurities.

The first step in becoming invincible is acknowledging that you many want the pleasure of a man, but that you do not *need* it.

Next comes the realization that you alone can create invincibility in yourself. You must never look to a man to provide it for you or to protect you from the struggle to attain it. Let's try an experiment. If you are currently in a relationship, use that partner. If not, use the last partner you had. First, explore each of the emotional dimensions listed below by preceding it with the phrase "I feel." Then put a check mark by either the positive or negative form of the feeling. After finishing the list, run through it again, preceding each emotional dimension with the phrase "He makes me feel" and marking it with an *X*.

I feel:
He makes me feel:

Sexy	Unappealing
Confident	Unsure
Strong	Weak
Worthwhile	Worthless
Smart	Dumb
Attractive	Unattractive
Interesting	Uninteresting
Useful	Useless
Calm	Anxious
Safe	Unsafe
Content	Discontent
Connected	Lonely
Sure	Doubtful
Effective	Ineffective
Enough	Deficient

Here is how to look at the results. Your level of invincibility is reflected by the number of checks made in the left-hand, "postive" column, while your vulnerabilities lie in the number of Xs made in the right-hand, "negative" side. Now count up your Xs. Examine any negative feelings that you have marked, for these need special attention. Look also at discrepancies between what you feel on your own and what feelings you look to a relationship to provide, for they reflect unwarranted powers you are giving to the man.

We all know that as children our feelings are shaped and molded by parental influence. But as adults, our state of well-being becomes our own responsibility. Hold only yourself to the task of creating internal harmony, contentment, and acceptance in your life. It is when you master this struggle alone that you become invincible.

Another exercise that can be helpful in determining areas of vulnerability is the following: stand in front of a mirror looking straight into your eyes and say "I want," over and over again. Pay close attention to the thoughts and feelings that occur to you. These are your wishes and dreams. How many do you feel can be given to you only by a man? How many can you manage to provide for yourself? To be invincible, you must concentrate on giving these things to yourself.

Giving Up Magic and Getting Something Real

An important prerequisite for becoming invincible is your willingness to give up magic. To do this, you must let some of your fantasies go. Fantasy takes up great psychic space and can be self-defeating. This is so for two reasons. Fantasy is comprised largely of wishes and can't stand up to the reality of day-to-day experiences. And second, fantasy is the working of our interior world, which is all too often comprised of unrealistic expectations, which inevitably leads to disappointment.

By far, the most common and seductive fantasies are the most dangerous. Fantasy and magic are easily attached to such real events as getting married, buying a house, having a baby. Women dream of their romantic future in detail. They know what kind of wedding they want, the house they want to live in, and how many children they want to have.

These milestones are often highly charged with symbolic meaning and exert a powerful attraction for fantasy. "I know if I moved in with him we'd be a lot closer." "I'm sure he'd be more attracted to me if I lost that five pounds." "I'm going to be so happy when I'm married." Thinking "I will feel" this or that fantasy is a prominent symptom of imbuing significant life events with solutional magic.

Men are particularly sensitized to a woman's fantasies and often see them as burdensome. A man described his thoughts this way: "She talks all the time about what it's going to be like after we get married. It sounds to me like she thinks it's going to be a whole other experience, which really worries me. For me, marriage is more the way things are now plus the piece of paper. I get scared when I hear her go on and on. I don't know if I can make her as happy as she thinks she's going to be." It's not the direction the man is concerned with, it's the amount of magic that's attached to the direction.

Invincibility is accomplished by letting go of magic and embracing reality.

❧

It is possible to understand how to win without neccessarily being able to do so.

BEING YOUR BEST DOESN'T NECESSARILY MEAN HE WILL BE HIS BEST

As we reach adulthood, we learn that we must depend upon ourselves to make our lives complete. When we are in love, however, we somehow forget this and make the error of expecting our partner to make us whole. In searching for love, validation, and respect, we must never forget that it is our responsibility, and ours alone, to bring this sense of completion to our lives.

Jessica couldn't have been happier in the early months of her relationship with Sam. Never had she seen a man with more energy or exuberance—which he directed toward her in amounts just short of overwhelming. He was bright, very ambitious, sweet, and funny. It wasn't that Jessica didn't also see chinks here and there, but even the little imperfections seemed endearing to her.

Jessica had turned thirty-five the day she met Sam. A few of her closest friends had taken her out to dinner to celebrate her birthday when in walked Sam with a man who was an acquaintance from her office. Jessica invited them both to join the group for cake and coffee, and as she was about to leave the restaurant, Sam had asked for her number.

Jessica had only recently begun to feel comfortable on her own after the breakup of her marriage two years earlier. She and her son, Mike, set up house, and all of her attention was divided between work and her young child. She hadn't been looking to get involved that day she met Sam, for she was feeling quite pleased with herself and more in control of her life than she had in years. But get involved she did, with high hopes that this man, who seemed to adore her, would someday be the partner she could settle in with for life.

As Jessica spent more time with Sam, she came to understand some of the reasons why he had never married. Although he would certainly deny it, Sam was wedded to his work and had been for years. His friends were complimentary toward her, telling her that she was the best thing that had ever happened to Sam. But, at some point, they also managed to sneak in questions about how she handled his singular focus on his work. She had thought his increasingly long hours were related to finishing the project he was working on, but she was learning it was his style, the way he always related to work.

As their relationship became more routine, Sam spent less time with Jessica. Less isn't quite accurate, for he wanted her nearby as he sent his faxes, read his newspapers, and made his business calls. Even when he was home on their weekends together, he was at work. Jessica tried to be supportive and made few demands on his time, involving herself with her own activities and doing things with her son, Mike.

Jessica had hoped that Sam would connect with Mike, who needed a strong male influence now that his father had moved to Seattle and saw him less frequently. But Sam didn't form that connection and was wooden and awkward around the boy. Jessica thought that perhaps with time Sam would relax and get closer to Mike, who looked up to him and was so in need of his attention and approval. When Jessica spoke to Sam about Mike, he told her he had never spent time with children and simply didn't feel comfortable around them.

Listening to Sam's words, Jessica felt a terrible pain for Mike. But instead of making Sam feel guilty or deficient, she doubled her efforts to spend time with Mike and do things that he needed. At those moments when Jessica had twinges of feeling sorry for herself, she would recall her life before Sam and how she had been just fine. She wanted, sometimes, to shriek and accuse him of being selfish, to dump his newly sharpened pencils, paper clips, and neatly organized papers on the floor, and cut his phone and fax lines with wire snippers. Instead, she tried to give herself what she needed. Until she could stand it no longer. Sam was shocked when she ended it. She hadn't even carried on and complained the way all the other women had who had been involved with him. "It wouldn't have done any good," she told him. "This is the way you are, and no matter how much a woman loves you, you don't have much to give in return." Sam had nothing to say. He knew Jessica was right.

The sad truth is that you may prepare yourself to be a kind and generous lover and still not be able to create a generously reciprocated love. That is why it is so important to be able to take good care of yourself. It is not possible to know the course of love until we are well into it. But the woman who makes her own life whole and worthwhile becomes invincible. And the invincible woman is able to detect the mortal flaws in a relationship. She has made sure she is not the cause and is able to leave before the experience becomes diminishing or destructive.

———

Invincibility always lies in the defense, while the possibility of victory resides in attack. A skilled warrior knows that when strength is lacking he must defend and attack only when strength is fulsome.

THE POWER OF BECOMING INTERNALLY GUIDED

In love, the protection against disappointment and hurt comes from making sure that you never find yourself playing out the dreadful role of victim. All of the events in our lives carry along with them the dimension of cause and effect, action and reaction, doer, maker, shaper and victim. In love, it is always to your advantage to place youself on the active side of that dimension. This is accomplished by learning to be guided from within.

Yet nothing like love draws us so powerfully to the other side, making us feel swept along, as if we are involved in something we need terribly and yet cannot fully control. In the context of love we are tempted to forget our internal guidance and feel as though our happiness and well-being are dependent not so much upon *our* actions, but upon those of *our partners*.

Love Is Not Necessarily about Change

By relinquishing control to our partners, we somehow feel that we have "changed" for them and expect them to do the same for us. A large part of this problem lies in how we comprehend and experience love. If we were able to please our parents and do what they expected of us, we were more likely to receive and predict their love. And through prediction, we gained some sense of control. To some degree then, love became defined as a willingness to change. *Our* change. For a child, this process is one of learning and growing, and change was a simple by-product. And as children, we were dependent upon our parents, and our compliance and willingness to change to meet their wishes wasn't only about love, it was also about our avoiding their disapproval and insuring their continued caretaking. Adults are not so dependent, and for the most part, they can be pretty resistant to any sort of significant change. And this is true quite independent of their love for you. Yet many of us remain stuck in the early model of love: "I changed for your approval, so that you would love me. I changed to try and make you happy." And mistakenly, we unknowingly apply this model to our partners.

Many of us sadly fall into the "if you were different, I would be happier" mentality. "If he really loved me, he would be willing to change," we think. Invincibility lies in not making this all-too-common error. The moment you allow your sense of value and well-being, your happiness, to become contingent upon someone else's actions and goodwill, you are in grave danger. The danger is twofold: the role you play is that of victim, and the power you confer to your partner is a natural setup for disappointment and anger.

Almost without exception, the things our partners do that begin to annoy, frustrate, or hurt us are not meant to do any of those things. Our partners are simply doing what comes most naturally; they are just being the way they are. The way they have *always* been. It is we who take their actions so personally, not they who intentionally inflict those actions upon us. The compulsively neat man who cannot have a magazine on the table or a glass in the sink and has to squeeze the toothpaste tube in his own peculiar way isn't trying to make you nuts, he is just busy managing his anxiety and doing all those things that help him in that task. That his fussiness makes you more than a little crazy is never the intention, it's only a side effect. The man who can remember everything having to do with work, but develops amnesia when it comes to tickets for a show, arranging a social engagement, or taking the responsibility for planning a trip isn't saying he doesn't care about you or your feelings. Those things just don't mean the same thing to him as they do to you. They are not on his mind, despite the importance they may play in yours.

To combat or avoid feelings of frustration and hurt, many women try to improve the men they're with. And, while children make accommodations for their parents, men don't typically change for women. Sure, you can rant and scream and blame and accuse, but in the end it will do you little good. Instead, you can become internally guided and invincible.

To begin becoming more internally guided, try exploring the following questions:

1. What is the complaint (something that bothers you and for which you hold the man in your life responsible)?
2. What specifically are your feelings about the complaint?
3. What do *you* do to make possible, cause, or perpetuate the issue?
4. What would you like to be different?
5. How would you like to feel?
6. Are you willing to give up blame and to assume some personal responsibility?
7. What can *you* do that will lead to a difference?

8. How can *you* achieve what you want on your own?
9. What actions can *you* take?
10. What have you learned about yourself from the experience?

Those most skilled in defense know how to hide in the deepest depths of the earth while those most skilled in attack move about in the highest reaches of the sky. In this way they are able to protect themselves as well as achieve a total victory.

MASTERING THE WHEEL OF SELF-DEFENSE

Those most skilled in emotional defense know how to step aside at times, to quietly work within themselves and gather strength. They have mastered the Wheel of Self-Defense. To do so, you must be willing to explore the presence of hidden fears and motivations. There is no better time to gather strength than during times of challenge or difficulty. Most of us would do anything to avoid adversity, for with it comes pain and confusion. This is particularly true in the context of a love relationship. But think about the positive value of reflective questioning for a moment. Questioning is like a signal fire forcing us once again to think through what it is we want and making us reexamine why we want it. Reflective questioning is the conduit for clarity. It forces us to make choices and take actions. Only in our willingness to face adversity can we gain the power to foresee problems and alter their course. Remember, if there's passion you can count on a little adversity.

The Wheel of Self-Defense

The Wheel of Self-Defense consists of spokes, each designed to support the wheel. Weakness in any of the spokes will create a weakness in the wheel itself. It is important to shore up and master each spoke, one by one, so that they may transfer their power to the hub, which of course is the unified self. The spokes of the wheel are:

Loss
Obstacles
Fullness of self
Foresight
Patience
Control
Resistance
Fear
Hope

LOSS

Loss offers us a time to gather strength. Loss takes many forms. It can be a real loss, where a relationship dies or moves on beyond our reach. Or it can be an anticipation or fear of loss that clenches our hearts. Regardless of which face loss wears, it offers us the potential for opportunity. That opportunity is for new actions and experiences.

Loss also poses two challenges. First, it tends to make us averse to taking risks. This is natural. Not wishing to be hurt or abandoned, we throw up protective walls and then forget we have placed them there. The walls become invisible to us, and only the shadows they cast remain. Most often, these shadows take the form of hyper-autonomy, distrust, or excessive pickiness. Each of these has the effect of creating and maintaining emotional distance. Their presence prevents the possibility of any intimate experience with a man, despite the quality of love he may offer. Find the courage to again begin to take chances. Trust is built only upon some amount of risk. Don't let a loss in the past block your chances for a loving present.

And second, the fear of loss may become attached to maintaining the status quo. This happens when we are afraid to give up something we know is wrong for us. We cling to the familiarity of the known. The protective wall surrounding this fear of loss also casts a shadow: disbelief. Because a woman doesn't believe she has the capacity to change or the mental and emotional toughness to weather the change, she may cling to a self-defeating pattern. A woman may stay rooted in a painful and destructive relationship because she doesn't believe she can create another one defined by more respect and generosity. It takes guts to move on.

Loss is an integral aspect of any life process, including love. To truly open the door to love requires that we be willing to face the potential of loss. Its occurrence in our lives cannot be avoided. Shed those things that are no longer fulfilling and affirming, for only in doing so do you make room for new experiences with greater promise. Their loss will be your gain.

OBSTACLES

At times we all may feel discouraged or blocked in our quest for love. But strength always lies in our choices. You may choose to see yourself as the recipient of bad luck and sink into the muck and mire of despair. Be overwhelmed. Become hopeless. Or you may see obstacles as learning experiences, challenges to be struggled with and mastered, possibilities to strengthen will and deepen personal understanding. Seen through this prism, each setback, each discouragement, each difficulty, even each failure becomes an opportunity to measure your character. Look at troubles as lessons, as puzzles to be solved. Look at failures as guides, for in their grist lies a greater chance for learning than success provides.

In the same way that muscles and resolve are strengthened by challenge and adversity, so too is the spirit of the heart. Obstacles and tests are toughening devices, and when seen as important sources of information, they can be richly rewarding.

Obstacles are often uniquely defined reflections of our personal development. Sadly, this is a fact we often forget. We try to externalize obstacles, ignoring the fact that they are *of us* and make believe they are imposed *upon us*. This shift from internal to external relieves us of responsibility and places it elsewhere. Assigning obstacles to chance, fate, or the bad behavior of a man gives power to magic and the conduct of others and robs you of a treasure that might be your own.

Obstacles are not only strengthening but they are also clarifying. As they occur in our lives, obstacles uncover new issues for us to master and force us to be more discriminating. As a teenager, you may have struggled with daring to smile at the boy you hoped might find you attractive. Or you may have had to lose weight. Hunger is good when you're on a diet. It means you're losing weight. Same thing with men. It is good to be in touch with loneliness if you want a partnership. It means you're going to go out and do something about it, hopefully. Later in life, the obstacles may shift to standing up to a controlling man or learning the more selfless love required in caring for a baby. Within our obstacles lies a lifelong process of learning about ourselves. Give up wishing to be free of such challenges, for at their very core they are really the ongoing expressions of our uniqueness and lessons not yet learned.

FULLNESS OF SELF

Anything that is sacrificed causes great pain and troubles you by its absence. When in the company of her lover, a woman may relinquish her strength, feeling that she must sacrifice it in order to maintain his love. But surely love cannot be threatened by strength, can it? Or a woman may fear that expressing her anger might rob her of a man's love. But if his love and acceptance are bound by the silencing of her emotions, can he really be capable of love?

Important and valuable parts of ourselves are cast aside for two reasons. Either they cause us shame or they cause us fear. The phenomenon of burying aspects of who we are often occurs first in childhood. We may bury a sense of adventure in an effort to please a timid or fearful parent. We may bury interests, aptitudes, and abilities in deference to what was shamed or affirmed in the swirl of our family mixtures. We may even have buried a basic sense of personal entitlement, leaving us attentive to the needs of others and neglectful of our own.

To love requires that *you* be there in the mix. Fully. This means that you must awaken any long sleeping parts of yourself and find the courage to bring them to the party. Relinquishing part of yourself may have been necessary to survive your family, but reclaiming those important aspects is just as crucial to the fulfillment of love. "I am neither ashamed nor afraid to be who I am" is a credo to be put into action in the conduct of your love relationship. Your fullest self is the greatest gift of honesty and trust you can extend. True protection is always about having free and easy access to yourself. Breathe life back into any silenced voices. Listen for them in the whisper of your feelings, in the silent jog of a memory, in the moment of a wish or dream.

FORESIGHT

How often, had your eyes been open, might you have seen the consequences of your actions beforehand? Take the time to listen to your inner voice and know the results of your conduct before you act.

"I knew I was going to wreck things," Sharon said. "It's not that I didn't know the consequences," she continued, "I just didn't seem to be able to stop myself." Sharon is referring to her relationship with Tom or, more precisely, how she is reacting to Tom's friends. Sharon and Tom have been together for months, have passed through that phase of having to spend every minute with each other, and have moved beyond infatuation. Tom has been wanting to spend a bit more time with his friends, and Sharon feels jealous and threatened. Ashamed and embarrassed by her feelings, she doesn't express them to Tom. Rather, every time he wants to see a friend, she says something to make him feel guilty or she picks away at the little imperfections she has discovered in his friends. She is pushing him inexorably away, and she knows it. And doesn't know it, all at the same time.

The value of prediction is our willingness to us it. Prediction is like insight; having it but not using it is a terrible waste. Foresight is a vision of the future, one of the highest uses of our intelligence. It provides us the ability to see ahead of time how events may unfold. Foresight is an opportunity for us to learn and master our next internal task. For Sharon, it is trusting her self-worth and finding the generosity to want the best for Tom whether he is in or out of her presence. Foresight is knowing that befriending his enjoyable experiences with friends enriches him and will bring him back to her.

Patience

It is impossible to force a rose to bloom. Patience acknowledges the organic nature of timing and its practice brings peace and contentment. We can throw a rock into a pond, but we have to wait for the ripples to reach the shore. Love is just the same. A smart woman sows the seeds of love and waits patiently for the coming harvest.

Why are we impatient? Sometimes we are impatient because we are used to getting our way. Or perhaps we have a very low tolerance for delaying gratification. We want what we want now, and if we can't have it, there will be hell to pay. That is simply being childish, and the only antidote is growing up. But more often that not, impatience is a reflection of insecurities. Impatience is another way of saying "I am unsure of my true value in love." You are impatient because you are scared. Women would like to get the commitment first and then go through the romance and fall in love. It's a very scary process, especially if you've done it before.

Impatience then is more about the feelings we want to avoid rather than those we wish to have. It is less about any aspect of love and more about avoiding discomfort. Patience allows love to have an organic form and takes the uniqueness of your partner into consideration. You should strive to develop patience, for it is your ally, a great source of strength.

Control

We wish to control others most when we feel somewhat out of control ourselves. A healthy man doesn't particularly like controlling women. Whatever you think you may gain in personal comfort by exerting control, you will lose in a man's ease and affection toward you. Men don't like to be controlled any more than women do.

Men resent a woman when they have to assert themselves against her control, and they resent the woman when they find themselves giving in to her control.

A warrior woman battles with herself, holding the simple goal of inner peace. Relinquish any attempts to control the man in your life and instead concentrate on a deeper understanding of yourself. When you have mastered your own issues, your need to control the man's actions will fade like the morning mist.

RESISTANCE

How can we know what is right for us and fail to acknowledge it? How is it possible to see the correct course of action and somehow fail to make it? Knowing and doing are sadly very different. "Doing" is "knowing" in action, and over a lifetime of learning, that requires change. We all resist change even though we may know unquestionably that it is good for us. The heart of resistance is doubt and our slavish attachment to the comfort of familiarity. Be willing to experience the unfamiliar, for in its virgin territory lies your truest potential for growth. If you hold as the only worthwhile outcome your personal understanding, then doubt no longer has a place. What are the positive changes you resist making?

FEAR

In love, the key is to create a victory before entering into battle. It is all too easy to pass up or ignore those auspicious moments when victory might have been yours and the battle avoided. Think about the important relationships you have had. Can you identify those moments when you knew something was amiss but were afraid to acknowledge it or didn't know what to do about it? Or those moments when some action on your part might have averted a problem? We can all come up with those moments, that convergence of events where the proper intervention might have prevented pain, frustration, and grief.

Why do we allow these moments to pass unheeded? Why do we fail to seize the initiative at the right time when waiting for the wrong time is always more difficult? At the core of this odd phenomenon is that vexing awareness: fear. Fear that we may be misreading the situation, acting selfishly, not giving our partner the benefit of doubt; fear that our actions may result in greater loss than gain. It is the fear we associate with any sort of trouble, making distasteful ripples as we have to face and deal with uncomfortable feelings and decisions. It is the fear of change and our tendency to hang on to the familiar, even when the familiar isn't good for us. It is the fear of being found deficient and lacking the proper leverage or real importance to carry off the intervention. And it is the fear that acting on the moment will expose our own faults in a way that silence allows us to make believe we can avoid.

Lisa found herself in the unenviable position of having one of her friends sit her down over lunch and ask what was wrong in her relationship with Jimmy. Perplexed at why such a question would arise, Lisa wondered aloud what her friend was talking about. Her friend leaned in close across the table and told Lisa, "I like Jimmy. You know that. But I love you, and I see him hurting you. At first, it was little things, teasing comments delivered with that charming grin of his. But they always have barbs attached to them. I watched as you would try and throw them off, hoping we didn't notice. Well, we did, and I know that they hurt you. Lately, Lisa, every time I see the two of you, Jimmy manages to get in some kind of shot, and I've got to tell you, they are getting meaner. We're all worried about you."

Lisa looked into her friend's eyes, knew she was right, and felt a sense of shame for having ignored something so clear that all of her friends recognized it. Lisa sat there with tears in her eyes, thinking back to that moment, months ago now, when Jimmy first turned on her. They had been at a dinner party with a small group of her friends when it had happened. Lisa had marveled at the host's smooth-running and spotlessly organized kitchen when Jimmy piped in, charming smile and all, "You ought to come over and give Lisa lessons. When she cooks, her kitchen looks like a tornado ran through it, and that's neat compared to her bedroom." Lisa was stung by his words but found herself fixated more upon whether he was accurate than on his inappropriate and hurtful choice of timing to lodge a critical observation.

That remark was only the beginning of a stream of put-downs all expressed, curiously enough, in a social context, particularly when they were among Lisa's friends. She had allowed a pattern to develop, one in which Jimmy felt safe enough to express his annoyance and displeasure only when there was company around. To alter this now well-established pattern would take going to battle to properly protect herself. If she'd had the foresight and courage to act in the first critical moment, her task would be considerably less daunting. Had she taken Jimmy aside after that dinner party so long ago and said, "What you did tonight is unacceptable. It hurt me and made me feel embarrassed in front of my friends. If you have a criticism to make or something you find annoying about me, I expect you to tell me when we're alone, and I promise I'll try and listen. But I want you to understand very clearly that I won't be with someone who uses a social gathering to express anger or some kind of critical judgment."

Recognize and seize the moment, for if you do not, your battles will be longer and more painful. A relationship is molded the way a potter shapes a vessel—the imprint of your firm hand in the still wet clay is essential. Protect your dignity and lay the foundation that will support and affirm healthy communications. Avoid at all costs setting yourself up for ways of relating that are inherently destructive and undermine love.

HOPE

Hope can be the bane of fulfillment in love, particularly when it is attached to someone else's conduct. Hope is the resistance to the way things are, the denial of reality. A love that is yours will come to you and offer itself. Hoping for its expression is more than simply useless. Hoping wastes valuable time and bring tears to your heart. Hope is unrealistic in the abstract (as in, "I hope I can find a kind, gentle hockey player") as well as in the specific (as in, "Steven is an artist, but I want him to make a lot of money").

Having the courage to plumb the depths of your personal understanding will create your only true and lasting defense. You will connect again to your inner self. You will trust anew your intuitive side, reaffirming your value and values. In giving up your resistance, you will conquer fear and doubt. In doing this, you understand that defense and attack are a unity and you have accomplished both.

❧❧

In ancient times, those seen as skilled in war won when it was easy to win. This was accomplished by creating the right conditions. Victories are never accidental nor left to chance.

MISTAKES NEED NOT BE REPEATED

Women can be successful in love by making few mistakes. They see the man clearly and are not undercut by their own weaknesses. They conquer obstacles by pushing self-defeating tendencies out of the way.

Consider your past errors with men. Study the great mistakes you've seen women make with men and study them well! Search deep inside for the part of you that is capable of making the same painful errors, the part of you that is vulnerable. "Not possible. Not those mistakes. I would never do this or that," you might say. Well, you could and probably would with the right man under the right circumstances. Yes, you! Find that part; it is there. It is there for all of you. The little gnawing fears and doubts that erode your confidence and allow you to take less set the stage for subtle abuse. It is there, and you must remove it.

How, you ask, is it possible to lop off a part of me that has been there forever, something I know about myself, have observed in action but don't know how to control? You crush the sabotaging part of yourself with the most important weapon you have, the only one you have ever had. You destroy it with your will.

Women so often give their best to those who deserve it the least, one of the most common mistakes. Why? Are women masochists? No! They give their best to people who let them down because they feel most known by them. Sadly, we never feel quite so seen, quite so known to the core, by those who see the best in us and treat us accordingly. We are the only ones who know our own worst thoughts, fears, and deeds, and we feel understood most by people who treat us as though they have shined a light into our darkest weaknesses, confirming that we have less rather than greater value.

30

We all drag along behind us unwanted baggage, but the trick is not to be tyrannized or defined by it. You deserve to be seen for the complex composite that you are. Trust the man who connects to your goodness and lets your strengths take center stage. And don't think less of him for not rubbing your flaws in your face; its not that he's stupid or blind, he's simply extending the acceptance of flaws he would like to receive from you.

Perhaps the most common mistake women make with men is to give away their basic entitlements. Healthy relationships carry with them a largely unspoken series of fundamental rights. It is only when these rights are honored that love, personal esteem, and uniqueness can be sustained over time.

LOVE'S ENTITLEMENTS

Take a moment and review the following list. First, precede each item with the statement "I *should* be entitled to." Place a check mark after each item that seems appropriate to you.

After you have finished, go back through the list, now saying before each item "I *do* feel entitled to." Now, put an *X* after each item that, in fact, you do feel entitled to.

Care (receiving basic concern and support)
Appropriate attention (to be listened to and heard as well)
Dignity
Respect
Acceptance (the right not to have to be perfect)
Affection
Privacy
Autonomy
Having other friends (nonthreatening relationships of your own)

Expressing and exploring your interests, opinions, attitudes, values

Free and responsible expression of feelings

Control (an appropriate degree of decision making)

These rights are fundamental to a healthy, loving relationship. You should feel entitled to each of them. Look at the discrepancies between the *should*'s and the *do*'s. Remember, a man can't take any of these rights away from you. Only you can disbelieve in yourself such that you give them away. A man isn't the protector of your entitlements. You are.

❦

Those truly skilled in the use of arms cultivate the Way and keep the rules. Only in this way can one govern in a just and humane manner.

Different cultures and societies have different rules. And following them brings more acceptance from the community and more strength for the individual. By knowing the rules, and adhering to them whenever possible, a woman strengthens herself against a surprise attack.

Warrior women successful in love have integrity and are governed by a strong sense of justice and fair play. They understand the full entitlement of the heart but never make men responsible for providing the wholeness, security, and validity they can create for themselves. The warrior woman knows well the five elements of love: passion, vulnerability, trust, respect, and acceptance. She practices them always in reciprocity, making balance the rule.

CHAPTER 2

PLANNING A SIEGE . . .
PREPARING FOR LOVE

Breaking the hearts of a hundred men is not a measure of being skilled in love. Finding a single man and treating him in such a way that both of you are enhanced is the true hallmark of excellence.

Accumulating a hundred victories in a hundred battles is not the measure of ultimate skill. Capturing the enemy's army without inflicting damages is the pinnacle of excellence. Nothing can be more effective or hold a higher priority in war than to grasp the enemy's most basic strategy.

—Sun Tzu

HOW WOMEN AND MEN APPROACH
SEX DIFFERENTLY

A man's sexual strategy is different from a woman's. In understanding these differences, a woman can protect herself and prevent heartache. Women often mistake a man's initial sexual interest in her for something deeper and more lasting. This doesn't mean that men are simply sexual predators and muddleheaded when it comes to their feelings, but it does mean that you must exercise certain cautions and grasp the fundamentals of their differing emotional makeup.

Ultimately, a woman and a man want essentially the same things from a relationship: warmth, acceptance, and companionship. Their approaches to achieving that goal, however, can take quite disparate paths. Most women need to feel the presence of some sort of *intimacy* before they give themselves sexually. Most men need to feel some *sexual connection* to a woman before they feel relaxed enough to give of themselves with openness and intimacy. Deeply embedded in both of these approaches is a wish to feel *safe*. A man's most vulnerable awareness is his need for a woman, and before he will allow that to be shown, he wants to make sure that the woman is drawn to him sexually. Only when he senses that she is, will he feel safe enough to take the first hesitant steps toward revealing his deepening feelings toward her, which he typically prefers to keep secret.

This isn't meant to imply that it is your job to throw yourself in bed with him. Simply understand the sequence a man is inclined to take on his journey toward a loving relationship. It is important to remember that we are all responsible for our own feelings of comfort and well-being. Trust your instincts and involve yourself with sexual intimacy at a pace you know to be consistent with your best interests. Show him your attraction without compromising yourself.

Part of the problem is that most men have a "wait and see" attitude when it comes to their romantic dealings with women—*wait* until they are involved with the woman sexually and *see* how they feel. Men can be utterly exasperating at this stage of a relationship. They want to feel important to you, but not too important. They want to get information while giving little in return. They want you to be interested in their life, but not intrusive. They certainly want you to be attracted to them sexually, but not too wildly or too soon, for that reads to them that you lack discrimination. They want you to offer exclusivity without necessarily demanding it in return. They want your easy availability without making any incursions into their freedom. They want the affirmation of your growing need for them without the slightest hint of your being needy. That's a pretty scary list of inequities, don't you think?

HOW TO CREATE SUSTAINED
SEXUAL INTEREST

Keep coming back to a man's primitive psychology: his caring grows out of *sustained sexual interest* (while for women, sexual interest grows out of *sustained caring).* In the beginning, women are more aware of the reasons why they like a man than men are for why they are drawn to a woman. For a man, the first few experiences of being together are primarily related to his awareness of physical interest, while a woman's attraction to a man is more layered and complex.

So how do you deal with a man's strategy when all he seems to want is to get you in bed? By following a foolproof set of guidelines. Your first task is to create sustained sexual interest. His strategy is to quickly express his sexual interest (and then often move on). Your strategy is to thwart that plan by slowing things down, by not allowing him to dictate the pace. But only slow some things down. Express interest and receptivity. Be kind, thoughtful, and giving. Let him get to know the strengths, texture, and richness of your life. Let him want you, but make him understand he really needs to get to know you before you'll give yourself to him sexually. Don't go to bed with him until you have first seen not only the promise but also the demonstration of his caring.

As you know, men value most those things that require work, challenge, and persistent effort. A man doesn't assign real importance to anything he can get easily. Let him work for you a bit. His effort will underscore your meaning to him. He needs to make those efforts in order for it to dawn on him that he's fallen in love with you. A man's desire will not be sustained if he is allowed to express and release it too soon. Take care not to get swept away by your own feelings (or fall prey to his insistent whining). Trust your head, not your heart.

HOW TO MAKE A MAN'S FEELINGS GROW STRONGER

The affections of a man can be won with little in the way of emotional upset if a woman remembers the second guideline: create for the man an atmosphere of safety and enjoyment without desperation.

This may sound easier than it is. Many women provide a generous measure of comfort and safety. For a while. The man waits for the proverbial other shoe to drop, the questions to begin, the definitions that are sought. Don't do it. Not too soon. Be smarter than the man. Stronger. If he is worth your love, he is worth the wait. If he cares, tensions and questions will be building within him just as they are within you. Let him be the first to make minor but telltale adjustments to your life. Let him be the one to utter the first words of love. Let him be concerned about why you're not pressing him. Most women let a man chase them for about two seconds and then spend months running after him and asking themselves what happened to his interest.

Some women only think they like being pursued, when in fact they seem to do everything they can to end a man's pursuit. Most women like to show all, tell all, and be all. You simply can't do that and still be chased. In love, women are the worst secret keepers, and yet when romantic love is new, holding the depth of your feelings to yourself is of paramount importance. It is natural to want to talk about how you feel in the early phases of love, but instead have these conversations with your best friend.

Salmon instinctively swim upstream to spawn. A man is just the same. Tilt the level of difficulty slightly in his direction and watch his efforts increase. He will be yours without trying. In fact, it is the "without trying" part of the equation that is the most critical.

❧❧

The tactic of waging war upon fortified cities is to be avoided when at all possible for this is where the enemy has focused his resistive force.

OVERCOMING A MAN'S RESISTANCE TO EMOTIONAL EXPRESSION

The worst thing a woman can do is to attack the point of a man's greatest resistance or to put his back to the wall. A man's resistance to acknowledging his growing feelings for a woman is like one of those Chinese toys you played with as a child. You put a finger in the end of the woven paper cylinder, and if you try to pull it out quickly, you can't. The harder you pull, the tighter the paper's grasp on your finger. But relax and the pressure on your finger eases.

Eliminate a man's resistance. You do this by acknowledging its presence and surrendering completely to its force. It is impossible for a man to sustain resistance when there is no counterforce being applied, for there is nothing for him to pull against.

Most men expect a woman to be the one to move the relationship along. Fast. Then they get prepared to dig in their heels. They are sensitized to the signs of being pushed and wait for the woman to declare herself, anticipating having then to declare themselves, often before they feel ready. Don't get drawn into this. Try to stay calm and contained.

If the man's resistance has been in place for some time, he will, at first, be suspicious of its absence. He will think you've merely tucked the issue away momentarily and will spring your wishes upon him once again as soon as his guard is down. But a man is easily lulled, and that is when the worry sets in. Men have greatest resistance in the areas about which they have the most mixed feelings and ambivalence. When a woman pulls on one side, the man tugs back on the other (reflexively: he feels this is the manly thing to do). When you stop pulling, not only does his resistance fade, but he also misses the position you took and gave voice to. Into the vacuum created by your voice's absence flows the other side of his ambivalence, the part he didn't have to give much thought or energy to, since you were providing it all.

Men know what is appropriate and healthy in the arena of love even though you may not hear those thoughts put in words. Men feel safer having a woman put words to those more tender, needful feelings. When deepening yearnings are no longer being expressed by the woman, the man begins to experience those same yearnings himself. Instead of resistance, as if by magic, you have the man acting toward you in exactly the ways you want. Now you might be thinking: isn't this game playing and just a little too planned and conscious? But why is it more acceptable to be fully aware of the winning tactics in bridge or chess than in love? It seems wise to be knowledgeable in the ways of all things, most particularly those of the heart.

Only after attacking an enemy's strategies are other actions to be considered. The next best is to act in a way that disrupts the enemy's alliances.

LESSONING THE POWER OF NEGATIVE INFLUENCES

Gaby knew exactly where she stood in the eyes of Sean's best friend, Lily, and it upset her a great deal. She understood the powerful influence Lily had over Sean and felt helpless when it came to thinking about how she might change this woman's feelings about her. At thirty-two, Gaby wasn't in the mood for a makeover and enjoyed her outgoing and ebullient nature. And the truth was that Sean enjoyed her as well, for she seemed a wonderful balance to his more reserved style. But Gaby also knew that Lily saw her as "too big and too brassy," descriptions she wouldn't have chosen for herself. After one too many declined invitations on Lily's part, Gaby had asked Sean if there was a problem. "I guess she just doesn't feel comfortable with you," was the extent of Sean's explanation.

There was no question in Gaby's mind that she couldn't simply ignore the formidable sway Lily held over Sean. What she did was to address the issue directly. Without ever attacking Lily, Gaby got Sean to talk about his relationship with Lily and asked how she had felt toward other women in Sean's life. As he talked, it was clear that Lily had managed to find something wrong with each of the women Sean had been involved with, and these seeds of doubt had become the nagging concerns that had finally caused him to pull away. It was during these conversations that Sean first began to understand his friend. "I've always felt that Lily loved me," he told Gaby, "but maybe too much or in too possessive a way. She would point out something that wasn't quite right in everybody I saw, and it made me feel blind or undiscriminating for not having seen it myself. I've never wanted to think about it like this, but maybe Lily just wants to keep me all to herself."

Things changed after those conversations, and Gaby sensed that Lily was slowly losing her pull. Gaby expressed compassion for the touchy dilemma Sean and Lily faced and went out of her way to encourage Sean to be understanding of Lily's possessiveness and fear of losing the centrality she'd held for so long in Sean's life.

Had Gaby attacked Lily directly, Sean would likely have gone to her rescue, and things might easily have blown up. Instead, Gaby shifted Lily's alliance with Sean, gradually using truth and his growing insight as the critical lever.

Sometimes a man will have a different sort of alliance—one that may have murky overtones like an old girlfriend he hasn't yet managed to let go of completely. Never tolerate a man's romantic contact with another woman regardless of how it may be disguised.

The goal of the general is to take All-Under-Heaven intact. The rule of preservation is of paramount importance. In general, the strategy for deploying an army is as follows.

Our goal is always to create a love that is clear and lasting. In order to do so, you must learn to use the power and leverage you have in your relationship to shape the situation to your liking. Here are the ways to use your strength constructively.

If your strength is many times that of an enemy, then send your troops in swiftly to surround him.

DON'T CONFUSE *YOUR* POWER WITH A *MAN'S* WEAKNESS

All love relationships must deal with issues of leverage. In love, "leverage" is emotional currency—that invisible commodity of exchange that defines power in the mix. Most of us have mixed feelings about power: we are uncomfortable having too little and equally uncomfortable having too much. Women in particular can feel uncomfortable when they sense the balance of power tilting sharply in their direction. For these reasons, it is important to think about leverage carefully.

When we care and allow within ourselves an awareness of our growing need for someone, we give away power or leverage. Being the recipient of leverage poses certain problems. A woman who senses leverage in a relationship can easily make the mistake of reading it as weakness in a man. We all know that no woman wants a wimpy guy, but when a man gives his love to a woman, transferring leverage is part of the process, a very natural part. Don't interpret your possession of leverage negatively or as a reflection of unhealthy dependence in a man. Embrace your power as a gift extended by the man, one that carries with it the markings of his caring.

Another problem created by leverage is the feeling of unbalanced control. While we all like to feel in control, having too much control can be unsettling. The reason for this is that control highlights our degrees of freedom and their counterbalance: personal responsibility. Our actions are reasonable, sensitive, and generous because *we* exercise the control to make them so. "I hate it when he lets me be mean and bitchy" is a feeling that comes out of unbalanced leverage. But shouldn't you be the one to be your own monitor?

In a healthy love relationship, leverage is dynamic and changing. One minute you have it, the next it's gone. Then it's back again. In love, that's the way it is, like a beach ball bounced playfully back and forth. In fact, the back-and-forth shift is what keeps feelings most alive. Enjoy your leverage; take advantage of its glow, knowing its presence allows you safely to move closer to the man. And should the discomfort of leverage become a concern, you can change it easily with your open expression of love and need for the man sailing the ball in a high arc back in his direction.

❧

If you possess double an enemy's strength, divide him.

If your resources are double those of a man's in strength, divide him. But what happens when, as is most often the case, your leverage is not significantly greater than that of the man, when you worry it may be slipping and you would like to accumulate a bit of power to be held in reserve? Separate him from the certainty of your love, for it will reduce by half his will to resist.

How does one go about doing this? Certainly not by threat or withdrawal. Not by being stingy with your feelings. And certainly not through crazy-making game playing. A woman's leverage is increased by a subtle shift in a man's sense of centrality in her life. Move him off dead center by reinvesting in the elements of your life that were in place before you met him. See the friends you may have neglected recently in your wish to spend time with your man. Give yourself the privacy and alone time you may have squandered in your willingness to accommodate to a man's wishes. These simple affirmations of personal privilege can't help but move him off center. When a man is nudged subtly away from the complacency of centrality, his energy will be directed toward regaining his position. His energy is your leverage.

If your forces are weaker or fewer, you must circumvent and avoid the enemy.

What to Do with Feeling Insecure

If you feel vulnerable, try pulling back a bit emotionally. It may be wise to regroup, take a little time, and wait until you have strengthened your position. Let's take a look at the balance of need. Love works best when both partners value the importance of the relationship roughly equally. Of course, we are all much more acutely aware of how we value our partners because our awareness of that value is defined by the constant flow of our feelings. How our partners value us may be less clear, although we have some idea based upon how they treat us.

Discrepancies are important here, particularly if you

sense that you value a man more than you think he values you. The greater the discrepancy, the greater the need for you to approach this dilemma carefully.

Discrepancies in his favor should be reduced immediately. Here is what you might try. Contain your feelings. Muster up the courage to do what is counter-intuitive. You feel the urge to close the gap by pressing, wondering out loud about the depth of his feeling, asking through word or deed for reassurance. You must resist these urges, as any will lead to disaster.

For a man, love itself is defined through what he *does.* Without these expressive and affirming actions (his, not hers) a man doesn't experience the specific range of emotions he interprets as love. These love-defining actions on the part of a man disappear in the presence of a woman's expressions of insecurity, however subtly they may be expressed. Let him make the telephone calls. Let him begin to talk about how he feels about you and what he wants. Let him wonder and maybe even begin to worry about the intensity of your feelings. A man loses focus on how he feels toward a woman the minute she starts going into detail about how she feels toward him.

The fastest way to elicit a man's love-defining actions is to pull back emotionally, just ever so slightly. Regardless of the depth of your interest, restrain your enthusiasm, letting *his* expressions of *your* value lead the way. There is nothing to lose using this strategy. If he is capable of caring, he will be compelled to show it. And if he doesn't, your sense of self-worth will not be damaged.

When troops are restless and untrusting, victory will be ever elusive. Thus we know there are three keys for victory:
1. A general who understands when to fight and when not to fight will win.

NOT FALLING FOR THE BAD GUYS

A woman who knows when and when not to love will be successful. She chooses to give herself to only those men who are also capable of love. No one knows who is capable of love in the beginning. No one knows another's true values or character right away, for initially, we all tend to show our better sides and are on our best behavior. But to an observant woman, important information about a man starts trickling in fairly quickly. Infatuation covers a thousand flaws, some inconsequential and some significant. Accept the little imperfections of course, but don't get seriously involved with a man who isn't right for you. Only the most careless woman says, "I knew he'd end up hurting me, but I just couldn't help falling in love with him." Take better care of yourself.

When they first started dating, a couple who lived in a suburb of Cleveland went to a Chinese restaurant for dinner every Friday night. (On Saturday night, they had a little bit of variety in their lives.) When they placed their orders, he always ordered a steak and a baked potato. Remember, this was in a Chinese restaurant. She went down the menu ordering something new every time and got to know what was inside every dumpling. A couple of times, she asked him why he didn't want to go somewhere else (this place wasn't known for their steak or their baked potatoes). He said he liked it because it was easy to park, there was never any traffic getting there, nor was there any problem getting a reservation. Plus, he had been going there with his parents since he was a kid. So she knew that he was a creature of habit before they got married, but she never thought it was that important. After seven years of marriage and one daughter, there have been moments when she silently screamed over how many habits he has and how rigid he was about them.

None of us have a crystal ball, but as you start getting to know the man, make sure you don't overlook, excuse, or explain away danger signs on his part. You may think you are immune only to find the inevitable: one day his bad behavior will be turned on you.

2. A general who knows how to deal with both superior and inferior troops will win.

NEVER ACT FROM WEAKNESS

A woman who trusts in her strengths and works diligently upon her weaknesses will do well in love. But all too often, we allow our weaknesses to make important decisions for us. The moment a weakness causes us to avoid something we shouldn't avoid or causes us to do something we shouldn't do, we have empowered that weakness. A weakness cannot be overcome if we let it dictate our actions.

"I think it's about time I started pressuring him to tell me he loves me, don't you think?" is a question a woman asked after being in a relationship for six months. Telling him how she feels and the direction in which she wants the relationship to go is acting from strength and being a model that the man might emulate. "Pressuring" a man is acting from weakness, and under those circumstances, who would believe his "I love you's" anyway?

3. A general who knows how to create and maintain morale throughout all the ranks will win.

A woman who acts in ways that reflect her worth and integrity will succeed in love. She will be treated with dignity and respect by men because she treats herself similarly.

⫷⫸

If you know the enemy and yourself, you needn't fear the outcome of a hundred battles.

Creating a successful love relationship requires asking yourself the hard questions. Though not equipped with shield or spear, a woman must build her strength and be clear—freed from past emotional entanglements—to be receptive to the experience of love. Whether you're in a relationship or not, take a few minutes and do the following exercises. Begin with a cleansing (designed to allow you to shed those negative thoughts and feelings that tend, at times, to plague all who enter love's arena) and end with a list of renewing affirmations. As you move through these exercises, err always on the side of responsibility and honesty. Daring to shine light into dark areas and attaining real personal clarity isn't easy for anyone, but there is no greater salvation or strength when it comes to loving and being loved.

CLEANSING

If any of the following are "things you tell yourself," now is the time to stop. Rid yourself of any of these self-defeating thoughts. Catch yourself as you hear yourself saying negative things in your head. Stop the words. Learn to turn them around into positive thoughts. If any of these descriptions apply to you, write down the statement in its positive form.

* * *

1. It's too late for love to happen for me.
2. Men are impossible, rotten, and totally incomprehensible.
3. Love is a luxury reserved for others and I should settle and be grateful for what I have.
4. Change within me is impossible.
5. There is something wrong with me to want more from love.
6. I'm not worthy of finding a fulfilling love.
7. My dreams and wishes are silly and shouldn't matter so much.
8. I am too afraid to risk what is necessary to find love.
9. When someone really knows me, I will be thought less of.
10. I am the victim of love rather than its ultimate creator and shaper.

PATTERNS OF ATTRACTION AND CONFLICT

Looking at relationships you have had, what are the dilemmas, problems, or conflicts that have recurred? It is important to understand these repeating themes, for it is *you* who bring them to your relationships. We may chalk up one occurrence to happenstance, two to misfortune, but any pattern, problem, or choice occurring three times is your contribution.

CHOICE

Who are the men you've been drawn to? What was it that attracted you to them? How loving were they? How sensitive to you? How giving? How exciting or dangerous? How open? How honest? How committed? Look for the patterns in your choices. Write down the similarities that repeat. These similarities are not thrust upon you by the men you've known; they are what you bring to the equation. Even if you think you couldn't possibly want that particular pattern or similarity, there is something within you that does or, at least, allows its presence. Be open to your unique contributions. Allow yourself to know them well. Embrace those aspects that are positive and root out those that are not.

CONFLICT

What problems did you have that were serious and threatening to the relationship? What sort of problems did he have that had an important impact on you? What were the issues you couldn't seem to resolve and talked about endlessly? What was the primary problem that led to the end of the relationship?

Again, look for the patterns and similarities. Write down the dilemmas and difficulties that have recurred in your relationships with men. Remember, the responsibility for these patterns is your own. Examine each carefully, trying to understand your connection to the pattern, what it is within you that sets you up for its presence and expression.

UNDERSTANDING FEELINGS

Fill in and complete the following sentences as they relate to your experiences with romantic love:

1. In love, my greatest attribute is _____ .
2. When it comes to taking chances in love, I _____ .
3. If I get close to a man, I'm afraid he will find out _____ .

49

4. When I get my feelings hurt, I _____ .
5. I get angry when _____ .
6. My worst fear is _____ .
7. When it comes to fighting, I _____ .
8. My biggest resentment is _____ .
9. When it comes to trust, I _____ .
10. What makes me most uncomfortable is _____ .
11. I feel valued when _____ .
12. Sexually, I feel _____ .
13. What can keep me from getting close is _____ .
14. What I find most difficult talking about is _____ .
15. What I have least confidence in is _____ .
16. What makes me feel guilty is _____ .
17. When I let myself feel it, I _____ .
18. What I don't seem to be able to make happen is _____ .
19. If my dreams came true, my relationship _____ .
20. I tend to sabotage myself because _____ .

What can you learn about your feelings? Their sources? How they work in your favor or against you? Which are you willing to work on, be more responsible for, to change?

A REMINDER TO YOURSELF

You've had plenty of opportunities to hear friends tell their stories and describe their experiences, conflicts, hopes, and wishes with the men in their lives. You've played the valued advisor, had distinct and practical opinions, known exactly what was going on and what should be done. Sit down and write yourself a letter as if you were that friend. Be as specific, perceptive, and honest as you would be if talking and counseling a dear friend. Be your own best friend. Look at yourself clearly, scrutinize your partner, and come up with the same sort of no-nonsense, useful advice you would lovingly offer a friend.

What did you learn? Where does this lead you in terms of things that might be constructive to do or try in your relationship?

STRENGTHS AND WEAKNESSES

List five strengths, things that you do well in a love relationship. For each, see if you can remember where you learned this strength, who taught you or modeled that strength, and how it has worked successfully in your relationships.

Strengths

Example:

Strength	Painfully honest.
Source	Mother.
How It Works Well for Me	People trust and believe in me.

Revel in your strengths, for so often we get stuck and only mourn our weaknesses. See how the composite of your strengths has created attributes about you that are lovable and to be valued. Lock these strengths away in a safe place to be revisited during moments of doubt.

Now, list five weaknesses, emotional glitches that work against you when you are in a love relationship. Try and find the source of that self-defeating tendency.

What do you know of its origins? Where and how did you learn it? When did you first notice it at work in your life? If you were determined to act in opposition to these tendencies, what do you think you might feel? What are the fears that keep these tendencies in place?

Weaknesses

	Example:
Weakness	Talk too much.
Source	Also my mother.
How It Gets in the Way	I sometimes tell more to men than they are ready to hear.
Fears That Bind It	I don't like silences with men; they make me too uncomfortable.

Take a close look at each weakness. Rather than juding yourself for it, figure out a way to begin to change it. Examine the fears that keep the weakness firmly in place. Changing a weakness is all about challenging fears. Remember that most fears are irrational and easily dispelled by simply moving into them. Select an item from the list you are willing to work on. Put yourself into the situation where the weakness is likely to be operative. Don't do the familiar. Tolerate the discomfort. Feel the transformation into strength.

HABITS

Habits are those things we have done so often and repeatedly that they require little thought. In essence, habits are reflexive and can serve us well (such as brushing one's teeth after meals), but they are often not very discriminating (we may brush irrespective of the meal we ate.) The lack of fine-tuning doesn't get in the way with our good habits, but it does with those that are bad.

Take a few minutes and examine the habits that influence how you are seen by men. Habits that influence how you feel about yourself in a love relationship. Which are your good habits? Which are habits you want to change? What are some of the negative things you do in a relationship that are reflexive vestiges of the past and are not linked to this particular man? Think through some of the ways these habits might sabotage the way you would like to be in a relationship.

A Lover's Affirmations

Affirmations are unambiguous statements that enhance our ability to say "yes" to ourselves. They are not directed toward the past and are intended to move us from the present to the future. Affirmations define the essential choices we all have within us but too often forget. They direct us to our most positive choices and actions.

1. I am willing to risk discomfort and be courageous in love.
2. I am willing to use my wisdom to lead in love.
3. I am willing to learn through my love.
4. I am worthy and hold within the potential for love.
5. My feelings and actions of love make me lovable.
6. I am allowed to honor and nurture myself as a loving person.
7. I acknowledge my strengths and will work on my weaknesses.
8. My love allows me to forgive myself and others who have hurt me.

9. Truth will free me and deepen my capacity for love.
10. I am willing to use my head as well as my heart.

As you say these affirmations, watch for the emergence of those voices that break in and mock, demean, or undermine positive statements about yourself. Don't ignore these voices, for they will show you how you block yourself. Learn to convert these negative statements into positive ones and add them to the list of affirmations. Look for the affirmation(s) that is most difficult to say (sounds silliest, least possible, most embarrassing) and write it down five times each day for a week.

CHAPTER 3

STRATEGIC ASSESSMENTS . . . *LOVE'S FOUR CONSTANTS*

Sun Tzu believed that the generals who are to be triumphant win first and only then go to war. What? How does this come about? Far from the battlefield, in the safety of their headquarters, wise generals make strategic assessments of their own strengths and vulnerabilities as well as those of their opponents. Only when they are fully prepared and certain of victory do they order their first attack. In the art of war, such strategic assessments lead to triumph. In the art of loving, such strategic assessments are a prerequisite for creating and sustaining a lively and fulfilling relationship.

The art of war is of vital importance to the state. It is a matter of life and death, a road either to safety or to ruin. Hence under no circumstance can it be neglected.

—Sun Tzu

HOW YOU CAN CONTROL THE PATH TO LOVE

You can be in control of love's destiny. However, this is not accomplished accidently. You learn to shape your love by being smarter: choosing well, maintaining your own sense of power, and creating a romantic connection. Being smarter in love comes from knowledge and the intelligent use of strategy. And this same thoughtful planning can deepen love into a healthy partnership and create a good marriage. Don't confuse strategy with blandishments or simple unsubtle "manipulation." Lovers have always employed strategy; it is quite simply doing what is natural but *better*.

We'll see that love is not a destination; it is pure process, the journey. The path to love is love itself. Don't make the mistake of defining it too narrowly, for it is comprised of all the myriad day-to-day events and actions along the way. Success comes from how well you choose, what you do, what you give. Yours is the choice to breathe life into love and in so doing make it flourish or, through self-involvement, to let it slip away. Become a skilled artist at something that will fill your heart with happiness.

The art of war is controlled by four constant factors. They are: heaven, earth, the commander, and discipline.

Heaven is:

Feeling absolutely loved and adored
Feeling known, understood, his soul mate
Being able to resolve differences effortlessly
Never feeling hurt or disappointed
Sustained chemistry
Fantasy
Infatuation

* * *

Heaven is a direction, not a destination. Like keeping your body fit, heaven is something you move toward and work on daily.

GETTING THROUGH INFATUATION

Infatuation can be deliciously thrilling, but real love follows a slower, more meandering course. How do you slow down your longings, your rampaging fantasies, your risk of making an absolute and irreversible fool of yourself? It's done by continuing your own normal routine. You saw friends, you went to the gym and to movies, you brought work home before you met him—keep doing it. He's not the sun in your solar system, he's just a new planet, maybe just a comet flaming by. Distractions will keep you from constantly thinking about him. Here's something you should know: he probably hasn't stopped his life for you, and he's not likely to be sitting by the phone waiting for you to call. This doesn't mean he will never love you. It means you are now a possibility in his life. Yes, it's tempting to get head-over-heels giddy and obsessed, but maintaining your own life and friendships can serve as a good reality check.

Many women find it difficult to compartmentalize their emotions. They can't make love all night, then go to work and forget all about him. It's not that they're overemotional, or needy, or deficient in some way. It's probably genetic, gender memory, an archaic survival mechanism. Once a woman makes love, she often becomes attached. It goes back to the earliest of times. Women had to know who the father of their child was, for he would then become the male who would help feed and protect her and their baby. Primitive woman got tunnel vision—all they "saw" was the man with whom they'd had sex. And that little bit of programming has proved pretty enduring. Yet so often, in spite of themselves, once a woman sleeps with a man, the ball is in his court. That's why—not to mention reasons of sexual health—it's best not to sleep with him until you know him, and know he won't disappear. Keep your longer term goal of loving partnership in mind.

Men are also, in many ways, as primitive as they were a million years ago. A man may think he is the master of his destiny, but his mind and body tell him to do two things: continue living and reproduce. Every cell is broadcasting these messages twenty-four hours a day. You think all the time he spends in the gym is first about issues of health and secondarily about looking good? Every trip to the gym is about reproduction. Having a good body will send out important signals of strength and health, which will increase his value in the mating world (women want a man who will give them the best progeny). You think that report he worked so hard on is simply about proving himself, getting ahead, and ego? It is about acquiring the skills and accomplishments that will make him more attractive to women. And that big screen TV? That's not just about seeing the football game better; it's also about having the biggest and the best, which is more exciting and seductive to women. (Women used to love the man with the biggest club and they still do: the Alpha male of the pack.) It's what every stock market purchase and tie selection is about: honing the skills and defining the image necessary to sustain life and reproduce it.

So many things a man does are related to making him more attractive and interesting to a woman. It's natural for all this to turn your head, but no matter how powerful his impact, don't let him set the pace for your involvement. Men are often only short-distance sprinters; they'll start off quickly and then abruptly hit the brakes. A woman should first go slow and only later begin to speed things up.

A woman comes to mind who you may think of as old-fashioned, an anachronism in this day and age. She believed that the way to a man's heart was through making love with him. She had only just met a man who drew her attention when he noisily moved his furniture into the empty apartment next to hers. That first night she brought over a jar of instant coffee (because she had seen someone do it on a commercial) as a neighborly greeting. The second night, despite some nagging misgivings, she offered herself, and he hungrily accepted. Thinking his loneliness would fuel a bond to her, similar offers were made on the several nights that followed. One of which was in the elevator. I'll leave the details to your imagination. On the seventh day, she rang his doorbell only to find it unanswered. Late that night, while alone in her bed, she heard the sounds of lovemaking through the bedroom wall they shared. Sadly, she had to listen and learn that sexual contact is often powerfully bonding for a woman, but much less so for a man. And now that coffee commercial makes her cry.

If you stay out of his bed until you are first in his heart, you will be the more protected. No matter how good women are in bed, men aren't enthralled with early availability and don't commit to acrobatics.

⊰⊱

Earth encompasses distances, danger, and security, whether the ground is open or closed and appraising the chances of life and death.

HOW TO MAKE SENSE OF A MAN'S NEED FOR DISTANCE

In order to understand earth, the more grounded constant in the art of love, let's first look at the notion of distance. When observing love, we must know how far or how close we are to our partners. Distance is an important dynamic in relationships. Most women are relatively comfortable with closeness, while men tend to be somewhat ambivalent about the amount of distance they maintain from the women they love. A man feels lonely, anxious, and detached when he is too far away. And, conversely, he feels engulfed, feminized, and suffocated when he gets too close. This is related to old, universal mother issues that make a man want to run when he begins feeling too dependent upon a woman and equally uncomfortable when he reaches the apex of his autonomy swing. These feelings, as well as the actions they spawn, are normal and naturally male. When a woman hears the words "I think this is all happening too fast" to her it is often the equivalent of "It's over." Any backward movement is likely to make a woman shaky, tearful, and furious. Remember, most women feel more at ease with closeness than men and find it hard to understand their seemingly erratic movements.

To add to the dilemma, women experience mixed feelings about closeness as well, but in their own fashion. Most women think they want to be the center of a man's existence. This is not so, even though they probably will never acknowledge this truth. Women often complain that men put everything else first: their work, sports, friends, even recreation. What happens after the first wave of courtship peaks and a man and woman can be in the same room without having their hands all over each other? Secretly, the woman feels relieved, but she will likely talk about feeling neglected. When a man is calling every other minute, a woman thinks, "This is too much. I hope he's not one of those dependent types I can't stand." But when he doesn't feel the need to call as much, she'll get scared and resent him for it. She'll also complain that things have changed, that he isn't as interested. A woman will feel uncared for if a man doesn't want to stay over, but she'll feel suffocated if she senses he needs to.

The truth is, left to their own devices, men would drive themselves nuts ping-ponging between closeness and independence. But throw a woman's contradictory feelings into the equation and things can get a little haywire. A woman wants a man to be open, but not too open; to be expressive and revealing, but mainly about his feelings of love for them—not about his anxieties about his work or his life. Women want a man to be close and connected but may be less comfortable when he shows signs of neediness. It's why love songs are anguished and why love stories all have a part where the guy loses the girl and has to camp out at the end of her driveway to get her back. Courtship is supposed to be hard because conflict and danger are exciting and create feelings of love.

Strategic considerations of survival also require us to reflect upon the critical issues of danger and security. We all know how dangerous love can be. Our emotions, our hearts, even our physical well-being are vulnerable. If you find yourself extraordinarily afraid to begin a romance with a new man, listen to your heart, for fear is very intuitive. However, this is a smart call only if the danger lies objectively in something you sense in the man and is not your own free-floating worries and insecurities.

Our basic unconscious wish to find someone who feels familiar is instinctively positive. But not all familiarity is desirable, so don't choose someone who feels familiar if, because of your childhood, you associate love with pain or the anxiety of turmoil. Familiarity can be the most dangerous of love's shadows. Karen grew up feeling as though she had to fix men. The first man was her father, a problem drinker who everyone in the house tiptoed around so as not to set off his volcanic and oftentimes violent temper. Karen didn't realize the power of this early template. As an adult, she found herself drawn rather consistently to men in some sort of trouble. She loaned men money and let them move in with her. She did this not because she believed they truly cared for her, but because they were in the middle of some sort of hard time. They needed her, and perhaps out of their need, they would find value and somehow come to love her. She handled these men's affairs, organized their finances, fought their battles, solved their problems. It was only when Karen finally realized there was something vaguely comforting and familiar about a man's problems that she was able to begin giving up her need to fix and rescue. But for Karen, this process wasn't an easy one. To give up the familiar meant giving up the comfort of the known and required finding new ways of seeing her value to a man. It required her risking the possibility of being able to form a connection with a man based upon something other than raw need.

It is only through the resolve to form healthy relationships with men that love can be found. Discard familiarity when it hasn't been kind or fulfilling. Trust your essential and intrinsic value, making them the center of yourself.

If what's familiar is positive, then it is a wise choice to

pursue and cherish a man who you feel you've known for a long time. An unfamiliar or "exotic" man may be dangerous, or at least promises to be more difficult to love. If you choose a man who is totally unlike you, you may never understand each other's hurts and angers. You may never be able to truly know or comfort each other. Men and women are different enough! Commonality of background, even in this fast-changing world, turns out to be a safe predictor of an enduring union.

Why Longing Gets Confused with Love

Another danger lies at the very heart of how we define or interpret love itself. Many of us confuse love with longing. If we had cold, unloving parents, as adults we sense love not by its presence, but by its absence—for us, longing may be all we know about love. But no matter how hurt you were by not receiving affection and approval from your parents, don't look for what is painfully familiar. Recognize this destructive pattern and stop repeating it. You deserve better. Don't settle for anything less than kind and mutual caring: actual, not fantasized. Go for the real thing—being loved, not endlessly wishing, wanting, and longing. And forget about that unavailable man. Let him make other women scream and smash their favorite china!

Which brings us to dangerous men. Women may have four dead bolts on their front door but then still often open their hearts and homes to dangerous men: men they know nothing about except what they've been told, men they know are career heartbreakers, men who appear and disappear like alley cats. Women can break a date with a nice, trustworthy guy on a last-minute call from some smirking cowboy.

Why? Because danger promises excitement and challenge. Of course, you know as well as I do that real love is not about cheap thrills. It's about safety, trust, comfort. Ask yourself—what emotions do I feel when I'm with him? If you're nervous, anxious, keyed up when you're together, and you cry and can't eat or sleep when you're apart, ask yourself: is this a good thing? Surely there are better ways to lose ten pounds!

The dilemma is that the trustworthy man doesn't stir the same intensity of emotion. One's personal soap opera just isn't as dramatic with a man who treats you right. Where's the cliffhanger, the ups and downs, the sheer terror and misery? Where's the riveting tale to regale your girlfriends with when they ask how your romance is going and all you have to say is, "Everything's fine with us"? But let's be practical and realistic for a moment. Look at the couples you know. Most good husbands are more kind than exciting, don't you agree? Now, correct me if I'm wrong, but Indiana Jones is still single. Like any good general, you must know when to move forward, when to withdraw. Remember that love comes with a warning label. It can hurt your heart and waste your years.

Whether a man is open or closed is also of importance. By open, I mean heart, head, and arms. You can tell if a man is open by how soon he introduces you to his friends, whether he admits that breaking up with his last girlfriend had something to do with him too, whether he invites you to his office or brings you home to meet his mother. Listen to his head and heart. Observe his actions and only then move into his arms. Watch, listen, assess.

I am reminded of a Frenchwoman who moved to this country and brought her French customs of loving with her. Jacqui loved passionately and intensely, expecting it would be returned. She kept a very clear head and a strong sense of what she wanted and what was not good enough for her. She would trust a man until it was clear that he was selfish or limited in his capacity to be loving to her. She had the confidence to expect more and the sense to move on. A halfhearted man should not be enough for any woman. It may delight you to know that she found a man who, even though they've been married for five years, still leans across the table at a restaurant to kiss her as they laugh and argue over their Bordeaux.

Choose your partner carefully, remembering that only love sustains life. The wrong partner will destroy you inch by inch, a thousand little disappointments of your heart and spirit every day. The right partner will give you love and make you feel fully alive.

❧

The art of war is controlled by a third constant: the commander. The commander stands for leadership and is defined by the virtues of benevolence, courage, wisdom, and sincerity.

BEING A LEADER IN LOVE

Kyle met Bonnie shortly after they were both out of college, and they quickly moved in together. He hadn't planned it that way, but Bonnie thought they could save rent money, since they were spending all their time with each other anyway. The apartment she found needed a lot of work, and Kyle deferred to Bonnie's choices of paint and wallpaper (although he didn't like the rose color she painted the living room walls or the flower prints she picked out). She would ask Kyle, "What would you like to do tonight?" He seemed rarely to have any preference for food or movie selection, although he frequently grumbled about the restaurant

65

or film she steered him toward. On weekends, he dreaded the 7 A.M. forages through various swap meets and often found himself alone at a refreshment stand, drinking coffee as she scampered off somewhere picking through other people's discards. (But he never planned or suggested any weekend activity on his own other than plopping himself in front of the TV for a day of football.) Bonnie went right ahead dreaming out loud about their future. She talked about her wish for marriage and wanting someday to have children. When she could get his attention long enough to ask him how he felt and what he wanted, all Kyle could seem to muster was, "I kinda like things the way they are." But he really didn't, and after a while, Bonnie didn't either. He woke up one Saturday morning surprised at the sun in his eyes and the note on her pillow. It said: "I've taken the train to N.Y. and will be living with my old roommate Linda. There's food in the fridge to last a few days, hope your team wins the playoffs. Don't bother to call. Good luck with your life."

You're the captain of your ship. Will you step forward to steer or will you drift on that deep blue sea of love? Loving requires active leadership. Forgetting this is a deadly mistake and allows love to move into uncharted waters without map or rudder. This doesn't mean you need to become Captain Bligh, but women are singularly adept skippers on this particular sea. You were born with the attributes of benevolence, wisdom, and courage.

Many men hate making decisions about love, although they certainly like putting their imprint on every other aspect of their lives. Perhaps it's because some men sadly equate a commitment to one woman with lost options, while women sense the opening of new possibilities as commitments are made. But if the man doesn't participate actively, he surely will be swept along by a woman's determination. Nature and a woman both abhor a vacuum. If a man creates one, a woman will fill it.

Leadership is not about control and getting to call all the shots. Many men seem to have a hard time getting this right. They squirm at assuming the responsibility of leading, but at the same time they need to feel in control. Come on, you can't let them have it both ways. Leading isn't all that difficult; it can simply mean that you are both actively involved and that you will create some of the fun and enjoyment in a relationship.

Be a model for leadership in love. This doesn't mean broadcasting or calling attention to this role, it simply means "showing the way" by example. You might just be surprised when the man catches on eventually and assumes some of the responsibility himself. (We can hope, can't we?)

How Women Humanize Men

With benevolence comes humanity, empathy, and the understanding of human frailties. Men need a woman's humanity and are in awe of it (despite the fact that they may never be able to tell you this). A man looks to a woman as both a model and an outlet for feelings and reactions he doesn't easily express. A woman humanizes a man. She makes his tenderness more accessible to him through her own comfort with empathy and compassion. A woman cries her tears as well as his, teaching him to be more accepting of the lump in his throat he hesitates to acknowledge.

The gift of empathy is not to be confused with pity or problem solving. No one appreciates empathy more than a woman. Just like men, women need someone to tell their troubles to. A man should take this as an honor, for it reflects a woman's wish to be understood. That's right, "understood." She wants a man to be a problem understander *not* a problem solver. But a man processes the interaction in a different way. For a man, problems are to be solved, not understood. It is easy to feel depreciated when a man steps in and gives unsolicited advice and the obvious solutions you could come up with yourself. Don't take this personally; he thinks he's doing something nice.

To most women, benevolence comes easily. Your own benevolence in love can be gauged by your ability to accept your partner's imperfections, your willingness to help him grow stronger and wiser through your warmth and kindness.

Which brings me to an important maxim about love: look for the good in your partner. In love, you hold the powers for pleasure and disappointment. However, too often we forget the wonderful, endearing little things that first caught our eye and made us fall in love. And how easy it is to get caught up in the inevitable annoyances that plague even the best of relationships. Don't look to find the bad in your partner; rediscover the good.

A young woman, Aubry, has a hard time seeing the overall good when the smallest cloud is hanging over her relationship with Scott, her husband of two years. Anything, no matter how minor—something he did or didn't do, something he said or didn't say—causes her to go ballistic. She fixates. It grows. She roars. She rages. She tears up his photograph. She pulls all her friends into the recounting of the incident as it gets worse with each telling. High drama and misery. Her mother told her to write out a list of Scott's good qualities—something to refer to when things weren't going well. So the next time Aubry found herself questioning the relationship, she went to her desk to find the list. It read: "He went to the drugstore to get me medicine when I was sick and couldn't lift my head from the pillow." That was all it said. The list was short. But it was enough to send her back into his arms.

Don't make the mistake of finding a great guy and then start picking him apart. Don't allow yourself to fixate on his imperfections. Don't complain about him to your friends—it's pure poison. Focus on the enjoyment of having him in your life and how you can love him more. Respect and encourage him more. Focus on the rose, not the thorn.

WHY MEN CAN BE COWARDS IN LOVE

Courage comes from having been to battle before and knowing it won't kill you. And it takes courage to risk loving again. It is courageous to love a person who is taller than you, hairier than you, someone who can make you pregnant. It is easy to act with confidence in moments of comfort and safety. What distinguishes courage is the willingness to act during times of uncertainty and emotional danger. Brave actions are those that you know are right for you. It is brave to insist that a man wear a condom. Telling a man that you're looking for a real relationship almost deserves a medal.

Men secretly admire courageous women who are clear about what they want. This is because many men have been brainwashed to think they shouldn't have to lead with courage in the concerns of the heart. Rather they should be a tough "guy's guy," focused on more important issues like the baseball standings and where the Dow Jones average is; that they should be a holdout, a rat, a heartbreaker, the irresistible bad boy; that they should only give in after a woman has worn them down; that they should surrender their independence only after having put up a valiant fight.

The truth is, most men back in to love and force the woman to take the more courageous stands. Women have been led to believe this is because women are more interested in love; that women need men more than men need women. You know that's not true, even men know that's not true though they're not likely to admit it. Men are embarrassed about their interest in love. Consequently, they allow women to feel nervous and exposed because they don't want to feel nervous and exposed themselves. "If anyone has to feel that vulnerable, it might as well be the woman" is how many men think (even at the expense of her feeling desperate and neurotic).

A lot of men are pretty cowardly when operating in the heart arena. But healthy men aren't frightened by their feelings, even when they are tender, gentle, or even needy. They don't make a woman pay for the courage of her directness; they are direct themselves. They don't force a woman to declare she wants a serious relationship; they say it first. And a healthy, loving man doesn't make a woman squirm and feel as though she has to beg for exclusivity. He offers it. Perhaps the bravest of actions a man takes is to make a commitment to the woman he loves without putting her in the unenviable position of coercing him into it.

LEARNING FROM THE PAST AND STAYING IN THE PRESENT

Wisdom comes from learning from experience. It is collected from keen observation, trial and error, and the accumulated learning only living can provide. An important aspect of wisdom is not to allow our past to ruin our present. Mistakes and past damage are high marks of drama and easily become fixed in our minds. When you look back, what do you remember most about your sister? The day she lent you her cashmere sweater or the day she socked you in the back in front of a boy? What do you remember most about your second love? The day you met him or the day he left?

We are the sum of the memory of our experiences. Smart women understand the thoughts and feelings that are attached to painful past events and can tell the difference between them and the unfolding present. Try not to blame your cold fathers for your tendency to love men either too much or too little. And don't hold your overly protective or warm fathers responsible for your tendency to love men too much or too little. Make sure you are moving forward and not allowing the past to shape your future. A woman cannot travel the path of love with unnecessary baggage.

HOW HONESTY ANCHORS TRUST

Being a leader in love means you must also master the attribute of sincerity: the core element of trust. Without trust, love cannot exist. (Obsession yes, habit yes, neurotic connection yes, love no.) Here's where a lot of men get into trouble. Men don't set out to be insincere or liars. They just set out to be expedient—insincerity is a means to an end. They don't intend to deceive, they deceive themselves. ("When I said it, I meant it.") Some men will say or do anything to get a woman into bed. Understandably, many women think men are not truthful, but it's more complicated than that. A man will often tell a woman what he thinks she wants to hear. But a woman listens to what a man says and takes it as gospel. And she will definitely hold it against him if he breaks his promises. A man should never ask a woman to give him her heart until he knows he can begin giving her his own.

It is easy to do what makes us feel more comfortable or secure at the moment. It is harder to do what is right—to be honest when it would be easier to hide, to give even though it's easier to receive, to understand even though the impulse is to judge, and to acknowledge your responsibility in a conflict rather than focusing solely on his. Strive to do your best and expect no less from him.

When evaluating the sincerity of his character, look more closely at what he *does* than what he *says*. Never make the mistake of feeling exempt from some fatal flaw of his you see, even though it is directed toward another. Is he afraid to walk past his old girlfriend's building? Does she speak highly of him? Does he honk and yell at old ladies who can't drive very well? Meet his mother. As your mother has probably told you, how he treats his mother will be similar to how he will treat you, if not now, then in the future.

The last of the great constant factors is discipline.

APPLYING THE ART OF DISCIPLINE

Discipline is the fourth constant factor that controls the art of love. By discipline, I mean developing control over conflicting emotions so the greater goal can be achieved. It is important to keep the greater goal (love) at the front of your mind. It is often difficult to do this when we are in the heat of battle and emotions take over.

One of the hallmarks of discipline is not to take

things too personally. In fact, most of other people's actions have very little to do with us. If he falls asleep, it's not because he doesn't want to be with you. He's tired. People behave in the ways they do for their own reasons and because of their own past experiences. It's only our own insecurity or narcissism, neither of which are very appealing, in a romantic relationship that makes us tend to assume everything is "about us." If he waits to say "I love you," it might be because he got into trouble for saying it too soon in the past.

Of course, it's hard to take yourself out of the picture. It is particularly difficult when a man said he would phone early in the week and it's now Thursday and he hasn't called. Of course you want to call him. Though calling him would reduce your anxiety of the moment, it would also now give him the momentum of control. Use all the discipline you have. Sit on your hands, or if you can't, have a friend come over and sit on the phone.

It's not that you shouldn't take initiative, and obviously, it's not that you shouldn't call a man. It's that conducting relationships takes self-control, pride, and a belief that your feelings and entitlements are important. If your best friend were asking advice in this situation, you'd tell her not to call someone who had broken a promise.

Be disciplined around giving and receiving. When giving, make sure to be fair. If you are too generous or too stingy with time or emotions, you will hurt your own cause. Being too generous is the usual problem with a woman. Don't give all your supplies to someone else.

If you take care of his entire life, he will have your time and his time as well. He will have your love and his love if he doesn't know how to give. There are certain litmus tests for his capacity for reciprocity: did he visit your grandmother in the old-age home after you've visited his seventeen times? Does he ever take your clothes to the cleaner, pay for them, and bring them back? Does he make the bed at your house? Receiving too much is not good for your head and heart either. Don't let him pay for everything, even if he's a gazillionnaire and your career requires saying, "Do you want fries with that?"

Many men have a hard time understanding the discipline involved in giving and receiving. A "gift" is something a woman *wants*. Giving a woman her freedom is not a gift unless she wants it. Giving her Sunday off because he wants to play golf is not a gift. Getting tickets to an off-road vehicle show is not a gift. Women want things that are hard for a man to give, like unrequested flowers, a card not on her birthday, or a back rub that is not necessarily a prelude to sex. They like a man who will get up from dinner and start clearing and washing without saying, "I'll help you with the dishes." They like a man who changes a lightbulb in the refrigerator because he notices it is out, a man who puts the toilet seat down when he's through, someone who tells her how good she looks without her having to ask. All this takes a lot of discipline on a man's part.

Most women want to be given the things that are hard for a man to give but don't want to hear how difficult it's been to give them. That spoils it. Women want a man to enjoy spending all day Saturday looking through paint chips, wallpaper samples, and upholstery fabric because he thinks the place needs to be spruced up, too. Instead of turning over with a grunt and saying, "Can we talk about this tomorrow?" after a quarrel, a woman wants him voluntarily to offer, "Let's talk this through and not go to sleep angry."

HOW NOT TO REWARD BAD ACTIONS

Many men try to be good partners and can't understand why women focus on their bad behavior and ignore the good. They come to this conclusion because "bad" actions stir up more intense feelings and concerns and are the ones that a woman needs to talk about. Men will do anything to avoid one of "those discussions." The truth is, men bask in the warm glow of a woman's approval. Many a rough edge can be slowly smoothed away by a woman finding those things a man does right and praising him generously.

The most deadly mistake women make is not their failing to reward good actions, but their tendency to reward bad ones. We offer a small story, of Serena. Serena lives in the flats of Akron, but this man she met stepped off the slopes of Mt. Olympus. Yet no one else saw his magic. When her friends rolled their eyes, Serena thought they were blind or perhaps jealous of her good fortune. He was a doctor for God's sake, a healer, a saint.

Although she had known him for months, his answering service was the only number she had for him. (So she could always get in touch with him, he said.) Serena never saw his house. (He was remodeling and wanted to surprise her when it was finished, he said.) Their lovemaking was always early in the evening, and invariably he had to leave soon after in response to an urgent page. By now, I am sure you know where Serena's story is going. She cried her tears alone, for even though she wanted him to stay, she understood that a sick patient needed his attention more than she did. Although he had told her that he didn't like surprises, Serena figured his birthday would be a good exception. Yes, with balloons and a bottle of champagne, she followed him home from his office. And yes, it was Serena who was in for a surprise.

She was flooded with relief and understanding when

he called the next day explaining a long dead marriage, martyrdom for the sake of the children, feeling tortured for having lied to her. And when he asked her to forgive him and let him come over, she did! That was two years ago. Last week, his third child was born, and he still stops off to visit Serena on his way home. She's in pain. She keeps hoping. Someday. Someday. So sad. So painful. Astonishingly, so common.

The purpose of punishment is never simply to inflict pain. Rather, its goal is the protection of your dignity. The best way to punish someone is to deprive them of you. If a man has behaved poorly, he can't have you or speak to you. Both simple and effective. To withhold punishment when it should be administered is to betray yourself. It is better to end a relationship for the sake of your dignity. Look at the reality of the situation and act on it. If he doesn't make you safe, don't make him feel safe. This is done by closing the door.

❧❧

These are the strategist's keys to victory.

Don't leave the work of love in your life to anybody but yourself. Step up to the challenge, for when performed with grace and character, loving is the most interesting thing we do in our lives. Never take yourself from the center of that experience. Love doesn't simply happen; you create its potential and sustain its presence. Hold these understandings close to your heart. Love is a process of deeds, not words; of actions, not intentions.

CHAPTER 4

WAGING WAR . . .
TIMING IS EVERYTHING

Victory is the main object in war. When the fight is long, your strength will be sapped and your treasure spent.

— Sun Tzu

HOW MEN FALL IN LOVE

Victory is the main object in love. If you do not accomplish this quickly, your strategies will be discovered, your weaknesses laid bare, and your spirit and resolve dampened. But what really is victory? All too often, women confuse proof with victory. Commitment certainly is confirmation, but victory in love with a man is a process. And that process is signaled by one overarching event: the man's emotional movement toward the woman.

Commitment often presents an artificial dilemma to many women. If properly understood, commitment need not be a problem at all. Too frequently, women allow their concerns about the depth of a man's love to tyrannize their conduct. Their insecurities are turned loose and result in one of those painful conversations when the woman asks for a confirmation of the man's caring. This is a dangerous mistake.

A man places no higher value on the relationship than the value a woman feels for herself. Insecurity damages that value and lowers the importance a man assigns to the relationship. For a man, there is no greater sign of a woman's insecurity than her need to push him for a premature commitment.

Here's the way it works:

If a woman contains her insecurities, a man will:

Be attentive
Feel uncertain about her need for him
Have peaked interest
Want to move toward the woman
Make a commitment

If a woman broadcasts her insecurities, a man will:

Be distracted
Feel certain and sure of her need for him
Gradually lose interest
Want to move away from the woman
Avoid any sort of commitment

Actually, men are rather simple creatures when it comes to love. But there is a trick! They are very different from women, and it is essential that this be understood. You see, men like to keep women a little off guard. They like to perpetuate the myth that women need them more than they need women. They feel safer that way, protected from their dreaded fears of dependency. Men fall in love as they move toward a woman. *A man connects to a woman as he pursues her.* It's always been that way: men do, women are. You've seen all those nature shows where the male of the species is preening, turning cartwheels, or clashing horns with some competitive adversary while the female waits quietly nearby, purring with discriminating pleasure. Well, men need to do the same sort of thing in a much more subtle, but no less important, way. They don't charge one another with their heads down or puff up brightly colored feathers; they court. For a man, the dance of courtship is choreographed in an emotional realm of promise attached to an unpredictable outcome, of fascinating potential swimming in a sea of uncertainty. Men like to win a woman's respect, her affection, and then her love. This active courtship dance, this process of winning the woman, is precisely the mechanism that sends the message to the man's brain that he is falling in love.

Falling in love for a man is about trying, showing, hoping, and proving, all of which are his attempts to close the gap he senses between him and the woman. For the man it is the very process of movement that says "I love this woman." If the woman closes the gap too soon, the man has no emotional space in which he can move in her direction. And no movement, trying, proving, or wishing means no messages to the brain that tell him he is in love. If there is no gap, his love connection to the woman lurches to a stop, and he thinks he has found a nice platonic friend.

Bonding is a continuous experience for men and a more discreet one for women. But most women don't understand this, since a man's process is so different from their own. Women are sometimes afraid that the man will get away if they don't catch him. Smart women know men like to catch women and not be caught by them. Men are acutely conscious of leverage and position. The needy woman automatically falls into a slot of lower position and risks being devalued. Warrior women contain their neediness and maintain the man's interest.

Men hate being uncertain and squirm in its presence, but nevertheless, they feel passion and driving interest when a woman creates it. Particularly when she can do it in small, measured doses. Women feel both safe and passionate when they are certain. Men do not. Men feel safe, but certainty pledged too quickly kills a man's passion. Warrior women are able to tolerate small amounts of distance, knowing this distance creates the space and sense of uncertainty a man needs to feel to continue bonding.

Commitment comes easily to the warrior woman for she has disciplined herself not to be betrayed by insecurity. Learn to wait for the man who is typically slower in acknowledging his deepening connection and need for the woman. A smart woman doesn't fall prey to her own vulnerability but instead is patient, creating the vulnerability of uncertainty in the man. She moves subtlety toward him and then away again, knowing this ebb and flow will fuel the man's interest in her. The man can then do nothing other than commit his heart to her, for her motions are sensitive to the rhythms of a man's desire.

❦

When your weapons are dulled and your spirits dampened, your strength wasted and treasure spent, other leaders will appear and take advantage of your damaged position. Then even though you may seek out the advice of the wise, none will be able to reverse what you have set in motion.

How Women's Patience Leads to Men's Proofs

A woman warrior's weapons are stealth, unpredictability, and patience. These skills will serve you well in handling a man as he zigs and zags toward his awareness of love and a woman's importance. This being said, it is dangerous to let your spirits be daunted and your strength sapped, for your position will be weakened. Conserve your precious energy. If patience is not practiced in the beginning stages of a relationship, the man will stop moving toward the woman and become rooted in place as surely as if his feet had been encased in cement. All women recognize this stuck point immediately, and a clever woman knows what to do to remedy the situation.

Tara didn't know what to think when Kevin seemed to take a backward step in their relationship, but she knew she had to do something. Tara had met Kevin when he was only recently out of a long and complicated relationship. In the beginning, she had been careful to keep things light, understanding Kevin had a lot to sort through. She also wanted to protect herself. In many ways, Tara thought Kevin was perfect—someone to see occasionally while she interviewed for jobs with law firms and studied for the upcoming bar exam. Whether anything came of this relationship or not was fine, and the last thing she needed, she told herself, was anything else that was too involving or demanding.

Their needs dovetailed nicely for some time, even including a respite when Kevin tried a reconciliation with his ex-girlfriend. It was a brief and failed experience, and when Kevin told Tara about his feelings, she felt for the first time that he was finally finished with that relationship and was ready to move on.

Tara began seeing Kevin again, and they resumed their easy pace. The bar exam came and went. And by the time Tara learned she had passed, she had already been hired as an associate with a large law firm. Kevin not only seemed to have moved on from his previous relationship, but, over the weeks, wanted to spend more and more time with Tara. Occasionally they went away on the weekends, and Kevin invited her to his hometown to attend the wedding of his best friend. There, Tara met Kevin's parents, whom she liked immediately. At one point, Tara was taken aside by his mother, who whispered to her conspiratorially how much she thought Kevin cared for Tara.

When they flew home late that Sunday night, Tara knew something important had shifted within her. Resting her head on his shoulder, she found herself thinking what a good father Kevin would be, having seen him playing and talking with a number of the children at the wedding. She even thought, for the first time, that she would like him to be the father of her children.

Kevin had wanted to stay over but hadn't planned ahead and brought along any clothes for work. Tara did something she had never done before; she told him to bring over some of his clothes and leave them there in her apartment. It was only after that conversation that she felt something shift in Kevin. It was imperceptible at first, but as the days passed, she knew Kevin had stopped pursuing her. Kevin was stuck.

Tara's instincts told her to move closer herself, ask him what was wrong, do anything to recapture the way he had been with her before. Tara had been at this impasse in a previous relationship and knew that her pressing him had only succeeded in driving him away. She was determined not to make the same mistake again.

Tara knew that what she had to do was counter-intuitive. She understood that the only thing she had done that was different was to try to close the emotional gap between them. At first she was hurt, but she reminded herself that this was Kevin's issue and not her own. She was resolute in not taking this personally. The first thing Tara did was to accept an invitation from a college roommate to come and visit for a weekend in Chicago. She had thought of turning down the invitation to be with Kevin, but she understood that he still needed a bit of time and distance to stay comfortable in the relationship.

Tara's sensitivity to the natural ebb and flow of a man's comfort with closeness was rewarded. Kevin still needed more time and experience in the pursuit mode, moving toward her. A few months later, it was Kevin asking if he could leave some things at her apartment.

Tara's experiences are not at all uncommon. Victory in love is in keeping the man moving toward you. As long as this is happening smoothly, the proof will naturally follow. Impatience is your enemy. Don't fall into the trap of interpreting a man's natural snail-like pace early in a relationship as something wrong. Expect it. Embrace its presence. Understand that the man is struggling with his wish to move closer to you. Know that for him to accomplish that movement means overcoming his fear of emotional closeness.

A woman who doesn't understand this will take the man's vacillations to heart and run the risk of pushing him away. She will become exhausted with her efforts and despondent with their futility.

Belief in your value as a loving partner is one of your most cherished assets. A slow-moving man's cautions are his own and not a reflection of your worth. Guard your value ferociously, for if you do not, your confidence will plummet and anxiety and doubt will take its place.

Men are sensitive to a woman who abandons her belief in herself and are prone to abandon her as well. A woman who feels diminished behaves in a diminished way and loses her attractiveness to a man. If that happens, he will be drawn to other women who may take your place. Then, even if you ask the wisest of your friends for advice, no one will be able to change the actions to which you will have contributed.

One who knows the disastrous effects of a protracted war can appreciate the importance of bringing it to an end quickly.

WHEN TO ERR ON THE SIDE OF SPEED

Any woman who has gone through the painful tug of war with an ambivalent man knows the dangers in that struggle, which brings out the most petty aspects of both women and men. While patience is important, undying patience is not. Knowing when to hold back and when to push forward is the trick.

Speed then is a very tricky variable. But there are some useful rules of thumb. Speed is important in the very beginning of a relationship, when it is important to set things on their way along a romantic path. Then, during the middle phase of courtship, speed loses its value and patience must preside.

At the beginning, speed is critical in establishing a romantic connection. A man needs to clearly understand and feel his attraction to a woman. If the relationship remains undefined for any length of time, a man will tend to drift and define the relationship himself as something other than romantic. Some men are especially prone to such murky slides and can leave women baffled and at a loss as to what happened. These men tend to be on the shy side and need more specific input from a woman. Men in general, and particularly those who may be a bit shy, need to be put in touch with the depth and direction of their feelings. And for this, a woman's assistance is greatly helpful.

Don't wait for a man to define the relationship, for more often than not, he may be waiting for you. Men are very dependent upon signals from a woman that reassure them that their interest is understood and reciprocated. How many of you have known a woman who has gone out to dinner with a man a number of times and yet still is not sure of his interest in her? At first she is pleased that he doesn't come on too hard and fast. She likes that he is respectful, self-contained, not all over her physically. Then later, she is confused and begins to wonder if he is attracted to her or simply enjoys her company in some platonic way. And, if more time passes without some definition, usually some sort of romantic physical contact, a woman often feels unwanted and increasingly puzzled about the man's intentions.

The man who is waiting for signals is equally confused. He needs a woman's encouragement to move forward (some specific acknowledgment of her interest). The man thinks that he is expressing the direction of his intentions by continuing to ask the woman out and waits for some signal in return. Make sure that you give it to him if you are interested and do it as soon as you become aware of your feelings. It is better to err on the side of speed in creating a romantic direction to a relationship even if certain mistakes are made. Creating a romantic definition puts the man in touch with your importance in a more focused way, which is essential for love to proceed and deepen.

RECOGNIZING A LOSING BATTLE

Once a romantic connection has been established, slow

things down. Enjoy the middle phase of the bonding process at a more relaxed pace. There does, however, reach a point where speed or movement again becomes crucial. This is during the third phase of courtship, which is after a woman and man have had a prolonged chance to get to know each other. This third phase is the time when feelings deepen and commitments are made. For a man, eighteen months is a rough guideline. If a man has been in an exclusive relationship for at least that amount of time, he should be ready. This is the moment to again speed things up. Doing this is necessary because there are some men who are not simply and naturally a bit slow; they are narcissistic and resistant to commitment.

This self-centered man differs from his plain vanilla, slower brother in two critical ways. He is more selfish in general and lacks an empathetic understanding of the woman's feelings and needs. This man not only makes women crazy, but he is often so clever that the woman can end up feeling as if it is her fault. This man should be recognized and avoided at all cost.

Wendy finally managed to corner Jack. Or so she thought. They had been seeing one another for three years, and she felt that some sort of real plan for the future was long past due. It wasn't as if she hadn't asked for it before, but Jack always seemed to find a way to worm his way out of it.

First, he had to pay off his lawyer for the divorce he had gone through shortly before Wendy met him. Next, it had been his children, who needed more time to adjust, even though Wendy felt as though she got along with them wonderfully and was more actively involved with them than Jack seemed to be. Then came a job change, which curtailed any talk of the future. Jack told her in anger one night that she was being selfish and unfair by not understanding how pressured these conversations were and how he needed all his energy and focus to make a success of the new job.

Again Wendy fell silent and tried her best to be supportive. But as the months wore on and his job became increasingly routine, she found herself brooding over the question once more. Thinking about it, Wendy felt that her needs always took second position to anything that was happening in Jack's life. He had taken her out of circulation and placed himself at the center of her existence while she felt that she orbited his as a distant and unimportant moon. So hurt and upset was she by his behavior that she found herself sniping at him in front of friends. During one particularly uncomfortable dinner out with another couple, she said to Jack between soup and salad, "So, Jack, why don't you tell me again why you're so squeamish about getting married. Maybe if Susan and Terry heard your story they could help explain it to me."

Jack gave her a tight smile, drained the rest of his martini, and shot back, "Why don't you tell everybody what your big rush is. I feel more like someone you're hustling in one of your real estate deals than someone you care about."

When the table fell silent, Wendy vowed never again to bring up the question of marriage.

Days passed before she broke her promise and broached the subject anew, detesting herself as she said the words. She was shocked by Jack's response when he threw up his hands and exclaimed, "All right. You've worn me down. I'll marry you, but we've got to work out some kind of premarital agreement first."

Having an exit contract negotiated even before the vows were said was not her idea of romance. Nevertheless, she went along with his wishes. If this is what it took to make him comfortable, she would do it. But as Jack became increasingly protective and self-serving in their bargaining sessions, so too did she. It wasn't until she heard Jack wanting to make sure that his two-hundred-dollar credit at a local department store would be added to his side of the ledger that Wendy finally understood just how small and withholding Jack was.

She heard how pathetic her voice sounded when she tried to get him to leave issues this small out of the contract. Couldn't they assume some fairness and rationality? she had asked him. When Jack said no, she knew it was over. Wendy walked out of his apartment and forced herself to hold her head up, trying to rescue some of the quiet dignity she had lost along the way.

〜〜

Once war is declared, waste no time. Move into the enemy's territory quickly. Timing and surprise are of utmost importance.

HOW TO USE AN ULTIMATUM

When the time has come for some deeper or more lasting acknowledgment of love, weigh the following very carefully. First, most women reach a point of feeling commited about twice as fast as do most men. It is always best to give the man a chance to bring up the notion of commitment. Second best is to broach the question of commitment and marriage yourself, but only after you already know the answer. And it is an *affirmative* one. The man hasn't been born who doesn't feel more passionate pulling than being pushed. The moment a man feels pushed, his heels dig into the ground the wrong way. All motion stops. And remember, it is motion on the part of the man that creates and is essential for his continuing to fall deeper and deeper in love.

However, there does come a time when love needs to move forward—when words should be spoken, promises discussed, and plans made. What happens when you've been more than patient, given him months beyond the time when you felt ready, and still the man has made no move toward commitment? This is what you must do: begin by expressing your feelings and wishes as clearly as possible to him. Tell him exactly what you want without putting any pressure on him to have to say anything in response. No pressure, for now. Not a hint. This should be done a number of times so that there can be *no* confusion about the depth of your feelings or your wish for a future with him. For most men, this is sufficient to cause them to examine their own feelings and move in a clearer way toward the woman.

But what, you may wonder, do you do if you believe a man cares yet still isn't able on his own to surmount the anxiety around commitment? This is a time when you might want to consider the use of the ultimatum. But before you do, consider the following: you may wish out loud any number of times, but you *cannot* use an ultimatum twice.

The ultimatum is a very bold and direct action. It rivets a man's attention unfailingly. Guaranteed. But a successful ultimatum also requires indirect action, which many women neglect. Having gotten the man sensitized, they stop with the ultimatum. Or worse, simply continue to apply more direct action—a big mistake. For example, a woman seeking a promise of marriage might say something like, "We've been together now for two years. I know making a commitment is hard for you, but I love you and feel ready. I want you to

89

think about it and tell me what you've decided, in say three months. If after that time you still can't make a commitment, I'm going to leave you and find someone who can." Then she immediately begins with an end-less interrogation of his thoughts and feelings, with-draws and pouts, or makes veiled threats—all just more direct action. Any man knows this woman is going to cave in and rescind the ultimatum in the end, for she wears her desperation on her sleeve.

Smart women do things a bit differently. Give the same ultimatum but understand that anxiety is your enemy and don't succumb to it. Contain your discom-fort and let the man struggle with his. Believe in the value of the love you bring to the relationship and the legitimacy of what you're asking him for in return. Put yourself at risk, trusting that either way the decision falls will allow you to move forward in your life. Smart women let uncertainty hang in the air like mist, under-standing that a man who truly cares will be affected by it. Be loving and present, continuing to conduct your-self in the way most consistent with being a good lover and friend. And even though a storm may rage within, you must maintain an outward serenity.

Smart women never make idle threats and are at peace with their call for a decision. They don't cajole, they don't probe, and they don't punish, for they realize that is counterproductive. They wait quietly and lov-ingly and let the man sweat.

At the end of the first month, give him a simple reminder that he has two months yet to go. After two months, let him know there is one month to go. Don't treat him differently, don't withdraw. Don't be cross and edgy. He thinks you've given him three months and doesn't see that each day that goes by may be a small torture. Don't panic. Keep being affectionate and generous with your love. Understand that his struggle is with himself and not against you. Don't crack.

So now it's time—"that" day is approaching. Don't draw attention to its arrival. Plan something simple where the two of you can be alone. He may not even remember that this is the day. After all, you're the one who's been keeping track. That's fine. Don't take it personally.

At the right moment, let him know that this is the day, the three months have elapsed. Tell him again very simply how you feel about him and what it is you want. Ask him if he's made up his mind. This is where you have to be strong, willing and ready to handle not just what you hope to hear but also the truth, whichever way it turns.

If the man loves you, he will make the commitment you've been wanting. Don't be put off by the fact that this isn't the most romantic way a man can acknowledge his love for a woman. If his answer is yes, he's won an important internal battle. He's thought about the value of your love and placed it above the trailings of his ambivalence.

Men only feel pressured by nagging, teeth gnashing, and the wordy barbs that make them ooze guilt. Men don't feel pressured by a simple time line and a clean request for a decision. Don't see him as having given in, or been forced, for that will only demean him and the love he brings. You didn't force him into anything; you asked him to choose something, to focus on what was of value and fulfilling in his life.

After he has professed his love and commitment, love this man and move forward with whatever plan seems most appropriate. Don't look back at the commitment with any sense of negativity. See it for what it was: a simple awareness and statement of appreciation and enduring value.

And what about the man who can't say yes, can't

acknowledge the importance of you in his life, can't take the next step? You know. You have to leave him and find a better home for your love. No, "Can't we just leave things the way they are for a while?" isn't good enough. Neither is "Why don't you move in here and we'll see what happens." If you get suckered by any of these tricky variations a man might throw your way, he's got you. And the back door, his freedom. If you succumb here, he will never believe you again. He'll know he has the upper hand, and he won't hesitate to use it. He will see your request for a decision as desperation, smoke. Your giving in, no matter how articulately he may plead for it, will never increase his love for you. It will damage it. You will be weakened, seen as someone who doesn't mean what she says, taken for granted.

You must not let this happen. Show him the back door. Ask for your key back. Don't see him. Tell him you don't want him to call. Don't talk to him. Don't talk to his friends. Don't call his mother. Don't make inquiries. Shut down your own friends as sources of information to him.

Do move forward with your life. If he comes to his senses, let him dream up something dramatic and clear enough to get your attention. Let it be a statement on his part that love has cleanly won. That he is ready. Anything less and you'll just be starting the painful cycle once again, and the credibility you've fought so hard for will be lost. Your belief in yourself will be shredded. Only you can prevent this from happening. Your love is the most valuable of commodities. Don't settle for a man who doesn't appraise it as priceless.

A country is made poor by a military operation that requires supplies to be transported a long distance.

TIMING AND THE DANGER
OF OBLIGATION

At what point do we tend to settle into our lives with our partners, get a little sloppy, forget the special nature of love? At what time do we forget that love is a gift and begin forming self-centered expectations? After how much time spent together does love shift from our wish to make our partners happy to our feeling that it is now their obligation to make us happy? When is it time to shift from giving to taking, from an awareness of our partner's well-being to an emphasis upon our own? When is it time to make our comfort, our feelings, our particular needs, the centerpiece of the relationship? The answer, of course, is never, but how easy it is to forget. The reason a man bonds to a woman is because she makes his experience in the world better. He feels stronger, safer, healthier, more secure and content than he does without her. These are the very same reasons a woman falls in love with a man. But all too frequently, we ignore this most basic of love's underpinnings.

Too often we forget that love is not ownership, not obligation or duty. Love is not unconditional, and it is not meant to be a solution to problems. Instead of feeling more comfortable and relaxed after a commitment, we all too often amplify our expectations and neglect the small but significant tokens of enjoyment that brought the love together in the first place. This can be a dire mistake, for romantic love is fragile.

Take Mark for example, a man who tried to do the right thing. He met Marianne two years ago, and over that time, they have become increasingly inseparable. From the first, Mark thought she was wonderful and couldn't wait to introduce her to his close friends and family. He wasn't withholding or elusive, and Marianne was comforted by his easy and direct style.

If anything, Mark pushed the speed of the relationship. Marianne, having been hurt quite badly in an earlier relationship and feeling more protective, trailed just a step behind. Mark never pressured her or tried to increase her pace. He told her how he was feeling and what he wanted as simply as he knew how. After the first month, Mark explained that he didn't want to see anyone else, and, after a few months, she had met most of his friends as well as his family. Marianne came to rely on Mark's reliability and counted upon his availability to be there for anything she needed that was important. Not one of her friends had anything but the most positive things to say about Mark, and as time passed, many asked her when they were going to get married.

It didn't come as a surprise to anyone when Mark proposed. Nor was it a surprise when Marianne joyfully accepted. But that singular moment created a change that was to have devastating consequences to the relationship. Marianne somehow forgot that love is voluntary, optional, ultimately conditional no matter what the stated promises may be. She began treating Mark as if he were a possession. Love no longer was seen as a gift but more as an obligation.

In the early days of the transformation, Mark chalked up the subtle shift in her behavior to her having been hurt in the past, and he tried to overlook it. But as time went on, Marianne squeezed Mark more and more tightly. She began complaining about his friends and even the modest time he continued to spend with them. She resented the evenings he spent on the Internet even though the majority of it was spent collecting research for a master's degree he was working on part-time. Then it was his mother, who he helped with voluminous loan papers when she decided to start a new business. Marianne forgot to comment on what Mark brought to her life and focused instead on what he took elsewhere. Rather than rewarding him for the real gift of his love, she punished him for his interest and involvement in anything that divided his attention to her.

Smart women take in the love they receive from the man and feel deserving of the connection they helped construct. But they don't become lulled or content with small victories but instead focus their strategies on the larger goal. The larger goal is always generous and sustained love. And to sustain love means understanding the necessity of rewarding a man's sensitive and loving actions. Sadly, Marianne lost Mark's love as he felt progressively more deficient and inadequate over time. Rather than feeling as though he were pleasing her, he saw only her unhappy face, letting him know that somehow he had let her down again.

MOVE INTO HIS LIFE, NOT INTO HIS HOUSE

Having secured a commitment of a man's love, move quickly to establish the evidence of your presence. Listen carefully to his life story and tell him your own and how he is included in it. It is to your advantage to integrate yourself into his life. Meet his friends. Spend time with them and allow them to know you, to see how well you treat the man, and what a positive addition you are. Be respectful and dignified with his friends, and they will repay you with their loyalty. Also, be sure to have him introduce you to his women friends. Befriend them if possible and never put him in a position of feeling as though you are threatened by them. Ask him about some of his old relationships. If any of these women are still a part of his life, make a plan to meet them. Find out from their point of view what led to the end of the relationship.

Get to know the man's family and make a special effort to establish a connection with his mother. This may be even more important should his mother be one of those particularly difficult sorts. Making sense of his mother will allow you to better understand the man's relationship with her. And the way he relates to her will have some distinctive collaterals with the way he relates to you. Don't believe differently, even if you can't find a thing in common with his mother.

Move something of importance into his house and ask him to leave something of like kind at yours. The commingling of property in the smallest of ways is a precursor to the blending that occurs later in marriage. Bring the distinctive colors of your personality into his home, warming it with your uniqueness. Put into his refrigerator the special treats that please you, letting him know the secrets of your delight. Pay attention to the things he likes and make a point of surprising him with them.

Treat this man who has fallen in love with you well. A smart woman's victory is her own secret.

🙢

The sole importance of a military operation is victory, not lengthy campaigns. Prolonged conflict is now profitable, and the general who understands war is the arbiter of the nation's fate.

The goal of a loving connection with a man is peace, safety, and contentment, never prolonged conflict. The arc of healthy, mature love is relatively swift, yet you must be careful to never sacrifice good judgment for speed. But neither should you confuse a man's elusiveness and withholding with the care you deserve.

Mature, healthy love is easy, not particularly complex. It is not an E ticket to Disneyland, not a screaming, white knuckles roller-coaster ride. It is not fraught with tangled misunderstandings, not marked with hurts and difficult apologies. Rather, love moves easily, with both partners making voluntary accommodations and concerted attempts to remove obstacles along the way. Remember: troublesome and painful courtships make for troublesome and painful relationships and marriages.

A love that begins as sweet and giving tends to continue moving along that same path. And a love born in drama and difficulty is destined to move along that same tortured journey. A smart woman appreciates the differences between these experiences and wisely chooses the sustaining and affirming love. This is called "winning a battle and becoming stronger." After all, victory is all that matters, and the warrior woman who understands love deeply becomes the final arbiter of the relationship's destiny.

CHAPTER 5

EMPTINESS AND FULLNESS . . . YOUR LOVER'S BRAIN: STRENGTHS AND WEAKNESSES

Even in Sun Tzu's times, other generals knew the basics of warfare. What set Sun Tzu apart was his uncanny grasp of human nature: the intricate layering of emotion, motivation, and need. He forced himself to look beneath the surface, asking why one approach worked while another failed. What he found didn't lie in the realm of spears and body armor; what worked was always embedded in a deep understanding of the human condition. Every successful tactic and strategy was anchored in an awareness of what makes people tick.

Success in love occurs when both partners are enhanced, no one is hurt, and a common goal of commitment is reached. This takes an understanding of the lover's brain, its strengths, its weaknesses, and how we may be sabotaged by it.

WHAT IS THE LOVER'S BRAIN?

The lover's brain is, of course, the same brain we all use in our ordinary dealings with other people with one notable addition: the bewildering complexities brought about by romantic love. First of all, the lover's brain is chemical. Sensitized by hormones, it gets influenced and intoxicated by surges of dopamine and acetylcholine and a variety of other neurotransmitters. It is also susceptible to adrenaline rushes accompanied by a pounding heart and damp palms, which we typically register as symptoms of fear. The lover's brain is as full of surprises as Pandora's box. It releases our wildest fantasies, our heartfelt wishes, deepest fears, and most private needs. The lover's brain takes its original shape from our past: what we saw, felt, heard, and received from our parents and, sometimes even more importantly, what we didn't see, didn't hear, didn't feel, didn't get from our parents. And the lover's brain is further refined by an endless stream of cultural influences—the media, books, movies, and songs as well as the kind of experiences we have had with the opposite sex. At the core, the lover's brain is highly emotional, and this lush, layered state makes it as vulnerable to certain weaknesses as it is capable of profound and generous strengths.

The three components of the lover's brain are personal awareness, emotional management, and emotional sensitivity.

Personal Awareness

Weaknesses	Strengths
Emotional denials or distortions	Clearly understands feelings
Unaware of impact on partner	Aware of your impact on partner

Takes things personally	Good emotional boundaries
Defensive	Takes in information
Gives up easily	Persists despite setbacks
Craves excitement	Seeks substance

Emotional Management

Weaknesses	Strengths
Inability to calm down after upset	Reassures and soothes self
Loses perspective	Retains perspective
Can't defuse negative feelings	Releases negativity
Expresses insecurities	Contains insecurities
Indulges bad behavior	Contains bad behavior

Emotional Sensitivity

Weaknesses	Strengths
Selfishness	Empathy and compassion
Misunderstands his conflict	Sees his conflict
Doesn't praise good actions	Rewards good actions
Doesn't punish bad actions	Punishes bad behavior

Let's see how some of these strengths and weaknesses can play themselves out in an everyday relationship dilemma. Kay and Al have been involved for just over a year and have what is really a very solid relationship. Kay met Al shortly after his sister died and was a wonderful support during a painful time in his life. As Kay's feelings deepened, she came to believe Al would be a perfect mate and father to her children. But lately, Kay has had some concerns she sees as potentially serious and has been rethinking her future with this man.

Recently Kay had an excited discussion with Al in which she described to him her wish to quit her job and set up her own business, a flower store catering to a downtown clientele. She had a hundred questions and reeled them off as they chatted over dinner. Even though Al had a business and accounting background and might have stepped in and offered to organize things for Kay, he instead suggested she take a couple of business courses and gave her the titles of books he thought would be helpful to her.

What Kay really wanted was for Al to tell her what to do, to simply handle the problem, to be protective of her the way her father had been.

Kay was angry, hurt, and felt diminished by Al's seeming lack of sensitivity and support. His unwillingness to step in and take over even led her to feel oddly unfeminine. Kay's own lover's brain had betrayed her, revealing weaknesses in each of the three components.

What Kay Did

Personal Awareness. Kay's emotions around her need for Al's protection were a distortion. She is exceptionally bright and capable of mastering anything to which she sets her mind. Kay's own family background led her to fuse vulnerability with femininity, which undermined her sense of female self. None of this, of course, made any sense to her intellectually, but Al's off-handed assumption that she could learn to set up a business on her own led her to feel tough and "more like a guy" than feminine. She was unclear about how she was seen by Al, whose actual perception of her was as very sexy, very female, but a female with strength and competency. He didn't see Kay as someone who was in need of his help. He knew she was quite capable of mastering her finances.

Emotional Management. Kay found it difficult to calm herself after the "books" incident and felt increasingly angry, hurt, and distant. She couldn't contain feelings of insecurity, complaining to him that he didn't care, that if he really loved her he would surely have given her the help she had asked for. And Kay lost valuable perspective making the issue emblematic of the whole relationship, which wasn't accurate. (Al had been very supportive of her when she had gone through a trying time at her work and had been a valuable sounding board in strategizing the negotiation of her new contract.)

Emotional Sensitivity. Kay had fallen into the common lover's brain weakness of all or nothing, leaping to conclusions that reflected her needs and expectations rather than a balanced set of truths. She saw the more obvious fact of his refusal to "protect her" but missed the deeper truth that he saw her as strong and not in need of his preempting her intelligence. Kay was critical and accused him of being cold and uncaring, using their differences for arguing, rather than for understanding. And Kay misunderstood or ignored his conflict, seeing only her own.

What Kay Might Have Done

Personal Awareness. Kay might have pushed deeper for more personal clarity and seen that her need for protection came from how she saw her father treat her mother and how he had related to her as a girl. Kay might have retained her sense of perspective and seen that the emotional dilemma was essentially hers. She might have forced herself to work it out internally (read one of the books Al suggested) rather than expecting Al to work it out for her.

Emotional Management. Kay might have taken a step back and reassured herself as to her strength and competency. She might have better contained her distress and insecurities instead of expressing them in ways that brought into question Al's love for her.

Emotional Sensitivity. Kay might have tried to better understand Al's point of view and, through discussion rather than accusation, move beyond surface truths to the hidden, deeper truths. Al had grown up with a mother he believed to be weak, which left him feeling unsafe as a child. The deeper truth was that he did have protective feelings toward Kay, but the expression of his brand of protection was to encourage her effectiveness. As a child, Al had seen his mother as ineffectual and self-deprecating. "Stupid old me" was his mother's favorite phrase, one he'd quickly learned to hate. His mother pleaded helplessness so often, she became an easy target for his father's irritation and derision. To feel safe himself, Al needed a woman whom he saw as capable.

Don't be betrayed by your lover's brain. If your reaction to a dilemma is emotional, question first your unique involvement—the confusing participation of issues spinning out from your lover's brain.

The army which is first to arrive on the battlefield and awaits the enemy is rested and at ease. The army that comes later to the field of battle and must hurry into the fight is tired. For this reason, skilled warriors make the enemy come to them and do not go to him.

—Sun Tzu

DEALING WITH DIFFERENCES CONSTRUCTIVELY

The woman who sees that a conflict is brewing and thinks about it clearly is best able to use her strengths. In love, we all must learn to deal with differences and, since romantic love carries with it the greatest potential for conflict, we wrap within its wings our most needful, tender, and hopeful feelings. We place in our partner's lap the wounds from our pasts, hoping that within love's embrace we will be healed. And we infuse love with the expectations we've been led to believe it can fulfill. Men do the same thing, and these superheated, overcharged forces, sometimes on a collision course, set in motion the unique patterns of conflict in a relationship.

Not only is some amount of conflict itself inevitable, but certain specific conflicts that reflect your uniqueness and the uniqueness of your partner are to be expected. How do you learn to recognize them clearly? Ask yourself the following questions and think about your answers carefully:

1. How do your natures differ in ways that you can see will lead to conflict?
2. What does he want, need, or do consistently that is in serious opposition to your wishes?
3. What do you want or need that he has a hard time accepting?
4. What insecurities (his or yours) are sources of friction?
5. How far can you move toward him and how far is he willing to move toward you? What is the real potential for change?

Denial is the greatest human tranquilizer and a most dangerous indulgence. Freedom from denial allows you awareness of where the difficulties lie. Insist upon only that which is possible, accept what is not. Harping on the impossible reflects only weakness and desperation on your part. If the issue is important enough, it is better to walk away than be reduced to futile complaints. Finding yourself lobbying for the impossible only weakens your position, leaving you endlessly reacting instead of acting.

If the issue is both possible and important, choosing the time and setting for a discussion gives you some distinct advantages. Such thoughtful planning allows you to be ready, to think through your point of view, and to anticipate the nature of his resistance. You know exactly what is at stake and what you are willing to risk. You are resolved. In this way, you cannot be caught off guard.

The Setting. Never choose the bed as a location for dealing with a conflict. This is the place you must reserve strictly for affection, and it should never be a place where you fight. Cars are also bad places, too confined, distracting, and dangerous if emotions run high. Choose some neutral setting, one that is out of the house if you can. A restaurant, a park, or even a quiet walk takes the conflict away from where you live.

Timing. Make sure you don't let yourself be impulsive and blurt something out just to relieve the tension of the moment. Timing should be when you are most calm and ready. Pay attention to the moods of your partner, when he is most relaxed and receptive as well as when he is most distracted or defensive. Bring him to the place and time.

If you are surprised by your partner and caught unprepared, it is an easy thing to handle. Just say something like, "I know this is important to you and because of that it is important to me, too. It's just that I need to think about this a bit. I don't want to say anything I haven't thought through. It wouldn't be fair to either of us. If you'll give me a few minutes, we'll sit down and talk all of this out."

Then think through your position. Know what supports both your dignity as well as the generosity and balance of love. And invite him to the discussion only when you are calm and ready.

An enemy will come of his own volition when he sees the possibility of gain. And an enemy is discouraged from approaching by the prospect of harm.

STAYING CLEAR ABOUT REWARDS AND PUNISHMENTS

Actions are encouraged by positive acknowledgments. Always make sure to go beyond taking the good for granted and complaining about the bad. Consequences in a love relationship should always be clear and predictable. Never be afraid to define them specifically.

Too often we forget the power of reward, which is the great shaper of most human behavior. We do a great number of things out of sheer randomness. We do things again and again because of some sort of advantage or reward, however subtle it may be. We feel better, safer, more effective, more male, more female, when we do certain things that enhance our comfort, and so we do them more often.

It is to your advantage to understand and enter this system of rewards, giving them freely when they are warranted and withholding them when they are not. The trick for a woman is in knowing what is rewarding to a man and not confusing it with what may be comforting or pleasing to you. Among some of the things men like to feel are: powerful, respected, masculine, capable, sexy, independent, strong, and so on. When you reward a man for something like his sensitivity, it is a good idea to couch it in a word or phrase a man can relate to such as, "It seems strong to me to hear a man talk about tender feelings."

Never be goopy in your praise of a man or you'll run the risk of making him feel suffocated. Never say something that is an obvious exaggeration or inaccurate, for the man will recognize the discrepancy and lose trust in you. And never say something you don't mean, as it may be interpreted as disrespectful and a manipulation.

It is important to remember the value of consistency. Don't tell a man you want him to be open with you unless you can handle his openness across the board. All too often, a woman wants a man to be more expressive in his feelings toward her, but then turns around and is uncomfortable when he begins to talk about other intimate feelings, worries, and insecurities. Be clear about what you want. If you ask for openness, you may get it.

Just as actions can be shaped and encouraged, so too can they be prevented. A woman can prevent an action on a man's part by hurting him. This is a powerful tool and should be used only with utmost consciousness and clarity. Many women punish the men in their lives because of impulse, petty annoyance, and hurt. This can be a serious mistake, since punishment should be reserved for only those actions you wish to prevent. Punishment is like shouting. If you yell and carry on about everything, nothing stands out as being particularly bad. For punishment to be effective, it requires you to be discriminating and make choices. In romantic love, we are sometimes afraid to punish when we should because we fear repercussion or loss. Be clear and trust in what you know to be right or wrong for a healthy relationship. Be brave and punish the wrong. Remember, the strongest punishment is letting a man know there are lines that can't be crossed without jeopardizing your love. If he crosses one of them, you know what you must do.

Punishable actions should be clear-cut. A man should know ahead of time what he will be punished for and even something of the nature of the punishment. Fidelity is among many of the actions that can be fostered and controlled by understanding these rules.

❧

To be certain of victory, attack where the enemy does not defend. To be certain of protection, defend where your opponent does not attack. So against a skilled warrior, an enemy does not know where to defend. And against such a warrior, the enemy does not know where to attack.

USING YOUR HEAD TO MELT A MAN'S ARMOR

Everyone told Ginny to stay away from Howard. He was too damaged, too hurt by the woman he'd loved who had run off with his best friend, the same man who had stood up for him in his marriage five years before. Howard was too self-destructive, far too risky. But there was something about Howard that charmed Ginny. Although others seemed afraid of his tough exterior, she saw it as a ploy to protect the pain he hid inside. "Be careful" was the admonition she heard voiced more than any other, although she never felt in danger. Howard was the one who seemed somehow fragile, living a lifestyle that included just about everything and anything except taking care of himself.

Howard blamed it on the "Irish thing," telling her that the sadness that swirled within him was just a little quirk in the genes following him from that "godforsaken island" of his ancestors. Ginny never tried to take his sadness away and allowed its presence without judgment. She introduced him to healthier foods without directly challenging the makeup of his diet when she met him. His cigars went voluntarily a few months after Ginny introduced him to the fun of in-line skating.

Ginny understood it was when he needed her most that he was least able to ask or put words to his feelings. She knew how the betrayal of his marriage had hurt him, leaving him encased in the armor that put in place a pattern of his leaving before he could be left. Still Ginny stayed, falling in love with the snapshots of vulnerability and tenderness she saw through the cracks in the walls he had erected. While others may have given up, Ginny remained through all his clumsy attempts at pushing her away as his need for her grew. Ginny understood his fears and made it impossible for him to want to leave because she never put pressure on him to stay.

Ginny wrapped herself in the only thing that is ever truly saving, the self-understanding that allowed her to see Howard's wiggles for what they were—not a reflection of his feelings about her, but the painful trail of a sensitive man who had been badly hurt. She saw all the tricks he used to protect himself emotionally, but Ginny acted in such a way that Howard never felt the need to defend against his deepening involvement with her. When it felt too scary for him to stay close, Ginny would let him move away for a while without questioning his obviously flimsy excuses. She had the wisdom to know that her letting him go with impunity was what allowed him to return to her with growing comfort and trust.

Ginny's greatest strength was her clear belief in the

power of her love. She made up her mind to manage the painful moments of discomfort and uncertainty by never taking the expressions of his fears personally. And her patience paid off; they have been married now for six years.

━❦❧━

A skilled warrior is so subtle and formless as to leave no trace. He is so mysterious as to be soundless. In this way he is the master of his opponent's fate.

THE POWER OF MYSTERY

Forever, smart women have carried about themselves a sense of mystery when they were around men who interested them. Everyone knows that mystique is alluring, and yet so many women seem to work systematically to eradicate it. It is a glitch in their lover's brain that tells them to do this. And they do so to their distinct detriment. Some women think the creation of mystery is a manipulation, something about which they needn't concern themselves. Some women see mystery as being in opposition to intimacy and go swiftly about crowding it out. And still other women are simply too self-conscious about retaining any mystery, and in their discomfort they need to reveal everything.

What is mystery? Female mystery is always about absence. It's about what you don't show, do, or need to say. You can't relate to a man the way you do to your women friends and retain even a wisp of mystique. With a man, sometimes it is better not to say something, not to do something, not to be entirely candid. But mystery is not in opposition to intimacy. In fact, it enhances closeness and makes it more discriminating. Intimacy is not about a glut of information. Never confuse the two.

110

Don't make the mistake of thinking that the more a man sees of you, the more he knows, the closer the two of you will be. The truth is that it is possible to know too much or have what you know pushed too close to your face. What is surprising to a man is often not what a woman says but rather what she does not feel the need to say. Surprise him by saying less when he is anticipating something more along the lines of a dissertation.

Men are intrigued by what they don't know, what they don't see or hear. Don't feel compelled to tell them everything that's on your mind or in your heart. Simply because it's there doesn't mean you have to divulge it all. Mystery isn't about secrecy but rather about privacy, and men like women who retain certain areas of privacy. Among those things men don't need to hear about are the heaviness of your menstrual flow or the new depilatory you've discovered.

Close your bathroom door when attending to your toilet. Don't let him see what you have to go through to look as good as you do. Don't get dressed in front of him (getting undressed is a decidedly different story). And seeing you in curlers, or any of its functional equivalents, is the absolute antithesis of mystery. A man doesn't need to know the nature of any of your ablutions; let them be your own private ritual.

Above all else, a woman should keep the source of her strength a mystery. She is bold in her actions toward a man at times even though she may not feel bold. At other times, she surrenders without his anticipating it, knowing the uncertainty it creates always gives her the edge. Men may complain about a woman's unpredictability, and yet its presence is fascinating to them. The reason for this fascination is that a woman's thoughts and actions are processed in a different way than are a man's. A man may feel comforted around strictly linear thinking, but he quickens to a woman's bursts of right-brain nonlinearity. Flash your intelligence and uniqueness. Trust and express your quirkiness, leaving him with a thing or two yet to learn just when he thinks he knows all there is to know about you.

❧

When you want to avoid battle, you may simply draw a line on the ground. Your enemy will be unable to attack because he will not know where you are vulnerable. Distract him and set him off in the wrong direction.

KEEPING VULNERABILITY
TO YOURSELF

No one in their right mind would broadcast their weaknesses, and yet that is exactly what so many women insist upon doing with the men they love. We all have both a logical brain and a lover's brain, and unfortunately, it is the lover's brain that so often betrays us. In our need to be loved, comforted, and accepted, we reveal our vulnerabilities rather than containing them.

Instead of keeping to themselves the issues that hurt and confuse them, many women provide men a diagram, show them specifically where each and every button is located. Intimacy is not an exposé of personal worries and insecurities. Talk about these issues with your trusted women friends as much as you need to, but at least early on in a relationship, leave discussions of these concerns out of your relationship with your lover.

Make your partner see your strengths as weaknesses and your weaknesses as strengths. Although Melissa had an extremely successful job in advertising, she had never gotten over a deep regret at not being better educated, a fear that had struck soon after she dropped out of college in her junior year. At the time, it had seemed a necessity. Her father had died suddenly, and Melissa was needed at home to help her mother with the younger children. She had found a job as a secretary at a large ad agency, and her drive and intelligence had allowed her to advance swiftly.

Meeting Martin made her focus on the future in a way she hadn't with the other men she had dated casually. Martin didn't know it yet, but he was the man she was going to marry. In so many ways, Melissa felt sublimely comfortable with this man. But the glaring exception was that old fear of somehow being seen as lacking or deficient for not having completed her education. And this feeling was exacerbated by the fact that Martin was well educated with a degree from Penn and an M.B.A. from Wharton. While Melissa had long since compensated for her truncated education by reading in a wide variety of areas, the nagging sense of inadequacy remained.

Melissa remembered vividly the first time Martin came over to her apartment. She was putting the finishing touches on the dinner she had prepared, and Martin was sitting on the couch flipping through the stack of magazines and periodicals on the coffee table. He had seemed pleased to find among them the *New York Review of Books*, a scattering of *Playbill*s she had saved, *Nature,* and the latest issue of *Scientific American*. He had remarked with a low whistle how nice it was to meet someone who took the time to read and think about things outside her field. "I've got to tell you," he said, coming into the kitchen, "I knew you were bright, but I had no idea you were interested in so many things. I don't often wonder if I'm going to be able to keep up with someone." Melissa smiled and said, "I'm sure you're not going to have any trouble at all," and refilled his wineglass. She had absolutely no need to tell him about how she had never really felt smart for having left college early.

Only you need to know your areas of vulnerability. Explaining them too early to a man will dissipate your power and focus discussions on your weaknesses rather than on your strengths. Such discussions are, at best, a shift in responsibility, which makes the man the arbiter of acceptance and, at worst, a disastrous definition of self where the emotional emphasis is upon negativity.

If you are able to determine your enemy's weaknesses while concealing your own, you can concentrate your forces while he is divided. Your enemy must not know where you intend to give battle, for in his ignorance he will have to prepare to defend against you in many places.

TRUSTING YOUR CLARITY AND PATIENCE

It is easy to be reactionary in a love relationship, easy to relinquish the powers of action, creation, and personal design, easy to become passive and watch idly as your experiences slide by, day by day. It is easy to abandon our logical brain (it reminds us that we are in command of the quality of our experiences), easy to slip into the lover's brain (in which lurks the dangerous delusion that, in love, your partner possesses that power, that he regulates the quality of your experiences). Conscious and mature love requires a woman to know herself as well as she does the man. This type of knowing extends to what it is you want, need, and expect at the deepest and least discussed levels of love. And it requires knowing what he wants and needs as well.

Tease out the man's aims and directions while concealing your own momentarily. This allows you to concentrate your energies while dividing his. If the man doesn't know where you intend to create some small change, then he must prepare and defend himself in a great many places, making it far easier for you to reach your own goals.

Tracy had been with Kevin for over two years and felt as though she knew him well, perhaps even better than he knew himself. Kevin was a rugged man and came from a controlling and religious family as strict with their beliefs and rules as they were about sex roles and patterns of communication. Although Tracy grew to understand and like his family, she also saw with sadness the mark of his father's stalwart rigidity on the amount of emotional freedom and expressiveness Kevin allowed himself.

In Tracy's mind, Kevin was wonderful—strong, giving, protective. And she loved his quick, self-effacing humor. She knew everyone saw her as fortunate for having such a man in her life. But there was something she needed that somehow didn't seem to fit in the mix of their experiences together. Tracy felt blessed, for no one had taken the kind of care with her that Kevin had. But some important part of her felt stifled. Kevin could give, but receiving for him was more than difficult; it was nearly impossible.

Tracy had a long talk with Kevin. She told him that she needed to have some way to express her protective feelings toward him, to be able to alternate in the role of giver and caretaker, to pamper him at times physically, to feel the delicious power of actively loving, which required him to be receptive. She saw how uncomfortable the discussion made him and noticed that instead of relaxing, Kevin seemed even more vigilant, even more in need of being firmly in control.

Not long after their talk, Kevin fell ill with the flu. He was sick enough not to put up much of a fuss when Tracy smeared the Vicks on his chest. This was the moment she had been looking for, and she seized upon it. Tracy came the next night bringing food. Later, she gave Kevin a back rub and even managed to massage his feet after only a halfhearted protest on his part. She loved the pleasurable feeling of giving and seeing him quietly enjoy it and take it in. Without calling any particular attention to it, Tracy continued with the massages after he had recovered and watched as Kevin relaxed more and more. She knew she had accomplished something important the night Kevin asked her for a back rub. After that, his walls fell quickly, and the love they shared moved into a healthier balance of real give-and-take.

Remember to always position the moment of change on your terms, placing yourself in control of the timing and setting. Don't forget that a man is most receptive when he is at peace and most resistant and defended when tired and stressed. Make sure to take note of and remember the leverage you have with a man. Never talk about it, simply apply it at the proper time. Most women underestimate the man's dependency upon them, for it is one of the few things a man hides well. Warrior women assume its presence and take it into the heart of their calculations.

Victory can be assured by understanding the enemy's plans. Agitate him and observe the pattern of his movement. Do something to create attention to reveal his strengths and weaknesses, his aggressive and defensive behavior.

THE VALUE AND DANGER OF TESTS

No one is better at devising more intricate and illuminating tests than a woman. And tests, at times, certainly can be important, but they should be of the right sort (coming from your logical brain), stated openly, and interpreted accurately. And women unfortunately don't always do this very well.

Allie has recently gotten engaged to a man she loves deeply. But being fiercely independent, she quickly ran into a conflict over decisions about her freedom to continue seeing her men friends at night and without her fiancé, Kurt. Allie thought she should still be able to go out with her men friends alone. She thought all this was perfectly normal and reasonable, but when she told Kurt she was going out to dinner with a man friend he had not yet met, Kurt reacted negatively.

Thinking about it, Allie had to admit to herself that this was some sort of test on her part. No one was going to tell her what she could do; that wasn't why she had chosen to get engaged, and she was angry at what she saw as Kurt's attempt to somehow control her. In her heart, she knew that she would react as Kurt had if he had come to her with the same request. "Oh, to hell with no double standards, there's nothing wrong with them when they are mine. I know what I'm doing. I trust myself," she thought. But the more she pondered the issue, the less certain she was about whether she wanted him to say no, or to be neutral and let her do whatever she wished. She wasn't sure whether she thought his saying no meant he cared more or less, whether a no meant that Kurt was weak and threatened or establishing appropriate boundaries, whether she was being manipulative or simply assertive.

It is important first to be clear about what it is you want. Don't create a test your partner can't win. And never tell him that you want one thing if, in fact, you want another. Some women will even behave toward a man in ways they don't want him to tolerate. "You wouldn't have let me keep on doing that if you really cared," a woman might say. She wanted him to say no without ever having let him know. A man thinks that had she wanted him to say no she would have said so. He feels duped.

Other women will put two things together that don't necessarily belong: "If you loved me, you'd do it." The joining of those two elements makes sense only to the woman. He does love her, but he doesn't want to do it, doesn't think it should be done. Or, out of insecurity, a woman might set up a situation she thinks is justified, but where a man is made to feel diminished and compromised: "Swear to me on your unborn children's lives that you were where you said you were last night," she might say. He was where he said he was but feels some important part of him will be lost if he complies with her demand.

The heart is fragile, even a man's. In love, a man is at his strongest and weakest, most capable of heroic acts yet also at his most vulnerable and exposed. Approval is high on a man's list, but in his desire to please, he is susceptible to manipulations that may damage how he feels about himself. Men are vulnerable to being manipulated because they *care*, not because they are *weak*. If it is a man's strength you are questioning, understand the nature of strength in love. The two measures are the generous caring and dignified protection of one's partner and oneself.

If you choose to test this strength in a man, then do it properly. First, a test should be appropriate, specific to the context and experiences of your life. ("If we were in a sinking boat with your mother, and you could save only one of us, which would it be?" is not a good test.) A man should know that the request, action, or question is a test, as it is unfair to let him fail without first letting him know he is being tested. Say it directly, something like, "This is a test." Interpret the results of the test accurately. If you say, "I really need you to stay home with me tonight, I'm feeling blue," and he does, you cannot then think of him as wimpy for having missed his monthly poker night. Remember, the only legitimate use of a test is to see how much a man cares, not how much he will let you get away with.

❦

Just as water has no constant form, there are in battle no constant conditions. And the warrior who can change and adapt according to his enemy is said to be divine.

Love has no constant shape or form. It exists as an invisible but dynamic form lying between you and your lover. Protect and honor your strengths and acknowledge and work on your weaknesses. See them both clearly. See the man in your life just as accurately. A man's apparent strengths are often his hidden weaknesses. Never be fooled or distracted by his bravado. Be compassionate about a man's feared weaknesses, for in those vulnerable arenas often lie the seeds for his real strengths. A warrior woman makes these discriminations correctly, nurturing the relationship to its greatest good.

Keep in mind the susceptibilities of the lover's brain. Know when your actions, fears, and expectations come from that mind-set and strive to position yourself with its strengths, for they are truly magical. Only when you are acting through the strength of your lover's brain can you be clear, emotionally calm, and sensitive in the love you give to your partner.

119

CHAPTER 6

ADJUSTMENTS . . .
ENTITLEMENTS AND
ACCOMMODATIONS

During times of crisis, the commander receives his orders from the civilian leader and is called to gather the army.

— Sun Tzu

THE PERSONAL STRENGTH OF FLEXIBILITY

Love comes easily for us when things are going well, but a whole lot harder during times of difficulty. This is when we need to reach deep within and gather our resources. We find someone to love and hope that our feelings will endure personal growth, changing circumstances, and the countless bumps life throws in our path. How can we fall in love and hope to keep it alive despite the inevitable problems that romantic relationships face? One trait stands above all others in protecting us. That trait is flexibility.

Flexibility isn't simply a gift you give in love to your partner. He is not the primary beneficiary. You are. When we bring another person into our lives we all

120

have to deal with differences—accommodating our partner's needs as well as our own. As we start rubbing up against those differences, we have two choices: rigidly digging in our heels or looking inside and seeing if the give should really come from our side.

Toby and Rich have been attempting a difficult feat: exploring a romantic relationship while starting a small business together. Toby ran into trouble when Rich asked her to be a little tougher in their business meetings and to be willing to make some of the unpleasant calls neither of them wanted to make because they required being forceful and assertive. "It's not fair," Toby complained. "You do that kind of thing better than I do." Rich replied, "I'm not going to be the bad guy all the time. It's as hard for me to do that as it is for you." Toby rallied and began making some of the "hard calls." The biggest winner in all this was, of course, Toby. She avoided Rich's growing resentment and, perhaps more importantly, learned to be more effective and confident about dealing with emotionally difficult situations.

What makes flexibility so valuable is that it allows us to change as circumstances change. Flexibility is not about the compromise of closely held values, it is about learning how to maintain those values by making the right adjustments called for by the situation. Whether you are only beginning a relationship or already long into it, flexibility is a skill that should be learned and practiced. Flexibility requires a firm fix on your core values, and they must never be abandoned. Never retreat from something you believe in, but never be rigid about trying to change something just because it makes you uncomfortable.

Proper planning takes many factors into account. Be aware of the uniqueness you are forced to deal with and set your course accordingly. Do not establish your camp upon low or difficult land.

MAKING THE RIGHT CHOICE

Love carries along with it the potential for a number of romantic pitfalls. Even though your spirit may be wild and adventuresome, always choose ease over hardship and comfort over weak knees. You are entitled to substance, which, unfortunately, is often misinterpreted as unexciting.

Invariably, at the end of a relationship, if a woman is honest with herself, she can describe with eerie precision the fatal flaws, which she knew were present from the beginning. Good fortune in love cannot be commanded or summoned. Rather, good fortune is founded first upon a good choice.

In love, the good choice is not grounded in excitement or drama. It is not one made more delicious by a man's elusiveness or mystery. Or by the tantalizing push-pull promise of a man's commitment fears. Good choice is never associated with any sort of abusive behavior, however subtle it may be. It is not about any of the things that may stir powerful, unresolved forces from the past. The good choice is rarely even about high passion. Get over it! This is the simple truth, and it's time you faced it.

Some women are fascinated by a certain amount of danger. Men obviously are, too, but while they tend to physicalize danger, women often look for it in their love relationships. And to the extent that this is part of the equation, women are more likely to be hurt. The sense of danger that may keep you on your toes in the early throes of love is going to make you crazy later on. Guaranteed.

Don't attach your feelings to a man who withholds the truth about his past, who needs you less than you need him, or who you feel anxious around. Don't extend your trust to a man who lies, even though it may not be to you yet, or to one who has deceptive aspects in his life. Don't give your heart to a man who feels good when you are feeling bad or one whose confidence is boosted by putting you down. Or one whose words are always more soothing and generous than his actions. Don't fall in love with a man who has an excessive need for control, for you will find yourself drawn into his orbit. And don't connect with a man who is afraid of being gentle, sensitive, and vulnerable even though such expressions may occasionally make you uncomfortable.

Time spent with any of these men will be wasteful and ultimately destructive. Read a romance novel or watch a movie about the woman who always falls for the outlaw or the guy with a wife he hasn't thought to mention yet. If you need this sort of excitement, live it out vicariously, not in the most treasured part of your life. Your love is your most precious gift. Don't squander it on the undeserving. There are times when you must use your head. This is one of those times. No matter how your heart aches, never linger for a moment in the company of a man who doesn't make you feel cared for, respected, and safe.

Concerning neighbors in adjacent territory, make them your allies.

COMMONALITY TAKES MUTUAL EFFORT

In a new relationship, areas of commonality should be sought and explored. It is good to stretch beyond the activities you do out of habit to see what new things you might learn through your experiences with the man in your life. Being a model for risking unfamiliar experiences will increase the likelihood that he too will make efforts to get acquainted with your world. Establishing common interests and concerns is an integral part of the bonding process.

The biggest blocks to commonality are resistance to change and keeping score. Be the first to offer to try something new. And, if you can, do it several times, trying to keep an open attitude about how the activity strikes you. Expect him to reciprocate in like kind. Don't keep score. If things begin to swing out of balance and seem destined to stay that way, try telling him clearly what it is you want and that his participation is important. It shouldn't take a lot of wasted months to discover the level of generosity you feel with the man and his in return. Pay attention to the balance of these things in your relationship.

In a marriage, common concerns can typically be grouped into five categories: sex, money, child rearing, the social calendar, and relations with family. Each of these areas should contain the involvement and participation of both partners. Sadly, many couples have sex together and divide everything else up. While these divisions may be efficient, they also increase the risk of resentment, misunderstanding, and loneliness. Even if you are better suited than he for certain activities, encourage his involvement, however modest. But this is successful only when you are willing to reciprocate. Accomplishing this means that you must remain flexible to the issues and activities that change with time and the natural aging of the relationship. Commonality is an ever evolving process. Continue to cultivate it as opportunities present themselves.

❧❧

Do not remain in barren or isolated lands.

PROTECTING YOUR UNIQUENESS

If the relationship lacks the man's encouragement and support of involvements that are important to you, take special care. A woman should not remain for long in such dangerously isolated positions. Don't give up meaningful aspects of yourself simply because their expression doesn't mesh with what a man finds valuable. Everything you do or are interested in need not be valued equally by the man. But, at the same time, you should never allow them to be trivialized.

Jenny forgot this and came dangerously close to losing a part of herself that contained great inner value. She and Andy have been together for three years, and she had gladly mirrored his organized and practical lifestyle because it felt safer and more secure than the somewhat chaotic and emotional family in which she had grown up. And Jenny had learned well; these days, she could out-organize Andy any time she chose to. Everything fit in her life. Each element had its own purposeful reason.

But something was missing. Jenny longed for some expressive outlet, something unfettered by the bounds of practicality. She signed up for a painting class, which created the first real debate between her and Andy. He wanted to know why. Why painting? Why at this time in her life? What possibly could she hope to accomplish?

Somehow simply wanting to paint seemed insufficient, but that was what she wanted and stuck to.

As the classes progressed, she found herself devoting more of her time and energy to painting. Even though Andy seemed to admire her work and pointed it out proudly to friends who came over, he kept asking Jenny where she thought all this time and effort was going. When Jenny couldn't come up with anything she felt sure would satisfy his penchant for practicality, she smiled, shrugged her shoulders, and reiterated how much she enjoyed the process. While that seemed quite enough for her, it only annoyed Andy, who retorted, "Fine. We can dig out the old card table from my garage and you can be one of those women who sets up shop in the park and you can try and sell your stuff on the weekends." "Maybe I will. What's wrong with doing some things simply because they are fun to do?" she asked, forgetting for a moment that *fun* was not a word Andy used often. He had given her an odd look and walked out of the room.

Sadly, after that conversation, Jenny stopped painting. She left the canvas she had been working on unfinished. She gave her paints along with a batch of old clothes to the Salvation Army. She felt as though Andy didn't think her particularly talented, and his thoughts about art were generally deprecating and trivializing. Andy didn't say a word when the easel came down and the paintings were stowed away in the back of the hall closet. Jenny didn't even know if he noticed.

Jenny had given something up. Something of immense personal value. She had done this only because she couldn't make Andy understand. He didn't relate to artistic expression in the least. Somehow Jenny made his approval more important than her own. In doing so,

Jenny split off an aspect of herself, which can only lead to diminishment of self and, ultimately, to a growing resentment. She had created a double loss.

What Jenny might have done was to keep on painting, trusting that enjoyment alone is enough reason to continue any healthy and constructive activity. She might have said, "I don't need you to think my paintings are great, but I'm not going to let you put my painting down because it's fun or because it doesn't seem practical or tied to making money." Jenny might have understood that defending her entitlement to "having fun" would have stood as a potent example for Andy of the importance of joy in life. Over time, her strength might even have illuminated how constricted and deprived Andy was and perhaps showed him other alternatives.

Those who are successful in life and love count not one single martyr among them. Under whatever circumstances you find yourself, trust and affirm your own uniqueness. It is no one's responsibility but your own. Assume it.

On deadly ground, fight.

STANDING UP FOR YOURSELF

Even in the best of relationships, there are problems that arise from natural differences and the personal changes we all make over time. It isn't effective to turn every dispute into a battle, for a man won't appreciate the difference between what is central to you and what is not. For this reason, he may diminish the importance of your reactions in general. Many a woman has been dismissed by a man as being "emotional" because she has failed to be discriminating about which issues she is willing to fight for. If you fight about everything, nothing stands out. Nothing will be seen by the man as important. And if you fight about nothing, you will be seen in the same way.

What is worth a fight? Your integrity and the unique expression of your values. If threatened, these core parts of yourself must be defended, since their loss can be a mortal blow. Even if your style isn't in the slightest way combative, you must summon the courage to protect yourself. You must adapt to this dangerous challenge.

There are typically only two reasons why a woman is afraid to fight. Fear. And fear. Either she is afraid that her rights aren't important enough to take a firm position on or she is afraid of the man. She worries that she will lose something if she dares fight: his love, his approval, or in some instances, his self-control.

Only you can muster the courage to believe that your feelings, needs, and values carry weight and deserve recognition. And only you can believe yourself to be resourceful enough to deal with any loss a man might throw your way. Remember one thing: the only mortal loss is your dignity and self-respect. Protect them. Never allow a man to think you won't fight for something that is central to you. It weakens the spirit and is a deadly message to send to a man, particularly one who may be controlling or a bit of a bully.

❦

There are routes not to be followed, certain troops not to attack, some fortified cities not to be fought for, territories not to be contested, and some civilian orders not to be obeyed.

ACCOMMODATIONS NOT TO MAKE

In love, there are paths not to be followed and issues not to be elevated to great importance. A warrior woman knows how to make these critical distinctions.

Laura wasn't about to make the same mistakes her predecessor had. Dean, her fiancé of six months, had had a hard time finding a woman he felt was compatible with his two live-in sons from a prior marriage. Dean's last relationship had ended badly when the woman he had been involved with couldn't seem to make things work with his boys.

Laura didn't anticipate the same hurdle. She liked the kids from the start and was determined to create a loving family unit. She would make the compromises. She would be the first to give. But as her wedding approached, all her plans and intentions were severely tested. Her work schedule differed from Dean's, allowing her to go over to his house an hour or two ahead of him. Inexorably, she was drawn into the day-to-day problems the boys presented. Their frequent bickering was something she wasn't used to, and while she instinctively resisted the role, she found herself going down the thankless road of playing cop, referee, and unwanted peacemaker. Both boys took turns complaining to their father when she appeared to side with one or the other. And instead of trusting Laura's connection to the boys, Dean began not so subtly implying that perhaps she was being too hard on them. Maybe she should lay off. Perhaps she just didn't understand what boys were like.

Then it was the boys' rooms, which she helped them try to organize, not just for their benefit but also because she couldn't stand the smell of sweaty clothes tossed under the beds, wet towels on the floor, and half-eaten snacks from the kitchen that never found their way to the garbage can.

Laura didn't mind doing any of this, but the more responsibility she assumed, the less Dean did with the boys, particularly anything disciplinary. What irked Laura most was the way Dean rolled his eyes whenever she wanted to discuss something related to the kids that he perceived as critical or when she asked for his support on some matter involving the boys.

When in the middle of one of their conversations, she heard Dean say, "Don't make me feel like I have to choose between you and the boys," she knew she had made some serious errors. Laura backed off. She tried to make the boys see her as more of a loving friend and less as anything they could construe as wicked stepmother. She closed the doors to their rooms, forcing Dean back in to deal with the mess. And she gave up her role of peacemaker, telling them cheerfully how she knew they would find some way to resolve the dilemma they were currently squabbling over.

Laura had learned an important lesson: there are some accommodations a woman needn't make, and that inaction can be every bit as effective as action.

WHEN NOT TO FIGHT

A man's actions, even though open to obvious attack, are not to be addressed at a time when there is a possibility he will fight back with fury. Nickie only wanted an answer. One that she could count on. After all, it was Ron who had first set in motion the plans to go skiing, and Nickie was simply trying to pin him down to some specifics. The problem was that Ron was having a hard time keeping up with a particularly demanding workload, and family complications involving his elderly mother made scheduling anything near impossible.

Nickie had been understanding about Ron's work pressures and let him talk for hours about how overwhelmed he was feeling lately. And she had been nothing short of wonderful with his mother when she had a small stroke. Nickie had made the weekly treks with Ron upstate to oversee his mother's treatment and spend time with her.

But Nickie felt herself succumbing to the stresses of the past months and needed some sort of a break. She wanted to get away, to spend a little time with Ron, to do something other than talk endlessly about problems. She thought about her own scheduling issues at work and decided she needed answers. Ron had called from work, telling her that he again had to stay late. When he called at half past ten, it was clear that he was upset and exhausted.

Despite her understanding this, Nickie brought up the ski trip, asking him for dates. Ron said, "Look, I'm fried. I've got a big contract that has to go out and I still haven't been able to put together most of the information I need. The person who's been responsible for gathering all that stuff just took off on maternity leave and my mother fell again and they're talking about putting her in a nursing home. Frankly, the last thing on my mind is going skiing."

"You know it's always something," she said, her voice rising. "You're the one who was so hot to go. I've gotten all the equipment together and I need to make arrangements at work. All I need from you is a date."

"Don't start up with me. Not tonight. All I had for dinner was Maalox and stale coffee. Oh, and I creased the side of my car leaving the parking garage. I'm not in the mood for a discussion."

Casting better judgment aside, Nickie plunged on ahead. But she wasn't prepared for the ugliness that

131

THE ART OF WAR FOR LOVERS

followed. She had made the mistake of choosing a time when Ron was feeling pushed to the limits to go after something she felt was totally reasonable. Normally, this wasn't anything that would trigger a fight of major proportions. But this night Ron was desperate, and desperate men fight desperately.

❧

There are five traits that are dangerous in the character of a general:

There are five self-defeating ways a woman can compromise herself from within. Each of the following should be thought about carefully.

❧

1. Those who are reckless and who don't value life can be killed.

COMPROMISING GOOD JUDGMENT FOR RECKLESSNESS

A woman can be killed by her recklessness. Literally. It is reckless to be with a man who is in any way abusive. This includes verbal abuse, as it is often a precursor for physical actions. If you examine the backgrounds of men who go on to kill women, one fact stands out: almost without exception, such men have a history of abuse with women. A slap is never just a slap. It is a forerunner of escalating violence. It is dangerous to be with a man who so poorly controls his anger. Such men should be left immediately.

Broadcasting Insecurity Is Reckless

But recklessness can take many forms, and each leads to heartache. It is reckless to let a man know he has the emotional leverage in the relationship even if that is the truth. Men respect parity and abhor discrepancy, particularly when it favors them.

If you find yourself feeling as though you care more for the man than you think he cares for you, keep this worry to yourself. Some problems are not helped through communication, and this is one of them. Talking about this dilemma will only have the effect of pushing the man away. Have your friends remind you of how terrific you are, how lucky the man is to have found you. Most often, this concern is only a passing crisis of faith created by meeting someone you have intense feelings toward and who you want to like you. It is your problem. Deal with it internally.

Not Insisting On Monogamy Is Reckless

If you are going to be sexually involved with a man make sure he's not sleeping with anyone else. A promise of monogamy should always be gained before bestowing the generosity of your sexual favors. Such understandings lead a man to take a woman more seriously.

If the woman's goal is the potential for continuity, she must lead the man to it. While men don't realize it as clearly or quickly as do women, they too want continuity. Men are drawn to women who insist upon monogamy, for they trust and respect them a great deal more. Men secretly yearn for an exclusive relationship, for it eliminates competition and reduces their performance fears. Even though they may be the last to admit it, men admire a woman who dignifies her body and heart, for such women are the true targets of a man's wishes.

Look beyond the heat of the moment, beyond the

insistence of a man's touch, and beyond the nagging insecurity that may send false messages. Trust in your own value, understanding that a sexual exchange is the acknowledgment and reward of a relationship in movement and never the cause of that movement.

Confusing Love with Longing Is Reckless

"My choices in men have been awful" is an all-too-common lament. And the focus is typically on the disappointing flaws, fears, and intimacy problems of the men involved. Of course some men are defective, but that's not the point! The point is your choosing such men. Why do women willingly place the gift of their hearts in obviously unworthy hands? Don't they see the danger of the situation? Don't they know who the man is until it's too late? Are they cleverly taken in by the man who promises one thing and delivers another? No, no, no! The truth is that such women don't really feel love toward this sort of man. Instead, they attach longing to him, confusing this dramatic counterfeit with the real thing.

Loving an unavailable man is an oxymoron. Love is about *having*, not *yearning* for something you wish you had. Love is about reciprocity, and unavailability is never reciprocal. You can find plenty of men who will make you nuts, but don't confuse that exquisite misery with love. It's not!

The inner workings of longing have nothing to do with love. The powerful pulse of longing is about either completion or feelings of inadequacy. Actually, those are both simply flip sides of the same coin. We seek to complete what we feel is lacking within ourselves. The magic you attribute to the uncatchable man is only the emotional containment you wish you felt and confuse for confidence on his part. And the underside of this coin is the responsibility you take for the failure of the connection. "If I were only prettier, smarter, softer, warmer, stronger, better, he would want to be with me. It's my fault, my problem, what I deserve," and on and on goes this train of thought. Here is the truth: longing isn't about love but rather about wishing for the impossible. That is why you choose the impossible man.

If love is what you want, if you have the stomach for it, then stay away from any connection that smacks of longing. If longing is in the mix, you've given up any sort of power in the relationship. You are fighting a civil war and pretending it is something else entirely. Smart women quell civil disturbances internally and don't mistake them for the real struggle at hand.

❧❧

2. Those who are too fixed upon staying alive can be captured.

COMPROMISING RIGHT ACTIONS BY ANXIETY

If cowardly, a woman will be destined to be dominated by her fears and will neither know or be known by the man. What makes someone fearful in a relationship? They allow themselves to become too self-centered or too partner-centered. Both of these positions are simply different faces of the same dynamic: the dread of somehow being found deficient.

The self-centered woman is afraid that making her partner's needs and feelings important will expose her own as being insignificant. She is afraid that if she stops shouting, "Me, me, me," she will be lost, her deficiencies revealed. The partner-centered woman hides her deficiencies in a different way. She masks her needs and feelings by making her partner the center, not daring to risk the outcome of expecting and standing up for equality.

It is cowardly to leave little room for *love-centered* experiences, which are defined by mutuality. This requires a balance of giving and taking. Your discomfort with either end of this dimension leaves scant space for the man in your life. It either crowds out his opportunities to receive or stands in the way of his capacity to give. In the end, love loses, and so do you.

It is helpful to occasionally take stock of the mutuality in your relationship. Mutuality in love is defined by openness, understanding, compassion, and generosity, all of which are compromised by anxiety. In a quiet moment, answer the questions that follow.

Openness

How open do you feel with him?

What are your secrets, the silent areas, pockets of shame, guilt, distrust, sadness?

What would you lose if you gave up your secrets?

How open do you think he feels toward you?

How comfortable are you in accepting his openness?

What balance is there to the ways you both deal with vulnerability?

Understanding

How do you go out of your way to try and understand him?

What efforts does he make to understand you?

What is the balance of taking the time and effort to try and understand rather than criticize or judge?

Compassion

> How do you express your compassion and sensitivity to his uniqueness?
>
> What does he do to communicate his tenderness and compassion to you?
>
> What is the balance between the way you extend and receive compassion from each other?

Generosity

> How generous are you to him?
>
> How attentive to his needs and feelings?
>
> What about his generosity? How giving is he?
>
> How well do you receive his gifts?

Pay close attention to balance: your willingness to both give and receive. If the balance is off on your side, take every measure to correct it. Risk giving or taking more. Love only lasts in balance. Do whatever you can to preserve it.

3. Those who possess quick tempers can be manipulated through taunting and shame.

COMPROMISING LOVE WITH TEMPER

If quick-tempered, a woman can easily be made a fool. An impulsive woman can be provoked to a rage and be made to say and do things that will not be in her best interests. One so easily angered is hasty and does not accurately weigh dangers and difficulties.

A too quick temper clouds judgment, reveals hidden sensitivities dealt with more effectively in other ways, and leaves a woman easily set up by the man. Such a temper never serves you well.

Anger is natural and healthy. It creates a veil for hurt when such an expression might feel too naked and exposed. And anger also stands guard around the boundaries of our self-respect and dignity, offering its crusty and reasoned protection. But a quick temper is different. Temper is anger stripped of the perspective reason gives to it. Temper is anger out of control. Instead of protecting one's dignity, temper erodes it. Instead of highlighting issues so that they might be resolved, temper hides them beneath a barrage of words and histrionics, making *your* conduct suspect. Temper is disorienting and distracting and can take you out of your plan and leave you at the whim of the man's.

<hr/>

4. Those who focus too closely upon honor can be disgraced, for they think of little else.

COMPROMISING SUBSTANCE WITH FORM

Honor as a value is, of course, to be cherished. Honor is a commitment to the core principles that form our character. Personal honor can't be bestowed upon you nor can it be taken away. It isn't related to accomplishment or performance, and certainly not to ease. Honor is doing the right thing, where action is connected to principle rather than to outcome. In essence, honor is about the integrity of personal conduct.

But honor carries along with it a shadow factor: false pride. "False" in that it is connected primarily to appearances. While honor is about *doing,* false pride is about looking at what has been *done.* Honor acts; false pride reacts. Honor does what is right; false pride worries about whether what's been done is right.

Always act from honor, for it elevates and dignifies

the spirit. False pride dulls the spirit and makes you vulnerable to embarrassment and disgrace.

When Helen met Dave, she thought for sure she had found the proverbial diamond in the rough. Accomplished in his own right, he had put himself through night school. The whole process had taken eight years, but during that period, Dave worked full-time to help his mother and three younger siblings after his alcoholic father had deserted the family. Dave was circulation manager for the magazine Helen had recently joined as a freelance writer, and she saw him as bright, decent, and generous, with a deep interest in the people around him. The two of them hit it off immediately and soon were spending much of their free time together.

Helen's relationship with Dave was a real departure for her. In the past, Helen's family had unrelentingly pushed her in the direction of men with money or who were from families they knew. Helen felt her parents' preoccupations were suffocating and the men they introduced her to were rather pretentious and boorish. Still she worried about the upcoming dinner with Dave and her parents, who had become increasingly insistent upon meeting this new mystery man in her life.

For Helen, Dave represented an attachment to issues and substance, a new freedom from the narrow, more socially driven focus within which she was raised. But despite her attempts to calm herself, Helen's stomach drew up tight as she and Dave pulled into the long driveway of her parents' home. Helen could feel the frost blowing off her mother and father as they both sized Dave up when he came in the door. And she was irritated when her father arched his eyebrows as Dave responded to a pointed question concerning which school he had attended. Dave joked about how long it had taken him to finally finish up at NYU. Her father went on to explain to Dave that most of Helen's friends had gone to school away from the city, at Harvard, Brown, and Yale. Then he asked about Dave's family. Dave described to them his drinking Irish father and Polish mother and told them how proud he was of his youngest brother, who had just started his own business as a plumbing contractor.

Helen could feel the burning judgment. She was familiar with their judgment and withered under its pressure. When they adjourned to the dinner table, Helen's mother took her aside, asking in a loud whisper, "Where in the world does he buy his shoes?" In the past, Helen might have been drawn in and laughed along with her mother or even made some jabbing comment of her own to appease her mother. Instead, Helen looked her in the eyes and said evenly, "I believe Dave told me he buys most of his clothes at the GAP," and then she walked into the dining room, leaving her mother peering haughtily down her nose.

It wasn't that Helen didn't feel some of the old attitudes well up within her, but she was determined not to allow her parents to influence her feelings toward this man. So when her mother's eyes locked onto her own after Dave stabbed a cherry tomato with the wrong fork, Helen smiled at her defiantly and picked up the same wrong fork and ate her own salad.

Helen knew she had won. Although her mother's eyes had asked, "How could you bring such an unworthy suitor into our home?" Helen didn't permit herself to be embarrassed and shamed by the superficialities that seemed to so dominate her parents' lives. She loved what Dave stood for and the kind way he treated her. Helen honored that and let the trailings of false pride finally fall away from her, feeling unburdened in the process.

5. Those who are too compassionate will be prone to rescue, troubling and exhausting themselves in the process.

COMPROMISING VALUES WITH
OVERBLOWN COMPASSION

If a woman is too understanding and compassionate, she may ultimately be exploited. A woman's capacity to understand and sympathize with a man can cloud her judgment at those times when she must be strong and hold her ground.

Men can't express their feelings very well, so the story goes. Women understand. Men are naturally less monogamous. Women understand. Men are seized by the fear of commitment and closeness. Women understand. Men need ways of blowing off tension and relieving the pressures and stresses of their lives. Women understand. Men can't do this and they can't do that. And women understand!

Understanding is where empathy and forgiveness intersect. It is the magic potion that soothes and heals. It is the shelter we all need from unfair and unforgiving forces. But understanding is also something else: it can be a deadly trap in which many women have become ensnared.

Traditionally, women have been the understanders, the mediators, the conciliators. Their role was to smooth over, adjust, make do. Events are not simply taken at face value, they are always seen within a broader context. And judged as such. As they relate to love, a woman places a man's actions within the grand brush strokes of his life—he feels this or does that because of the forces or people acting in his life, historic or contemporary. A woman understands. All this certainly is great for the guy, but what about the woman?

The proper application of understanding requires a knowledge of limits. Your own, not his. How much will you understand? What are the boundaries of your understanding? If you understand too little, he will feel unloved and unaccepted. If you understand too much, you may be taken advantage of and exploited. Understanding must be earned, and it is earned by a man who is responsible. Only then is it warranted.

A responsible man is one who is courageous enough to struggle with his issues and one who attempts to be honest with you as well as himself. A responsible man is one who tries to learn from his mistakes, not one who simply expects you to understand them. Time after time!

A common trap for women is being too understanding too often. This is a costly mistake, for it condones and perpetuates bad behavior. Men may not ever tell you this, but they don't respect an environment in which bad behavior is permitted. Be generous in your understanding but guard its boundaries well.

These are five fatal flaws in a general and are a disaster for the entire army.

These are the five serious shortcomings in a woman's approach, and any breakdown in a love relationship is the inevitable result of one or more of them. Look honestly at these vulnerabilities within yourselves. Most people look helplessly at their own imperfections, feeling swept along and overwhelmed by them. They know all too well the unfortunate outcomes attached to these flaws, but somehow they can't find the courage to begin dealing with them. Don't allow yourself such passivity. The compromises of recklessness, temper, fear, false pride, and giving to a man indiscriminately shouldn't be ignored—they should be reckoned with.

What is needed is a vision. While most people simply deal with the reality before them, the true key is that reality can be shaped, bent to your own design. To do this, your plans and actions must come from your Highest Self—that domain of greatest integrity, honesty, and love. A vision is not fuzzy but something that is clearly defined, something you can put easily into words. A vision is something that is always a little beyond the grasp of everyday events; it is loftier. In that way, a vision is a direction to move toward rather than a specific destination. A vision is flexible, accepting, encompassing, disciplining. It embraces your strengths and weaknesses as well as those of your mate. It elevates to the highest position your willingness to give, seeks to be a model, teaches always through actions.

What is your vision of love? Try taking the time to think about it. Reduce it to real words rather than an abstract swirl. Condense it to a few short sentences, then to a single sentence or phrase. Now put it into action. Live it in the conduct of your love. Watch how it begins to shape your experiences.

CHAPTER 7

MARCHES . . . DIFFERENCES, PLOYS, AND OTHER OBSTACLES TO OVERCOME

After the blush of infatuation fades, we settle in, expecting love to deepen in a smooth and forward-moving way. But the problem is that forward movement in love often uncovers a lot of things that lay buried beneath the layers of "best behavior" and partial blindness that characterize the early days of a relationship. It's not that we don't expect transitions, we just expect them to be easy. It's not that we don't anticipate the discovery of differences or that certain glitches will emerge, we just hope our little kinks will be adored and theirs will be worked upon. We even expect occasional conflict but not stubbornness or stinging accusations hurled back in our direction. And we've all struggled with our own version of self-doubt but assume it will melt in the warmth of our love. After all, they did fall for us, didn't they?

In love, everything about us, from our earliest days on, is dragged instantly into the present. Love lays bare

144

every aspect of ourselves, every old wound, every emotional cranny, good or bad. And love reveals the same unfiltered material of our partner as well. Romantic love is the mingled pairings of our mutual histories, strengths, flaws, and idiosyncrasies. We anticipate that the path to love will be straight, unblocked, and true. But it is smarter to be prepared for a few hairpin turns and surprises along the way.

Most of us believe that good intentions are all we need to solve the problems we will encounter. But we need more than good intentions. We need to understand the most effective positions to take in certain situations should they arise.

The general who fails to exercise careful planning or takes his opponent lightly will be defeated. When moving the army, pass quickly over mountains and stay close in the valleys. When making camp always find a place which faces the sun. Never camp on high hills. Find gently rising land where you can see the surrounding country. Always fight going downhill, never climbing up.

— Sun Tzu

BREAKING THE EMOTIONAL IMPASSE

The mountain is the symbol for impasse and challenge. We all hope for easier, more gentle passages, but mountains occasionally block all worthy paths and can only be mastered when they are seen for what they are and approached correctly. It is important to pass through mountains quickly and not linger long, for they are treacherous and portents of great danger. Mountains in a relationship are tests of personal understanding, resolve, and inner beliefs. One should deal with

145

these tests quickly and move into friendlier terrain. This is done by being painfully honest with yourself— the only effective weapon for avoiding an uphill struggle.

Kate, a successful woman in her midthirties, had to acknowledge she had reached an impasse with her husband, Will. His drinking, which had been an occasional problem, had accelerated radically during the past year. Her expressions of annoyance had turned into a dread of his coming home drunk once again. And her concerns deepened into fear, not simply for herself but for their two young children.

When Will refused to go to AA, Kate found her way to an Alanon meeting herself. It was filled with people trying to cope with the drinking problems of loved ones. Sitting there in the drafty, smoke-filled meeting hall, she listened and thought about her situation. She knew she loved Will and cherished their times together when he was sober. She truly believed there wasn't a sweeter person she could have for a mate. The thought of losing him was as devastating as the lurch in her stomach hearing him later that night fumbling with the lock and key and cursing.

Kate knew only one thing. She couldn't stay in this place of darkness and uncertainty. The next morning she sat Will down, telling him first how she loved him and how worried she was for all of them. As she spoke, she was sure he had heard these words before, probably many times. But this conversation ended differently. As he got up to leave, Kate took his hand and said, "I've made a decision. I can't live this way any longer. You know I want this marriage to work, but it isn't. Not with your drinking. I can't change that. I can't make you stop. Only you can. I'll forgive you the illness of your drinking if you continue, but I won't stay with you. Now it's time for you to make a decision."

Kate knew she had to act decisively and not out of fear. The impasse was weakening her spirits and slowly eroding her love for Will. They separated in the days following that conversation after Will came home drunk again.

Months later, after Will had stopped drinking, he called and told Kate how it was her strength and self-protection that finally gave him the courage to see what he had done to himself and the family. When Will called next and asked Kate if she would go to an AA meeting with him, she knew Will was going to survive and that their love would as well.

Bonnie faces a different sort of impasse. She has been involved with Doug off and on now for nearly three years. She describes Doug in less than glowing terms to her friends, leaving them all to wonder why she is so determined to keep him in her life. Doug, now in his early forties, has never married or, for that matter, ever been in a committed relationship. Every time she and Doug seem to be getting closer, he somehow manages to dance away, leaving her feeling stymied and powerless. He wants things to stay the way they are: loose and uncommitted. And she wants something more.

Bonnie has permitted this impasse, and the stalemate it has created blocks her vision and pains her heart. She hasn't learned the value of fighting downhill. Only then will she know if the campaign has intrinsic value or is simply the challenge of the hill. A warrior woman seeks no less than the knowledge of this distinction. Personal goals are worthy of struggle and mere hills better left to rock climbers.

But perhaps the truth is more complicated. Women

who thrive on closeness don't put up with a man's waffling for very long. To do so feels too empty and unfulfilling. Bonnie fills in the gaps with hopeful fantasies and endless excuses for Doug. She feels more at ease with the agony of wanting something that can't be than with the certainty of a real commitment. She controls fantasy, while real love is controlled by experience. At some level, Bonnie would rather "imagine" what it would feel like to be loved than to take the chance of being loved in fact. That way she holds on to her dreams without ever having to turn them into the rockier path of reality, never having to expose her own doubts about being lovable. While she doesn't know it, Bonnie diminishes the men who have cared for her for that very reason. To accept love, one must first feel worthy of it. Bonnie's own mixed feelings about closeness are hidden, lost in the shadows of the man she's chosen. She's drawn her secret tight around her, seeing only the mirage of her misplaced adoration.

There is danger in such adoration, for it tends to be obsessive. Mature love is an accumulation of valued experiences and is strengthened over time by mutual trust, acceptance, and safety. Obsessive love is an accumulation of valued fantasies loosely held together by powerful but ultimately disappointing experiences. The recipe for both certainly have common ingredients but in very different proportions.

What Bonnie needs is a hard and honest personal accounting. If she is looking for bittersweet torture or the impossible mountain to climb, Doug is the right choice. He will no doubt call after their latest breakup, and she can plunge back into another emotional tug of war. But if she is seeking the kind of love that leads to committed intimacy, pursuing Doug will get her nowhere. The problem is hers. The conflict is hers. And the choice is also hers. Only we can break the impasses we create.

⊰⊱

Stay away from water. After crossing a river, move far away from it. When an invading force crosses water, do not meet it in midstream. It is advantageous to allow half of the enemy's forces to cross and only then deliver your attack. Take position on high ground facing the sunlight and upstream from the enemy.

TRANSITIONS: BRINGING YOUR PARTNER TO YOUR SIDE

Rivers are the great metaphors for transitions and important decisions. When your partner begins to cross a river do not meet him at the water's edge. Make sure he has committed fully to the crossing before engaging in anything that would create conflict.

Transitions are times of change. Sometimes momentous change. During these moments we are aware of our feelings, but sometimes we forget that our partners may also be having strong feelings related to the change. If the transition is one that is important to you, let it be the one thing you focus upon. Concentrate your energies on making it happen. Don't muddy the waters.

Rose forgot this lesson, which put her wishes into serious jeopardy. She and Bill had been married for four years, and at the age of thirty-six, she had finally succeeded in coming to an agreement with Bill on getting pregnant. Both of them had been talking about wanting a family from the earliest days of their marriage. Both had continued to pursue their careers, believing the time would come when they could slow down and seriously address having a child. It was shortly after Rose's birthday that her age suddenly struck her as ominous. She had felt as though she had plenty of time, and now she had visions of aging eggs and hourglasses with the sand running dangerously low. Rose brooded over her thoughts for a few days and then began a series of talks with Bill.

At first, he was a bit surprised, thinking that in worrying about her biological timing she hadn't taken his feelings into account. Rose was taken aback by his seeming insensitivity. Tearfully, she explained to him about her sudden fears of waiting too long and of not being able to get pregnant. They sat for some time that night going over in detail all of the elements that would change forever if they created a family, and in the discussion, Bill found himself reconnecting to his own long held desires to have a child. His concerns were primarily monetary. What sacrifices would have to be made? What would it mean to give up one of their incomes, at least for some time after the baby was born? Would taking a maternity leave jeopardize Rose's career? They had both gotten used to living on a dual income and, despite their efforts, hadn't managed to save very much over their years together. But when they went to bed that night, Bill was exchanging possibilities for names with Rose even though she knew he was still struggling with his own worries concerning the timing and seriousness of making a responsible decision.

Then Rose fell into the trap of complicating the issue. Instead of letting him get used to the notion that now was the right time to start trying to get pregnant, instead of allowing Bill the time to make the decision and to feel as though it was also his own, Rose chose to throw into the mix other things that were on her mind. She talked about how strongly she felt about getting out of the city and finding a more wholesome place to raise a child. Their two-bedroom house was too small, she told him. Rose wanted to buy something larger with a proper yard. She related how important it was for her to spend time with the baby, hoping they could find some way for her not to have to go back to work indefinitely. And then fell the fateful last straw. Rose revealed her secret wish for her widowed mother to come and live with them for a while, which Rose thought would be good for her and the baby.

Rose was shocked when Bill pulled back altogether. Rather than continuing to be receptive, he threw up resistance to the whole notion of having a baby, leaving Rose hurt and confused.

What went wrong? Nothing that Rose wanted was inappropriate. She simply hadn't allowed Bill the time to make his own internal adjustments, to fully invest in the choice to begin a family at that time. She had not allowed him to cross the river of significant change, but instead she had met him in midstream, causing him to pull back to the other side.

In crossing salt marshes, your task is to get over them as quickly as possible because of the lack of fresh water, edible plants, and the exposure to your troops.

OVERCOMING SELF-DOUBT

Move across salt marshes speedily. Do not linger in them. The salt marsh is the metaphor for personal doubt, a human condition with which we all must struggle. Most personal doubt has little to do with who and what we are in the present. It's like an alarm bell clattering away years after the burglar has gone. The seeds of insecurity you may feel today were planted

151

long ago. What keeps these feelings in place is your unwillingness to let go of them, to let them be reshaped by new experiences. Clinging to them isn't hard just on you, it's hard on your partner as well. Nagging doubts lie in the way we see ourselves, not in the way others see us. Doubts are our burden to bear, our discomfort to deal with, and as such, they have no useful place in the interpersonal domain, where they only confuse issues. But unfortunately, it is in the interpersonal arena that most people broadcast their insecurities. Unfortunate because the antidote doesn't lie there. And it is doubly unfortunate, since believing that someone else can reduce our worries only sensitizes our mate, allowing them to see, and often confirm, our worst fears. Or, if that doesn't happen, our partner simply becomes exasperated by having to constantly deal with our negative self-absorption.

Judith worries about her looks. She has always done this for as long as she can remember, perhaps because she grew up with a mother everyone thought beautiful. Judith always compared herself to her mother and never felt she quite measured up. This is a story she related about an incident on the way to meet her fiancé's parents for the first time.

They were in the car, and she couldn't help herself and pulled down the visor to peer into the reflection again. Ted glanced over and reminded her that this was the third time she'd flipped down the mirror.

"Enough already, you look fine," he said, hovering on the edges of annoyance. He didn't understand. Judith hadn't met his parents before, and this was important to her.

"You didn't say that when you picked me up," she told him. What he came back with was, "I did too. I told you I liked your dress."

He really didn't understand. She wasn't her dress. He thought she was unattractive. She knew it. She said, "I know my dress is okay. I just don't know how you think *I* look." She hated that desperate sound her voice got and pushed the visor closed. Then they had an all-too-familiar give-and-take:

"Jude, I think you look great. You know that."

"You only say it when I make you."

"No one's making me say anything."

"You know what I mean."

"No, I don't. If I tell you you're pretty, you think I'm being patronizing, and if I assume you know it, you feel neglected or some goddamned thing."

Judith bit her lip and scrunched over, seeking the protection of the door. She couldn't stand these conversations where no matter what he said she always ended up feeling worse.

"I see how you look at other women," she offered accusingly.

"Everyone looks at everybody. I see you checking guys out. Doesn't make me want to run out and get hair plugs."

"Getting a little bald is sexy, having no cleavage isn't."

Suddenly the brakes were screeching and he pulled over to the curb.

"If you thought all I was interested in were big tits and a pretty face, you'd hate it!"

"Don't be so sure, not if they were mine."

"Jude, I think you're perfect."

"Yeah, but you don't really think I'm pretty, do you?"

Exasperated, Ted pulled back into traffic. Judith didn't feel one bit better.

We live in a culture where appearance is obviously highly valued. It is natural to have certain concerns over how you look, for that is how we are often judged, at least initially. But Judith's focus on her physical appearance is excessive. Is this simply the necessary by-product of one too many glamour magazines? No, this is something far deeper.

Judith is an attractive woman, not necessarily a *Cosmo* cover candidate, but attractive nevertheless. In fact, attractive women seem to be those most vulnerable to concerns over appearance, for such concerns are symptoms, not source material. And unfortunately, there is always a doctor who is ready to haul out a scalpel to tinker around with someone's symptoms.

Here is the pattern: Judith feels unattractive and doesn't know quite why. She only confuses things by hoping Ted might calm her worries, but secretly she knows that no string of compliments can alter how she feels, even though she is compelled to continually elicit them. She feels terrible about herself and is rapidly on the way to making Ted feel the same way. A most self-defeating and negative spiral.

The dilemma is that her problem has nothing to do with her physical appearance. To deal with this, one must be committed to going to the source. A woman feels unattractive because she has unattractive feelings. And these feelings have very little to do with the way she looks. Rather they are linked to past anger, hurt, disappointment, and rejection. She doesn't know how to change these "unattractive feelings" so she attaches "attractive" to something else, something she can have an effect upon and some control over—her appearance.

Excessive concerns around appearance always have to do with old wounds. "Old" means childhood, and "old" typically means parents. And above all, "old" means internal—an issue you're stuck with and must work through from the inside out. Don't make a man's approval the agent for change. This will not help.

The problem is that changing how you look won't necessarily change how you feel, when how you feel doesn't have to do with how you look. Your value to those who are important to you, which is the only true beauty, is never based on appearance. It never was. Your value is based upon your impact: the expression of yourself infused into the life and experiences of another person.

Your value is not enhanced by a silicone chin, saline implants, or liposucked hips. Don't run down that dark road. The antidote to self-doubt is tearing your attention away from appearance and refocusing it on the more substantive aspects of your being—the doing, acting, giving, creating facets of who you are—your real gifts. These are the experiences you can control and shape in a way you couldn't as a child. And it is through these experiences that peace and esteem flow.

An army always chooses high ground over low and sunlight over shade. In this way the army nourishes its health and, at the same time, occupies a strong position. The army that makes itself less susceptible to disease is said to be sure of victory.

PROTECTING PERSONAL FREEDOMS

High ground has its foundation in ethics and morality and will serve you well. Low ground is characterized by a meanness of spirit and selfishness. You should never allow yourself to be the target of such conduct. In a man, such conduct often emanates from anger and self-loathing.

Beth has been married less than a year and already

has made the mistake of pulling a shroud of darkness around her. It started early on in their relationship and was done, she told herself, out of loyalty to Edward, the husband she adored. During their occasionally turbulent courtship, Beth's best friend, Naomi, had made a few critical remarks about how Edward treated Beth. To support her position in a conversation one night, Beth told Edward what Naomi had said. Instead of attempting to understand Naomi's natural protective instincts, Edward took her words as a personal attack. He told Beth that Naomi couldn't be a real friend if she didn't encourage the relationship. Edward's complaints about Naomi accelerated to such an extent that Beth finally gave up having her over to the house and neglected to tell Edward when she saw Naomi for an occasional, now secret lunch.

Then Beth's family came under scrutiny. In Edward's eyes, Beth's mother and father didn't call enough and weren't generous enough. This conclusion gave Edward the license to step in, making it difficult for Beth to feel free initiating her own phone calls or sending little gifts home to the family. Rather than standing up for herself, Beth began communicating with her parents using E-mail at work. And despite the fact that Beth had the considerably higher income of the two, she hid the money she sent her kid sister for college by circumventing her checkbook and sending cash.

Was Edward simply an ungenerous and controlling man with little sensitivity to her feelings and needs? Perhaps. But Beth was a confederate by allowing it to happen and by permitting the secrets that stole the sunlight from her life, which set up the inevitable resentment that followed. What might have been different if she had insisted on being direct, honest, and forthcoming? If she had set appropriate and protective

156

boundaries for herself? If she'd had the courage to hold her ground rather than sneaking behind his back?

A smart woman dares to believe in the high ground, loves the sunlight, and shuns the shade. In this way she nourishes her spiritual and emotional health and occupies a firm position. To hell with the man who can't handle that.

❧❧

When you encounter "Heavenly Wells," sunken land enclosed by steep heights, do what you must to avoid them. Likewise, "Heavenly Prisons," narrow passes with a covering of brush must also be avoided. "Heavenly Nets," terrain where troops can be cut off and have no clear way out of danger, must not be entered. When you see "Heavenly Cracks," impassable ravines or lands that are low lying with natural pitfalls and enclosures, be sure to march with haste away from them. Do not approach them.

AVOIDING LOVE'S COMMON PITFALLS

There are four common pitfalls a woman may encounter in her love of a man:

1. *Heavenly Wells.* Having heightened and unrealistic expectations of men.
2. *Heavenly Prisons.* Having hidden fears of intimacy that block closeness and fulfillment with men.
3. *Heavenly Nets.* Being set up to give too much to men and demand too little.
4. *Heavenly Cracks.* Allowing hurt, distrust, and anger from the past to color current actions.

Having Unrealistic Expectations

Beware of the bottomless well of unrealistic wishes that

become attached to a love relationship. Heightened wishes come from our belief that a partner should be capable of meeting all our needs if they love us.

So, you may ask, how do you know which wishes or expectations are appropriate and which are not? Remember that the most generous aspect of love is fundamentally accepting your partner. That is how love begins, isn't it? You wouldn't have gotten involved with him if you hadn't thought he was pretty wonderful in the first place. It's only later that our discomfort around sticky little differences and our need to tinker with small changes rise to the surface.

Reasonable demands made in a healthy relationship are for equality, tolerance of differences, and the upholding of mutually agreed upon commitments. All other wishes run the risk of being more self-serving than loving and, over time, can inflict damage to a healthy relationship.

Having Hidden Fears of Closeness

A prison of lonliness can be created by fears of real intimacy. There are no bars in this prison although it can surely isolate you from the riches of love. Our capacity for closeness rests upon a foundation of self-worth, trust, and acceptance. Fears of intimacy can easily be hidden, which poses a difficult dilemma, since no problem can be addressed and worked on if it isn't first acknowledged. Here are some of the signs that intimacy may be an issue for you.

Are you consistently attracted to elusive men? Men who create drama? Men who you suspect have intimacy problems themselves? Women are drawn to such men because they too share this fear. They can hide from themselves by pointing to the man, who may have the more obvious problem.

Is it hard for you to trust men? Be vulnerable around them? Reveal your inner thoughts and feelings? Can you combine friendship in your love relationships? Ease? A lowering of barriers? If not, feelings of inadequacy may block your potential for intimacy with a man.

Do you feel comfortable with a moderate degree of dependency on the part of a man? Allow him to talk about his insecurities without seeing him as being weak or diminished? Can he be fully open with you? If not, such restrictions may bar you from the textured experiences of a loving relationship.

Giving Too Much of Yourself

When a woman's feelings of worth are not well grounded, she is susceptible to covering them with a disguise of generosity. We all have a sense of what makes us valuable in a relationship. It might be brains, looks, personality, the expression of character or values, accomplishments, or myriad other attributes. But if you don't feel good about yourself, you may be tempted to overdo—to give, provide, and defer your own needs to such an extent that the relationship is out of balance.

The woman who isn't sure of her value often hopes to camouflage that fact by giving too much to the man. This pattern is self-defeating. Such a woman doesn't test her worth by demanding balance but allows the man to take her for granted, which only deepens her bad feelings about herself.

Holding On to Old Hurt and Anger

Perhaps the most confining predicament is having sustained negative feelings toward someone you also want and need. The past hurt, anger, or distrust we bring to a new relationship creates the painful and confusing dilemma of ambivalence. Trapped in this life-depleting situation, a woman often feels unwilling to give up angry feelings and equally unwilling to stay away from the gender to which they are attached.

The smart woman looks for the source of her anger and is sure not to carry it over from relationship to relationship. She dares to express her appropriate anger clearly and practices the cleansing release of forgiveness.

She faces all of these issues within herself and tries not to impose them on the relationship, for they reflect internal concerns about which only she is responsible.

If you uncover many obstacles placed in the undergrowth, their purpose is one of deception.

GIVEAWAYS OF MEN'S DECEPTIONS

When many obstacles have been placed in your path, it is for the purpose of deception. When a man gives elaborate reasons, excuses, rationalizations, and faulty explanations for his whereabouts this is most often a sign of trouble. A dalliance should never be permitted. This is a time to be particularly vigilant.

A sure sign of an ambush is the sight of birds rising in flight. If there are steep embankments or ponds covered with water grasses or hidden by reeds or deeply forested mountains with thick undergrowth, you must explore these areas with special care. These are the areas where ambushes can be easily set.

AVOIDING AN AMBUSH

Ungrounded complaints on the part of a man are often signs of impending trouble. When such grumblings are only occasional, they may simply signal a passing mood or transient irritability and are probably best ignored. But if his complaints are expressed relentlessly, beware of being led into a fight.

Don't make the mistake of getting caught up in the specifics, for he will have succeeded in ambushing you. Look carefully between the lines and into the tiny spaces between words. Ferret out the hidden meaning of his complaints. Listen for the emotional theme he may not be able to express in words and respond only to that.

Try and put the emotional theme into words as clearly and simply as possible. If he had a point, be graceful and acknowledge it and respond to him as honestly as you can. If he is being unreasonable or distorting facts, trust your instincts and stand firmly in your position.

Look beneath any unusual compliments, flowers, and gifts that break typical patterns. When you sense moodiness, withdrawal, or depression, look for its underlying source. Any changes in sexual habits, particularly those preceded by either unfounded complaints or wishes for specific novelty, should be explored. The old adage chides women for being the last to know when a man is having an affair. This is incorrect. Women are not the last to "know," but they are, all too often, the last to "see." Denial descends like an opaque veil during times of greatest threat. If a man spends any considerable or unnecessary time with another woman, he is sleeping with her. The only exception is if you thoroughly understand the man's vanity or that of the other woman and it would not be feasible on either part.

❧❧

When you see that groups of armed vehicles have moved out and taken a position on the enemy's sides, he is forming his troops for battle.

HOW TO READ A MAN'S RESOLVE

A man frequently plays out the role of reactor in a love relationship. The woman acts and the man reacts. This has little to do with his strength or weakness, but with a woman's more active awareness of what she wants or what she wants changed. It isn't that men don't know what they want, it's that a woman's needs in love tend to be more crisply defined, better articulated, more complex. This discrepancy is responsible for men, more often than not, being the respondent to a woman's actions.

So when a man initiates an action, the woman needs to perk up her ears a bit. This is particularly true if the man precedes the discussion with a phrase like "We need to sit down and talk." Men don't like to talk, so when they invoke the communication word, they are serious and rather desperate.

Being serious doesn't necessarily imply that what he has to say is reasonable or justified. Simply understand that the "We need to talk" signal is a preface to an agenda he has thought through, mulled over, and come to some resolve about. For you to win on such an issue will require an equally steely resolve on your part.

Look carefully at the language of the enemy. If he comes to you in humble terms but the army continues its preparation for battle, you can be sure that the army will advance.

WHEN *NOT* TO LET YOUR GUARD DOWN

When Linda announced it was time for her parents' annual visit, her husband, Ralph, promised to be on his best behavior and do nothing disruptive, which had been his pattern in the past. In bed that night, Ralph spoke to Linda with some contrition about his past antics and explained once again how he'd felt hurt by her parents' slights and seeming disapproval of him before their marriage. But that was long ago, and Ralph told her in a soft voice while stroking her hair he was even beginning to like her mother a bit.

Linda was taken aback by this conversation. She was so pleased when Ralph didn't start with his usual complaints and the angry pouting that typically preceded her family's visits. Linda was even more pleased when Ralph announced the following morning that he would be happy after all to make the arrangements for the surprise party Linda was planning for her parents. He even volunteered to make the invitations on his computer at work. He had changed. He would show Linda.

But as her parents' visit drew near, Ralph had made none of the promised preparations nor had he designed the invitations. Linda offered to step in and help, even to take over if it seemed too much, given Ralph's busy schedule. "No," he told her. "There's still plenty of time. I told you I would get it done and I will. Just trust me." Linda did, much to her regret. When she finally did relieve Ralph from his duties, the place they wanted to book for the event was already taken. Ralph never even got the invitations together, telling Linda that the printer at work he had planned to use couldn't print on the card stock she had purchased. Even the special cases of wine he had promised to buy fell through the cracks. Linda had to do it all, and he had the nerve to feel injured and misunderstood when she expressed her disappointment and anger toward him.

When setting up guidelines with a man, it is important to understand his intentions even if they are hidden. When he speaks to you in humble and conciliatory terms but continues to behave in the same way, he does not intend to alter his position or change.

❧❧

When the enemy's talk is deceptive but the enemy advances in an aggressive manner, you can be sure he will soon retreat.

CALLING A MAN'S BLUFF

Most women seriously underestimate a man's emotional dependence upon them. And in doing so, they undervalue the strength of their partner's connection to them. This can be a mistake because it gives to the man the power of the bluff, a favorite and well-honed male technique.

As a rule of thumb, the more dependent a man is the more likely he is to employ the bluff. The reason for this is that men generally feel uncomfortable with their strong dependency needs on women and will try to disguise them. The bluff is a man's way of saying, "I don't need you, I don't need your approval, and I certainly don't need your permission. You need mine." The more blustery a man is, the more likely it is that he is bluffing. The bolder the assertion, the more outrageous the threat, the stronger is his wish to hide his need for you.

The best way of dealing with a bluff is to understand its emotional underpinnings. By doing this, you refuse to take on the man's anxiety, which is his hidden purpose in using the bluff. He is feeling a bit out of control and uncomfortable and he wants to wiggle away from it by transferring the discomfort to you. Don't fall for this understandable but deceptive practice.

So when do you call a bluff? A bluff should be called after considering two factors. First, your conduct should be reasonable, appropriate, and above all, feel right to you. And second, the principle you are upholding should be more important to you than is the man's approval. Remember the story of Beth, who stopped communicating with her parents regularly because of Edward's bullying complaints? After thinking about Edward's position, Beth decided to again do what she felt was right: she started calling her mother and father when she wished to speak to them. One day after looking through the phone bills, Edward came across the long-distance charges Beth had made calling her parents once each week. Edward was particularly agitated and went off on a tirade about expenses and her mother and father not calling Beth as much as she did them. The episode culminated in his shouting something to the effect that he wasn't sure what he was going to have to do if Beth didn't promise to stop.

Beth stood and looked directly into his eyes and said, "What's happening right this minute is unacceptable. Absolutely. I love you, Edward, and I hope you don't feel as though you have to do anything. But I'll tell you this, I intend to call my mother and father as often as I want to, as often as I believe to be reasonable. I wouldn't ever interfere with your staying in touch with your family and I won't tolerate your trying to control my talking to mine. This is what I'm going to do. You do whatever you must."

Edward grumbled a bit under his breath, but nothing was ever said again about Beth's calls to her family.

When the enemy's messengers speak in tones that are apologetic, understand that they are stalling and that the enemy's troops are tired. When the enemy sees an advantage and doesn't have the energy to take it, it is a sign that his troops are exhausted. If you see his troops leaning on their weapons, they are hungry. And when his officers are inconsistent or short-tempered, they too are growing exhausted.

KNOWING WHEN A MAN IS READY TO SEE YOUR SIDE

When a man speaks to you in apologetic terms that don't ring true, he is fishing for time and trying to regroup. This is a tactic used in an attempt to get you off the trail. But more importantly, it is a signal that you are close and he is wearying. In a dispute over an issue, there are certain predictable signs men give off when their stubbornness is beginning to flag. Pay attention to these signals because they indicate his possible early retreat and resignation. The critical edge this provides is that you will know he is close to giving in long before he knows it himself.

An empty but clearly stated apology is often the first crucial crack to appear. You hear the tinny tones in his voice, observe the uncomfortable body language, see how his eyes subtly shift away as you look to meet them. He isn't sorry and you know it. Don't let yourself get taken in by his transparent attempts to distract you through his less than truthful words.

Another indication of fatigue is his failure to take advantage of a situation in which he could clearly do so. It is often easy to mistake this tactical error for a change of heart, when in fact the omission is simply a time-out the man is hoping you won't notice.

A third sign of his tiring is moodiness set off when you raise an issue of importance. When he is irritable and short-tempered, he is nearing exhaustion. When he relinquishes personal comforts and smugness, he is desperate. And when you overhear him complaining about his plight to a friend, he has totally lost confidence in his stance.

When a man leans on tired and flawed arguments, he is weakening. Now is *not* the time to let your own energy be depleted. He is ready to resign his position.

When a Man Calls for a Truce

Don't let yourself get lulled into thinking you've solved a problem just because a man comes asking for a truce. In a dispute, a truce is saying, "Let's not get into this for a while," it's time-out, a break, a temporary recess, but it's not a resolution. Most men don't ask for a truce when they are close to agreeing with a woman. They ask when they are trying to buy more time to bolster their argument or hoping the woman will forget about the issue and a decision won't have to be made.

If you find yourself saying yes to his call for a truce, understand it doesn't mean he's any less committed to his position. He's just dug himself a foxhole he can sit in for a while thinking about his next move. Set a date for when the discussions will resume and know that you'll have to be the one to remind him when the time comes.

If the issue is extremely important to you, remember that his stalling tactics favor his side rather than yours. Instead of a "truce," you're entitled to say, "I know this is hard for you to talk about but let's keep going until we've come to an agreement on this."

Don't Get Caught Up in Being Right

In love, being "right" garners no particular advantage. Don't make your moves or base your conclusions on the basis of righteousness. Think about your need to be right. Your insistence upon this choice may ultimately doom you to being alone.

The road to love is not all that treacherous. Love flows through mutual dignity, respect, and acceptance. Side-tracks should be avoided because they chip away the cornerstones of love, which must be preserved if it is to survive.

Self-righteousness is often a cover for rigidity and its jealous protector: control. Be respectful of each other by understanding the subjective nature of being "right." Only strength is to be found in your willingness to yield, acknowledging his differences and their entitlement for expression.

To read a man accurately is a woman's greatest gift to him. Consider and make note of his dreams and unexpressed wishes as clearly as you see his fears and imperfections. Stand as staunchly for what is good for him as for what is good for you.

CHAPTER 8

TERRAIN . . .
RESPECTING BOUNDARIES AND TERRITORY

The ground can be described on the basis of its natural topography and be divided into six groupings: accessible, entrapping, questionable, constricted, precipitous, and distant.
— Sun Tzu

Love relationships are played out in their own special domain. We all want to move comfortably around on this magical stage, hoping to feel valued and secure. But this invisible terrain possesses its own unique dangers and detours as well as its easy, open stretches. To move along the path of love avoiding as many bumps and bruises as possible requires a real understanding of this unseen world.

Territory is as specific as sides of the bed and as abstract as the freedoms you extend to a partner or assume for yourself. Issues of territory can raise the hackles of the most mild-mannered control freak, sending them in a frenzied rush to nail things down. But territory is also the playing field upon which generosity and compassion are expressed. Learn to recognize the emotional underpinnings of territory, looking to the advantages as clearly as you do the hidden risks.

❧

Territory which both you and your enemy can move within with the same ease and facility is called accessible.

KEEP GIVING WHAT YOU WANT TO GET

Territory in which both the man and woman can operate with equal ease is called "accessible." A relationship has the greatest amount of accessible territory at the very beginning. This is a time when boundaries haven't yet been established or expectations put firmly in place. It is a time of generosity and revelation, which creates a vibrancy and sense of aliveness. It is also unfortunately a time when small deceits can hide the potential for pettiness, demand, and possessiveness.

Accessible territory is about freedom, the ability to be and express who we really are. That's who we show each other in the beginning, our most giving selves. Why do we then so easily abandon this most gentle realm of love? Why do we forget the joy of giving and start worrying about what we are getting?

The answer is quite simple. We look to love for more than it can provide. We ask it to complete something within ourselves when only we can do that job. We ask love to affirm only that which we can affirm. We demand too much of love and feel depleted by it. We demand too much because we focus upon receiving instead of giving, on actions we can't control rather than on those we can.

We forget that the excitement of love comes not from what is done for us but from what we willingly and joyfully do. Accessible territory has no staked claims upon it, no rigid fences. It is defined more by what isn't there than what is. Self-centered actions pollute these empty spaces and crowd out precious freedoms. Act to guard the freedoms of your partner as you guard and respect your own. In love, it is in the empty spaces we dwell. If your bowl is filled with expectations, jealousies, and disappointments, there is no room for anything else to flow into it. Instead of adding to the mix as many people do, remove a selfish demand each day. When your bowl is empty, it cannot help but be filled by the presence of love.

Expect nothing less of your partner, for why else would you love him?

Territory that is easy to move into but difficult to get out of is referred to as entrapping. Even though the enemy may attempt to bait you into attacking, do not, for there is no advantage. In entrapping ground, attack only if the enemy is unprepared and at half strength.

WHY SOME ACTIONS CAN'T BE TAKEN

It doesn't take spending much time with a person to begin to know what they are sensitive to and what would hurt them. Most of those things we know generically, for they are similar for all of us. But we each also have our own unique vulnerabilities where a word or an action can cause lasting harm. This invisible emotional space is easy to move into but unfortunately nearly impossible to retreat from.

Entrapping territory is the meeting place of two painful vulnerabilities (yours and your partner's) as they collide head-on. Most of us don't deal very well with hurt. It causes us to focus, if only for a moment, entirely on our own pain. It makes us forget to look also at our partner's position. Emotional pain can be the source of easy blunders from which it may be difficult to recover.

We can't retrieve or redo any of the hurtful things we may say or actions we may take. How many of you have said or done such things? Yes, we all have. While it is natural to lash out when we have been hurt, it is not loving to do so. Nor is it at all understanding. In love, most of us are hurt not by the intent of our partners but by the all-too-human struggles they have *with their own issues.* Our hurt is a by-product of their struggles and difficulties. But it is in this murky domain that lasting damage can be done.

Eva and Jason had been married just over a year when she stepped into entrapping territory. It was a first marriage for her, while Jason had been married once before and had two small children. The past couple of years hadn't been easy for Jason, who had gone through a very difficult divorce, and his attempts to integrate the children into his life with Eva had had all the predictable rocky moments.

Eva loved Jason and worked hard to get the children to like her. And she did her best to be generous and supportive of Jason when his ex-wife, Julie, moved to a distant suburb, making it much more difficult for him to see the children. Eva swallowed her reaction to the kids' requests (from their mother she assumed) that Jason buy them shoes and clothing even though the child support he was paying stretched their own funds to the limit. Eva even went along with Jason having the children over each weekend, despite the fact that having them there on their only days off encroached upon their time alone.

Eva could see how guilty Jason felt for having been the one to leave the marriage, particularly when his son would tell him how their mother would cry and say that she didn't understand why Jason had left them all. Eva could also see that it pained Jason when the kids so obviously snubbed her attempts to be affectionate with them.

Eva found herself not just looking forward to the long weekend she and Jason planned to spend alone together, she was counting on it. The call came the night before they were to leave. Julie was sick. Couldn't get out of bed. She wanted Jason to take the kids, as he did every weekend even though the plan had been in place for some time now. When Jason said no to her, she had screamed, "Your father doesn't care about any of us. He won't help me out and he doesn't want to see you." Then she slammed down the phone, leaving Jason devastated.

Eva, who saw Julie as horribly manipulative and destructive, sat seething, waiting to see what Jason would do. When he uttered the words, "I think I'm going to have to get them," she went ballistic. What Eva wanted was to feel loved, to feel as important to him as his children were, to have him deal more forcibly with Julie, who seemed so present and intrusive in their lives. Eva was hurt. Terribly. What she shrieked without thinking was, "I can't stand this anymore and I don't want your goddamned children here with us all the time. Maybe you should just go back and try and make it work with Julie."

The second the words had flown from her mouth, she knew what she had done. She had set feelings in motion in Jason that she couldn't alter, in spite of her protests of not meaning the awful things she said.

In love, there are some words not to be spoken, some feelings not to be expressed, some actions not to be taken. Be aware of those sacred spaces in a relationship that are not to be entered, for there is no return.

Territory that is advantageous to neither you nor your enemy is called questionable. It must be remembered that even when the enemy invites your attack to march away. When half his troops have followed, only then may you attack with advantage.

WHY SOME THINGS CAN'T BE DISCUSSED

Questionable terrain is that territory where information, specificity, and detail serve no useful purpose. How often have you heard questions such as, "So, what was your wildest sexual experience?" "Come on, you can tell me." "You really don't like my mother, do you?" "I hear women say that size doesn't matter, but I want to know what you think." Or, "You've never told me about your old sexual experiences. I'd really like to know." Sure.

The answers to such questions lie distinctly in territory that shouldn't be entered. Don't let your partner trick you into stepping a foot into this soggy ground, for there is only quicksand here. There is no advantage to being explicit or giving details about certain things, particularly when you are dealing with a man.

Women are often capable of handling more honesty and detail than men are and can make the mistake of forgetting this important difference. Men may pretend they can deal with your honesty without a meltdown, but don't fall for such a pretense. A man may seduce you into divulging detailed information and then turn around and use it against you.

Most women want to know facts and feelings. Most are not threatened by the man's past, believing and trusting in the quality of the present. A man may ask you for the facts, but he really doesn't want to be given them. He asks for information when what he wants is affirmation.

The task here is in recognizing questionable terrain. Listen for a man's need for reassurance even when it is hidden in the disguise of a question. For a man, the two most obvious areas of questionable terrain are family and sexuality. His mother is still his mother and only he is free to tear her down. Ever. And men don't want to know about your sexual experiences, especially when it comes to numbers or gritty details, even though they are often compelled to ask. A question such as, "So, how big was he?" should only be answered honestly if he was smaller than your partner. "Twice your size," may be closer to the truth, but there is no advantage in saying it. Neither is there an advantage in saying, "But you're the more sensitive and giving lover." To you, that may be a heartfelt compliment. A man, however, will neither appreciate nor process it as such.

Honesty and openness must always be placed in context. Expressing something simply because it is true carries no advantage. Truth is always defined by the greater context. The greater context is fleshed in by subtext, the hidden question, the unexpressed need for reassurance. Even a woman more tolerant of honesty who asks a man what he thinks of her in bed probably wants to hear affirming words rather than a detailed, blow-by-blow comparison of how she measures up to the other women in his life.

Constricted territory is land made up of canyons and narrow defiles. If you occupy such land first, you must deploy your troops fully and block the roads and passes. But if the enemy has already sealed off the terrain, do not enter.

PERSONAL FREEDOMS TO PROTECT

If you don't establish boundaries that guarantee your freedom, they may be drawn up by the man in your life. And when they are of the man's design, they are all too often defined more by the level of the man's insecurities than by his trust, more by his need to control than his generosity.

Lucy is a woman who made the mistake of getting caught in the narrow spaces of love and became enslaved by her partner Arthur's worrisome fantasies and failure to take responsibility for his own discomfort. Here is her story as she told it:

If anyone had ever told me it would come to this, I wouldn't have believed them. Not me. Never. Not with what I know, not with what I've been through. The crackling fire didn't warm me and the Vivaldi didn't make my spirit zoom the way it once did. Even the inviting aroma of roasting garlic and rosemary turned bitter in my mind when linked to the coming shame.

Arthur pointed, and we were escorted to a table at the back of the restaurant. Arthur did the usual—deftly positioning himself and offering a chair to me before the maître d' made his move. Grinning that charming smile of his, he asked for the wine list as we sat. I was facing the wall. I always face the wall when we go out.

"You don't mind, do you, hon?" he asked, flashing a smile and a hand across the table touching my cheek. "You know how I like to be able to look around."

"It's me you're talking to, Arthur," I said.

The smile faded, replaced by dark rumblings of an approaching storm. Something all too familiar. Then, just as suddenly, his mood brightened as he darted away and began chattering about some mindless event at his office.

My body was there. My head nodded at roughly appropriate times. But I was elsewhere. Somewhere far away. A safe place. It felt dangerous not to gather the distance close around me for without it I was afraid I might start screaming. Or worse yet, want to kill him.

"I asked you where you were today," he said, breaking through the drone.

"What?" I heard myself say across the chasm.

"I called you twice this afternoon. Where were you?"

I wanted to shout, Fucking my brains out you asshole! Instead "I told you I had to go to a meeting downtown today" tumbled meekly out.

"Oh yeah," he grunted plunging back into his salad.

I found a small spot on the wall behind Arthur's head and lost myself in it. It felt like a reminder of the prison I'd allowed him to create for me. Starring at this spot helped me keep it all together. I knew if I started unwinding, I'd surely spin out of control.

"Something wrong with my hair?" he asked, chewing the remnants of a roll.

"No, Arthur, nothing's wrong with your hair," I mumbled.

I suppose at first I was flattered by his jealousy. It was endearing and made him seem sweetly vulnerable, reminding me of how my cat used to mark his domain. But then everything escalated. We couldn't go to a party without Arthur gluing himself to my side. The simplest friendly exchanges with a man were met by endless interrogations until it was no longer worth looking, smiling, or talking with anyone other than Arthur. Then the phone calls during the day, his suspicions disguised as interest and concern.

And now this. We can't go out to dinner without me sitting facing the wall. He says it's because he likes to look around, but I think he's worried about who I might be looking at. I gave into it, hoping for a little peace and now I wonder what territory he'll try to gobble up next.

Lucy made a critical error in allowing Arthur's possessiveness to set the tone of the relationship. Out-of-control jealousy is a process in which the woman always participates. In order not to fall into this trap, a woman must not tolerate double standards. Double standards tend to widen with time rather than merge because they are all driven by insecurity. Lucy is not viewed by Arthur as accommodating but as someone needing restrictions to control her behavior. Lucy's willingness to "give in" doesn't appease Arthur, it simply confirms his worst fears. In his heart, Arthur "knows" that if Lucy weren't guilty and weak willed with men, she would never put up with his crazy, inappropriate demands.

As far as precipitous terrain is concerned, you must move quickly to secure the sunny heights and there await the enemy.

THE POWER OF GOODNESS

Placing yourself on the sunny slopes has to do with approach. It is advantageous not only to know what represents goodness on an issue, but also to approach it with grace and compassion. A "right" position can be approached either from a place of light or from the darkness of anger or frustration. There is no advantage in approaching an issue from the shady side, even if your position is lodged firmly in the technicality of correctness. Goodness is a combination of doing what is right in the right way.

Pat was forced to deal with an especially difficult decision in the first few months of her marriage to Norman. Late one night, Norman told her that his oldest boy (who was just beginning his senior year in high school) wanted to come and live with them. The boy was having problems in school, and Norman's ex claimed that she could no longer control the boy, who had already had a couple of minor skirmishes with the law. Pat saw that Norman himself was struggling with the dilemma and her heart went out to him. But she also saw the arrival of Norman's son as an ending to the quiet bliss of their marriage.

Part of her wanted to say no. To try and get the boy help. To suggest something to support the boy's mother so she might feel strong enough to keep him with her. To make Norman feel selfish and guilty for bringing the product of a long-dead marriage into their house. To do anything to keep the boy from coming. But Pat also knew enough about the circumstances to know the boy needed his father's steadying influence now more than ever. Pat didn't have to hear "only for a year" to settle on what was the right thing to do. Not only did Pat say yes, she also embraced her choice with a resolution to make Norman's son feel welcomed and loved. It is interesting to see the magic worked by open, outstretched arms.

When you are at a considerable distance from an enemy who has configured his troops to his liking and which are a power equal to your own, it will be difficult to provoke him into combat. There is no particular advantage to attacking from this position.

LOVING WITHOUT NEGATIVE ANTICIPATION

In love, "distant ground" is territory that has not yet been defined. It is only seen as defensive to occupy territory that the man has not yet contested. Don't be the first to make this unloving blunder.

Negative anticipation is the enemy here. This "worst-case scenario" thinking is the emotional form of generalization. We all generalize because it makes learning more efficient. But while generalization is necessary and constructive, its emotional cousin—negative anticipation—is not. Negative anticipation is fear based on and largely a product of past experiences. And it is destructive because it takes your partner out of the equation and puts your fears, dreads, and worries in his place.

Dialogue allows both partners a voice. Negative anticipation is a monologue with the only voice being your own. The danger in a monologue of anticipation is that it robs your partner of his voice and, in its absence, tends only to confirm your concerns rather than tempering or dispelling them with the reality of his thoughts and feelings.

Negative anticipation is to be avoided. Don't bring your baggage into the sanctuary of a new love. If he is not to be worthy of your love, let him demonstrate that deficiency himself. You needn't supply anticipated problems of your own construction. It is hard enough to keep a relationship clean. Don't be the bearer of unnecessary debris.

Ten Outcomes Not to Anticipate

1. Don't anticipate rejection. Understand that caring about yourself is contagious.
2. Don't anticipate opposition. Believe that nothing can stand in the way of your loving, reasoned actions.
3. Don't anticipate censure. Trust that your fullest self can be expressed.
4. Don't anticipate perfection. See how your mistakes can be forgiven and corrected.
5. Don't anticipate difficulty. Trust that you can solve meddlesome problems while they are still easy.
6. Don't anticipate abandonment. Trust that being alone with yourself is more sustaining than an unworkable union.
7. Don't anticipate failure. Learn how its appearance can be another opportunity for growth.
8. Don't anticipate danger. Know that worry only sets in motion forces that fulfill it.
9. Don't anticipate disrespect. Only you need to be at peace with your values.
10. Don't anticipate comfort. Understand that only then will you be fearless.

It is never too late to rid yourself of negative anticipation. Here is a good exercise to try as an alternative to the ritual New Year's resolutions. Find a comfortable spot where you can sit or lie and close your eyes, relaxing for a few minutes. Let yourself visualize walking slowly along a forest path. Ahead through the trees is a lake filled with warm, clear water. Move along farther, stepping into the water. As you move deeper, say, "In these waters, I shed the anticipations that dwell within me." As you move slowly deeper, say, "In these waters, I am cleansed of anticipation and in my naked-ness, renewed." Bring to mind a specific anticipation you are willing to let go of. Release it, knowing its presence is not protective.

❧

There are five types of disasters a general can bring upon his army. None of these calamities is brought about by natural causes, but by his own errors. These ill-fated and unnecessary outcomes are: insubordination, sinking, collapsing, chaotic, and beaten.

In order to avoid failure a woman must stop seeing herself in the following ways: weak, ambivalent, impulsive, unfocused, defeated. Each of these tendencies should be understood and avoided. You hold within your own hands the clay of love. Shape it wisely.

❧

When the soldiers are strong but the officers that command them weak, the army will be insubordinate.

THE IMPORTANCE OF TRUSTING YOUR VALUE

When insecurity is strong and your belief in yourself is weak, the result is a kind of internal insubordination. The only people who don't occasionally have concerns over their attractiveness, value, and lovability are apparitions, not mere flesh and blood mortals. For most of us, depending upon mood, situation, and maybe even the time of month, we may feel self-confident one moment and dodging the nagging darts of doubt the next. This is the normal ebb and flow of esteem with which most of us struggle.

Mistakes in love can be made during periods when feelings run high and intense, but your belief in yourself sinks mysteriously low. How we value ourselves is our internal territory and a domain we must learn to protect. Experiencing a lapse in your inner beliefs is often a signal for reflection and nonaction. Any actions taken during these predictable moments run the risk of appearing desperate to the man. Take a moment and step back. This may be one of those times when doing nothing is a whole lot better than doing anything. How many of you have asked the question, made the statement, taken the action that you knew showed weakness and yet were compelled to go ahead and do it anyway? We've all done that, haven't we?

In love, there is no aspect of trust more important than the trust in basic inner worth, no trust more fragile and none more connected to the value you assign your lover. The higher you value him, the more you want him, the more vulnerable will be your belief in yourself. It is easy to be spontaneous, alive, even a bit daring with someone you aren't particularly drawn to. You aren't risking anything, so nothing feels as though it's in jeopardy, right? These experiences are rehearsals, priceless opportunities to experiment and find out what you're like with a man. Don't go numb when it comes to the real thing. Those experiences have only one purpose: building trust with what you *like* about yourself with a man you *like*.

There is nothing more fascinating to a man than a woman who is confident, nothing that makes him take more notice. A confident attitude creates interest all on its own. A man feels safer with a confident woman and believes his choice is a good one because she exudes a sense of spunky value about herself. A man values a woman no higher that she values herself. Act boldly, and bold feelings will gradually follow.

You've worked hard to learn what is right for you.

Trust that knowledge when it counts the most, when it's most difficult. Resist the temptation of the impulse you know you'll only pay for later. Believe in your value. You needn't act simply on how you feel. Even if your confidence is flagging, act as if you're confident anyway. You are imprisoned by negative feelings only if you permit it. Step outside the bars and do, say, and be what you know to be right for you, not what may seem easiest.

Here is a good exercise to try when you feel that first flutter of anxiety, that slow drip of mounting worry or its more charming counterpart, drama and excitement. Create a dialogue. Talk to yourself as if you were your own best friend. Step aside and listen to the explanation of the situation with all its hopes, fears, and excuses. Then write on a piece of paper what is in your best interest to do. Not the easiest, the best. Use your intelligence, sensitivity, and knowledge of love.

Now for the tricky part. Put that plan into movement (yes, this means doing and saying things to the man you love). Behave *as if* you are confident and the confidence *will follow*. Guaranteed. Only if you are willing to do this will you be well trained in love.

When the general has no moral toughness or cannot discipline properly, when his orders and guidance are not wise, when he provides no consistent rules, and when he permits the formation of the troops to be sloppy or disordered, the army is in chaos.

How *Your* Code of Conduct Defines the Terrain of Love

It is important for all of us to have personal rules for how we act in the world. And these rules should be independent of our partner's behavior. Always encourage your partner to grow into your guidelines for conduct. Never bend to his level if it is below yours. Stooped postures tend to become permanent afflictions.

Before you can lead your partner into following your rules, you must have them clearly established. What do you stand for? What do you bring to love and what do you want from it? What do you push yourself to do even if it makes you uncomfortable? What do you prevent yourself from doing even if stopping yourself creates a similar discomfort? How responsible are you for your own sense of value and well-being and how much of that responsibility is projected onto your partner? How generous and trusting are you of yourself? How generous and trusting with your partner?

Most of us don't put in the time and effort to address questions such as these. In turn, we then have only fuzzy notions of where we stand, what we bring, and what we can reasonably expect from love. Moral toughness is about character. And character is never fuzzy. Character takes positions and knows where it stands.

Entering into a love relationship with maturity requires character. Ask yourself the difficult questions. Avoid easy, reflexive actions. Be disciplined. This means taking yourself out of a reactionary mode and placing yourself into a revolutionary one. Have the vision to bring ideals to your love, for without ideals as fixed points to move toward, there is a tendency to slide into the accidental and, ultimately, the mediocre.

Let the man be elevated by what he sees in you. Define your own code of conduct and strive to live by those guidelines. When a man acts in a way that is consistent with what you know to be best about love, let him know. Appreciate him openly. And when he does something that is undermining, be as specific and surefooted with your disapproval. Let him know how you feel and why.

The danger in not having thought through a code of conduct for love is that your own lack of definition gives the man unnecessary license to be sloppy and inconsistent in his treatment of you. If you don't know where you stand, neither will he. If you don't define boundaries, he will not know when he has stepped across one.

Always try to prevent hurt and confusion. Work on yourself first. One positive, character-driven act on your part is worth more than a thousand good intentions.

❧

When a general is unable to estimate the strength of the enemy and attacks a large force with a small one, or knowingly allows weak troops to engage strong ones, or when he fails to use his elite troops at the point of attack, the result is rout and defeat.

WHEN LOGIC AND CURIOSITY ARE YOUR ALLIES

If a woman brings only her feelings to a dilemma, she is making a serious mistake. She needs more firepower. In addition to her feelings, a woman needs the strength and reasoning of her intellect. Never throw a weak argument against a man's strong resolve. Use your finest assets, the combination of your emotional and reasoning powers. Anything less can easily result in defeat.

Marybeth's story is a great example of what can be gained by listening to reason rather than swing into emotion. Marybeth loved to be held after she and John made love. The contact and physical closeness was wonderfully comforting and anchored her emotional closeness to him in a way that sex alone never did. John's tendency was to leap up immediately afterward, light a cigarette, grab the remote, or run to the kitchen to make himself a sandwich. Most of the time when he pulled away, Marybeth would choke back her hurt, despising the odd sense of weakness she felt. She would not be reduced to begging. She had her pride. But at other times, she would get upset, sensing he was about to jump up once again and break the spell. Marybeth saw the look on his face, a mixture of guilt and, as time went by, a growing trace of resentment.

It was the subtle resentment that got her attention and caused Marybeth to change her approach. One night after lovemaking, Marybeth did something different. She refused to get upset. Instead, she talked to John. Not about her feelings and not about his selfishness. Marybeth talked about his discomfort or, more precisely, encouraged him to talk about it. She let him know that she understood this was a real issue for him and that when she was clear about it, she knew it had little to do with her and everything to do with him. With her help, John began opening up a bit. She wanted to know and understand; she wasn't reacting emotionally. It was this night that he told her a story she had not heard before, one that he only just then recalled himself.

When John was fifteen, and in the midst of his confusing hormonal rushes, his mother and father divorced, and John remembered his mother as being moody, depressed, and needy. John had enjoyed her company in earlier days, but now she seemed cloying and overbearing. Feeling lonely, she would come into John's room at night and sit on his bed to talk. John hated the fact that his eyes so often found the outline of her breasts against her nightgown and hated even more that he would get aroused despite himself. Pinned in by the wall on one side and his mother on the other, he felt trapped, suffocated. And this feeling was amplified when she would inevitably ask him for a hug. John wanted to push her away and escape, wanted desperately not to hurt her even further, wanted to slit his wrists for having to feel any of this.

By telling this story to Marybeth, John understood for the first time why the pairing of sexuality and affection was so troubling to him. It brought up the anxiety from so long ago of comingled affection, arousal, taboo, and feeling trapped. And the telling was freeing. Over a period of time and with the opportunity to put his feelings into words, John got steadily more and more comfortable with the blending of closeness and sex.

In addition to her heart, Marybeth used her head. Instead of interpreting the problem as hers, she stood back and saw that John was having trouble and that his trouble was quite independent of her. It was her clarity and reasoned help that allowed him to grasp the source of his feelings. And it was this process that brought the two of them closer together.

❧❧

When a general advances, he does so without seeking personal power. And when he withdraws, he is not concerned with avoiding punishment. His only purpose is to protect the people and the best interests of the civilian government.

EXPANDING THE BOUNDARIES OF COMFORT

Love is not about the singular needs of the woman, nor

of the man. Love is the embodiment of the relationship, the "we," the unifying synergy comprising the two of you and has its own needs. Many of us hope for love to deepen, but we relate to it only in terms of how it serves *our* needs. We ask ourselves, How does this relationship make me feel? Success in love is embedded in the health and solidity of the union. The real question should be something like, how are *we* doing? Is the relationship, the marriage, the love between us, flourishing and well served?

The needs of the relationship exist in the fringes just beyond the edges of our comfort zones. It requires a stretch to see and attend to them. Being smart in love requires looking beyond what feels comforting to you and takes looking at what makes the union comfortable. What sustains the union is sensitivity, generosity, and freely given accommodations. Dare to be a model for stretching beyond the comfortable, knowing that he will take your lead and stretch back in your direction.

How do you do this? By enlarging the boundaries of your comfort zone. Make a list of your lover's likes, wants, or needs that make you nervous, uncomfortable, itchy. He likes to hike and go camping; you don't go anyplace that doesn't have room service. That's on the list. He likes magazines piled up haphazardly on the coffee table; you can't stand the morning paper not being in the trash can by 9 A.M. That's on the list. He likes Springsteen blasting; you prefer Mozart as just audible background. That's on the list.

Be honest with yourself and be specific. Withhold fanfare. Work on reducing some of these differences by moving toward him. Stretch. Give. Your movement will not only nurture the love between you, it will also be personally expanding and illuminating as well.

When a general treats his troops as he would his own loved sons, they will follow him anywhere and even be willing to die for him.

HOW FRIENDSHIP CREATES LOYALTY

When a woman treats her partner with loving acceptance, she can be assured of gaining whatever capacity for loyalty he possesses. Acceptance creates openness and the greatest amount of shared territory. Openness is how two people stay in touch, know what they are feeling, and understand when things go wrong. Openness is the by-product of acceptance that leads to the most important ingredient in lasting love: friendship.

Emotional disengagement in a love relationship is, most often, caused by a breakdown and failure of friendship. Friendship fails to thrive or is damaged by chronic judgment and criticism. Although men may seem incredibly insensitive, they are in fact upset rather easily, especially when they feel the stinging disapproval of their mate. Men, often lacking the expressive range women possess, may simply become a little quiet, attempting to camouflage their hurt. Men can be so successful at this that women don't realize the depth of the man's hurt feelings.

If the man continues to feel your disapproval, his disengagement can quickly become a way of life. He pulls back, anticipating criticism. If a man doesn't feel that he can be open with you, he will find someone with whom he can. (This is the most common setup for a man having an affair.)

Men crave friendship with a woman, perhaps even more than a woman needs it with a man. The reason is that most women have closer and more intimate friendships than do men. Many men tend to be loners. They may have business acquaintances or even guys they play golf with, but no one they are particularly close to or open with. This is why men are so hungry for a real friendship with a woman. The easiest way to get a man to open up to you? Befriend him. Like him. Accept him, and the barriers fall.

Some women are hesitant about establishing the close bonds of friendship for fear that this will automatically rule out a passionate relationship. Nothing could be further from the truth. Friendship is the underscore upon which the melody line of passion is played and sustained. Make your man your friend. If you encourage his openness with your interest and acceptance, then he will be yours for life.

If a general is indulgent with his troops but is unable to control them, if he loves his men but cannot make them obey his commands, he has turned them into spoiled children and made them useless.

A LITTLE FEAR ON A MAN'S PART IS *NOT* A BAD THING

It is the secret mixture of abundant love combined with a pinch of fear that sustains the bond of passion. If the woman is the only one being kind and accepting, then the man will become arrogant and cannot be counted upon. And if a woman is uncomfortable with discipline and afraid to use punishment, then the man will become spoiled and have no respect for proper boundaries. Romantic love, even mature romantic love, is not unconditional. We all give up that notion as we learn (sometimes kicking and screaming) the conditions and consequences attached to adult love. We would all like to believe we might find a place where love will last forever, but romantic love is fragile and kept alive by a vigilance to discipline.

Many women feel more comfortable being kind and understanding than being tough. They would rather be held than to have to hold a firm line. Sometimes women make the mistake of being too focused on the man's needs, pushing their own into the background. They have convinced themselves that to hold on to the man they must suppress their feelings and blur their boundaries. Instead of this being an equation for success, it is a blueprint for certain failure.

A man thrives on a woman's generosity and understanding. But his love is kept alive by seeing how she creates and sustains his respect for her. Every man must know in his heart that you would prefer losing him rather than your dignity. When a man doesn't know that crucial fact, he will cross lines that shouldn't be crossed, and you and the love between you will suffer.

The only antidote is finding the courage to be a loving disciplinarian. Never allow a man to be disrespectful to you. Never allow a man to think that any kind of lie or deceit is acceptable. Never allow a man to hide behind lazy excuses or explanations for his bad behavior. Show me a man who is crazy mad for a woman and I will show you a man who gets absolutely crazy if the woman is mad at him. Don't fail to use your anger appropriately, for it is the guardian of dignity and preserver of respect.

When a general who is wise in war moves, he makes no mistakes. When he chooses to act, his resources are without limit.

PROTECTING THE TERRAIN OF LOVE

Most of us know far more about love than we ever put to use in our daily lives. We have the important facts, we've had the experiences, the hundreds of conversations with friends. Many of us would rather keep on learning and keep on talking, as if being good at love in the abstract is what it's all about. And that's part of the problem. Too often the wisdom we have is wasted because we don't exercise the will to translate it into the real actions of love.

Love is about conduct, not intention. Love is about what *is,* not about what you *wish.* It doesn't matter how much you know, what counts is how much of this knowledge you put into use. Many women are afraid to use their knowledge, afraid to put into action the very things they know implicitly serve and protect love most effectively. It's not that they don't know what to do, they're afraid of doing something wrong, afraid their actions will hurt rather than help them. They don't trust their own wisdom, the very knowledge they've worked so hard to obtain.

A woman who is smart about love makes few mistakes because she believes the advice she would lovingly give to a friend enough to take it herself. Her words concerning love are not descriptions of what someone should do, they are descriptions of what she does. She doesn't make mistakes because she would rather do something right than complain about something wrong. She doesn't make mistakes because she doesn't let her decisions be influenced by ease, comfort, and soft-minded thinking. She does what is right. She invests in foresight, leaving hindsight for the less stouthearted. She thinks before expressing her feelings, never valuing the immediacy of emotion over thoughtful judgment.

A smart woman doesn't act when nonaction would be more effective. She doesn't push on when surrender better serves her purposes. She never broadcasts her power simply for the sake of listening to the thunderclap it creates, and neither does she assert her leverage when it isn't challenged. The smart woman praises to affirm and punishes only to teach rather than demean. She contains her energy, knowing that when she chooses to act, her resources will be limitless.

This is why I say: Know your enemy, know yourself. Know the ground, know the weather. In this way your victory will never be in question for it will be total.

Never indulge the false illusions, should's, or ought-to-be's in either yourself or in the man. See him as clearly as you are willing to see yourself. That is the only reality worth your energy. All else is useless and must be rooted out. It is always better to seek a generous heart than to throw yourself time and again against one that is scarred over or closed. Cast aside your wishful filters. Only by knowing yourself, your man, and understanding the terrain in which you play out your love, will victory be ensured.

PART 2

GAIL PARENT'S
TAKE ON THE BATTLE
OF THE SEXES

From a Woman Who's
Fought in and Survived the Trenches

Chapter 9

On the Use of Spies . . .
Help from Friends

There are five kinds of spy: the local spy, the inside spy, the reverse spy, the dead spy, and the living spy. When all spies are at work, no one knows what they are after—this is referred to as organizational genius on the part of the general and is valuable to the leadership.

—Sun Tzu

There are five kinds of spies you can call upon to equip you with information about a man. You'll find useful spies among your family, your friends, his family, his friends, his former relationships, his business colleagues, and from people who know you both well.

GETTING INFORMATION FROM THOSE WHO CARE ABOUT YOU

It may sound harsh to recommend the use of spies. It won't feel wrong or manipulative if you realize that in love relationships, *spy* is being used as a word for friend, his or yours. Friends have always been employed to help find out information about a man. To gather this information you need spies; don't try to do it yourself. Cheryl, a thirty-four-year-old who fell madly and stupidly in love with Harold, ended up going through his garbage to find clues about his life. Not only did she spend a lot of money on scented soaps to get the smell off her hands, but Harold caught her one day elbow-deep in his coffee grinds. She was so upset at the time, she didn't have the presence of mind to say, "Have you seen my diamond earring?"

Local spies are people drawn from your immediate support system. Don't complicate matters by asking too many people to help you, because they'll begin comparing notes with one another before reporting to you.

Enlist your best friend to check out some facts about a man, especially if the relationship is in its early stages and you're unsure of how you could fit into his life and he into yours. For example, it may be difficult for you to ask a twice-divorced man whether he will ever consider marrying again. However, a good friend can find out how he feels about marriage in a light, curious way. "Are you enjoying your freedom?" is a question she can ask right before she asks him to pass the salt. Also, it's actually easier for him to tell your friend the truth because he can be more relaxed with her on some issues than he can with you. He knows he's not hurting her.

If you're part of the new dating generation, anywhere from nineteen to thirty-two, there's a good chance you'll need a spy just to find out if you are really dating or not. In today's society, many people of the younger generation refuse to use the word *date* at all. Therefore a young woman can see a man five or six times and still not know whether they are dating, beginning a friendship, or doing business. This is because men and women in this age group get together for dinner, for movies, for sports, with neither party calling it a date. It's done with such casualness that there is total confusion as to whether the two of you are going to get together. Usually this confusion starts with a question such as, "Do you want to grab a bite and talk about it?" ("it" can be anything from talking about business to participating in tennis). The good news is that neither party knows if it's a date, however, neither party is daring enough to ask. You're going to have to send in a local spy to see if he thinks, it's a date, or if he thinks that you think that it's a date. The uncertainty never ends. Her opening statement should be, "I hear you're seeing (your name here)." Then, pray that he gives her more information.

When the relationship is still new and shaky, you will want to know some specifics about him. You may want to uncover his whereabouts and with whom he is socializing when he's not with you—things like, where he was last weekend. Since it would be awkward for you to ask him to account for his actions, have your spy do it, even if it's in your presence.

Let's say your spy and the man she's dating end up in a restaurant with you and your new guy. If you want to know where he was last Saturday night, have your friend bring up the subject by talking about where she was. This is an approach used by professional spies. They talk about themselves, then include the mark in the conversation. So to spy, your friend brings up what she did last weekend. "The rain gets me down, so I rented six movies on Saturday," she announces when she feels the time is right. "I watched old musicals until *60 Minutes* came on Sunday night."

Hopefully, the man you're interested in will get involved in the conversation. He may say something like, "I was happy not to be in town for the bad weather. A group of my friends from college get together and brainstorm once a year. This year it was in New Orleans, and the weather was great." (It may not be quite as smooth or as easy as this.)

Inside spies are drawn from the man's inner circle of friends. They end up working for you, but this kind of infiltration isn't easy, since his friends are automatically loyal to him. One thing you don't want to do is fool around with the male bond. *However*, remember that they want to see him happy. And if they feel that he will be happy with you, they will be very helpful in trying to make the relationship work, even if it means giving you information about their buddy. They're the ones who will let you know that he's the kind of person who likes to be pursued or the kind who needs time alone. They will let you in on personal traits that would take years to find out about on your own.

It's important to know them because they are the friends who have seen him in relationships with other women and are the most likely to know what his patterns are. Get to know them by being friendly. This will help you in two ways. It will make the man you're with feel good that you have taken his people in and they will inform you if they feel you're accepting of them. You are going to have to be a shrewd tactician; first you must learn who his local spies are (male friends, platonic friends, siblings) and how they rank in influence over the man you are investigating.

Inside spies are wonderful message carriers. You can tell them things like how much fun their buddy is, and they'll carry the message back. You will be able to convey your happiness and caring for their friend indirectly, which might, at the beginning, be easier for you, since there are some things that are too difficult to tell a new man in your life. Also, coming from a friend, the words carry more weight. Since he's known him longer than he's known you, the information will feel even more real. (They can also be carriers for less vital information, such as telling him that you really love being cooked for and adore gifts of cashmere sweaters. Many men are relieved to know what you want for gifts. They are not natural shoppers the way women are.)

Inside spies are invaluable. Listen to them. The story of Allison and James proves that theory. Allison was asked out to dinner by James, which may seem like a normal occurrence, but it was nowhere near normal. The two had broken up about five years before. He had moved from Illinois to Arizona. (It's always a relief when the man you've broken up with moves out of the state you're living in. You can pretend he's missing in China.) When he called to say he was coming to Chicago and that he would like to see her, she said yes, thinking that it would be harmless. It was only after Allison agreed to go out that James revealed he was coming back to his hometown to find out the result of a case that had been in and out of court for over six years. He stood to win $1,200,000. Allison was shocked that she would be with a man she hadn't seen in five years on one of the biggest days of his life.

Allison knew someone who knew someone who was with the law firm representing James's case. When she met with him, this lawyer didn't know what the chances were of winning, but he did know that it was an obsession of James's and that his firm had suggested that he accept an out-of-court settlement. When she told her friend's friend that she was having dinner with James the night of the decision, he laughed so loudly that Allison was drizzled on and people four tables away heard him.

The end of this story is not pretty. Allison, being Allison, decided that she could deal with the situation. In other words, she wasn't listening to her inside spy. The minute she walked into the restaurant, she knew the news was not good. James was sitting at a table and looked so morose and so angry that even from a distance she felt his hand would break the glass his scotch was in. The maître 'd led her toward him, and with each step, she saw the corners of his mouth creep more and more downward. He didn't want to talk about it, he said, so for the rest of the meal they talked about harmless, unimportant things. She made him smile once and considered it her greatest victory of the year. (She was still attached to him.)

But months later, he's still in depression, and Allison hasn't heard from him once. She now knows the facts: he had won the case but was rewarded far less money than he expected. The moral of this story is simple. Revere your inside spies, even if they spit when they laugh.

In the following case study, the names of people and their dogs have been changed to protect the privacy of the individuals. Hannah is now a clever tactician at managing inside spies and in interpreting what they say. She never needed one more than when she met Donald at a dog run at a large New York City park shortly after she moved into his neighborhood. (Yes, she did have a dog, a golden retriever named Pamela, but it's not a necessity. Going to a dog park without a dog is common practice now.) Donald was boisterous and friendly, louder than his black Labrador, Louie, and very willing to talk about himself. By the second time they met, she had found out he was in his mid-thirties, divorced, and a successful, self-made businessman. (The only downside seemed to be that Louie kept stepping on her feet.)

"Donald pursued me," Hannah said. "He'd call me at work every day at ten in the morning to tell me the joke of the day. After three weeks of a phone-and-dog-run relationship, I got to like him, but I wasn't physically attracted, so I wanted to keep him as a friend." Donald continued his pursuit, inviting Hannah over to his apartment. She went because she enjoyed this big man with his big voice and large gestures. (She wore boots to protect her feet from Louie.)

Donald talked her into taking a costly rug he no longer liked. But she kept refusing his advances. She wouldn't even go out to dinner with him.

Enter Donald's brother and sister-in-law. She accepted an invitation for dinner with Harris and Natalie, figuring she wouldn't be alone with a man she wasn't interested in romantically. The evening should have been instructive for Hannah. She and Natalie exchanged looks a few times when Donald displayed sibling rivalry in a very boyish way. (She didn't realize it at the time, but she was bonding with a future spy.)

Two months after they met, Hannah and Donald wound up in bed. They cuddled one night, probably because he wore an I AM A FEMINIST T-shirt. (That's a trick, by the way.) Once that happened, she felt she had to exchange kisses. The truth is, Donald was not a bad kisser, and a kiss is *not* just a kiss. When it happens, men and women are allowing each other the kind of intimacy that sparks a huge change in the relationship.

Having sex with Donald was, for Hannah, a surprisingly intense experience. There were even feelings of love. (Unfortunately, after this type of experience, especially if you've known the man for a while, few women escape stirrings of love. It's not your fault, even gyne-cologists will tell you that women excrete a certain hormone that causes their bodies to plan the next fifty years, if only for the next twenty-four hours. It's not that men don't want love, all people want true love. The difference between men and women is that men as-sume it is guaranteed they will find love, so they want to play as much as possible beforehand. But women are scared to death that they never will, so however much they may want to play, they'll give up in a heartbeat for any glimpse of true love.) You have to believe Hannah accidentally left a bracelet on his bedside table and called him the next afternoon to see if he would be home that night so she could pick it up. He said something predictable—"You didn't have to leave jew-elry to come back"—but in a mocking way.

"When I got my bracelet," Hannah said, "he walked me to the door and said he was busy that night, and could we see each other Tuesday. I agreed, but I left feeling miserably sad. I kissed him only because I felt it would be an issue not to." Why don't men understand that saying "I'll see you next Tuesday" is a major insult? What's even worse is: "We'll get together soon." Vague-ness stings. Fortunately and unfortunately, it's a power-ful weapon to use. If a man asks to get together on Friday night, and you respond, "Let's see how we feel on Friday"—he'll feel the sting.

Hannah needed information from Harris but didn't feel comfortable calling him. As she walked to the park with Pamela, feeling guilty that she hadn't taken her to the park for several days, her eyes concentrated on the sidewalk. When she looked up, there was Natalie, Harris's wife, going in the opposite direction. Because women bond quickly in times of war, Hannah told

Natalie that she had been to bed with Donald and that he had been acting cold ever since.

Basically, Natalie said that Donald shouldn't be allowed to even mingle with the opposite sex. She said that this was no secret and that everyone who knew him knew that he had tortured his ex-wife. Hannah was relieved to hear that he was rotten to other women and not just to her. It's always comforting to know that you're not a man's only victim.

Hannah was grateful for Natalie's information, and since she generally liked her, Hannah invited Natalie to lunch the following week. (Spies should always be repaid.) Thanks to Natalie's information, Wendy ended her relationship with Donald before any further harm was done.

If you're smart enough to get information from inside spies, don't assume it's false. Consider the following points:

• You can easily learn certain facts about a man from him: what he does for a living, what year he graduated from college. But the true nature of his emotional life and his patterns with women are known by the enemy camp *before they are known to you.*

• Inside spies are instrumental at telling you, in direct terms or by suggestion, exactly who the man is and how he is likely to behave in the future. However, you have to assess the situation further because they may have their own agenda. Listen to them and also observe the man you're interested in to see if the information makes sense.

• When you are sure your inside spy is either neutral or favoring your camp, use that person to contact other inside spies you are not acquainted with or do not know as well. You will then be able to know how a majority of the people around him feel about him. There was a man in Chicago whose friends called him "Scott Free." It was a perfect nickname and a danger signal to women. He should have had a warning label on him from the surgeon general's office. He truly was harmful to a woman's health.

Reverse spies are recruited from a man's friends and members of his family who want to find out what you think of him and of the relationship. (They are his inside spies.) Since these spies talk directly to you, be on your guard. Be aware of any tricks or attempts to trip you up that they may use to get you to spill information you may not be ready to reveal. (That you fall in love easily is not the type of information your new boyfriend needs to know. He won't feel special.)

Two ways to spot a reverse spy are: someone within his circle takes a sudden interest in you and makes a casual date to have lunch, to play tennis, or to go shopping. Assess if they want to be with you or pump you for information. A second ploy involves one of his reverse spies calling you under false pretenses. Say they call "for a friend" about a specific bit of information that only you would know. If many people would know this information, he's sending out his spies to get close to you.

The use of reverse spies may work to your benefit. You can drop any detail to them that you want repeated. Anne had such an experience with Todd. He knew Anne well enough to know that she'd be more likely to open up to a woman whom she had never met than to a man she barely knew. So he sent in his friend Melanie to find out if Anne felt their new relationship could lead to something serious.

Melanie called Anne, using a request for advice about breaking into public relations, Anne's profession. They met for a drink, and Melanie established herself as the eager student and flattered Anne.

Soon Melanie was relating information about Todd that Anne would not have been comfortable asking about. Melanie filled her in on Todd's last relationship, a three-year engagement that ended a week before their intended marriage. (She should have been more concerned that his engagement lasted for three years than that it ended a week before the wedding. Three years is a long time to be engaged when it's not wartime. That the wedding didn't take place can simply mean that one or both people realized they weren't right for each other and that the person who would be most upset would be the caterer.) Melanie let Anne know that Todd was very fond of her and that she was nothing like this last woman.

Anne's antenna for the tactics of reverse spies tuned in to what Melanie was really saying: *Do you care about Todd?* The subtext also included: "I'll tell him if you do." Anne purposely leaked that she liked him, and that she hoped to keep seeing him. Then she decided to use the power of the reverse spy and give Melanie some information to carry back to the enemy camp. She said, "I'm really not good with possessive men. If only he would take it slowly." Todd pulled back a bit. After only one drink, during happy hour, Anne and Melanie solved a large problem, let Todd know what he needed to know, and got free hors d'oeuvres.

• When you spot a reverse spy, do not reject them; be open to contact. They may provide you with the information you need for your strategy.

• Do not criticize a man to his spies. They will defend

him if they love him and excuse him with explanations if they like him. Reverse spies will always report back to him, judging you difficult or demanding or backbiting. *Remember, they are his friends, not yours.* Don't confide in them. Don't say anything you don't want to get back to him.

• If he sends one or more of his children in as reverse spies, judge the man, not the child. He has no right to use his children whether they are five or twenty-five. "Do you love my daddy?" is a question you should never hear. Don't be seduced by reverse spies fished from his gene pool. And do not pump his children for information about his feelings, finances, or habits.

Dead spies are meddlesome troublemakers who feel they must insinuate themselves into your affairs and cause friction. Be on guard for this branch of the spy network. They are interested in your business for their own good, not in helping either side. When a *dead spy* takes aim, he hopes to permanently harm you and/or the man in your life. Dead spies trade in rumor, gossip, and false information.

Beware of the dead spy in local spy's clothing. They will try and convince you that they are in your corner, but they are really working for themselves. Is a platonic friend of his or an ex-girlfriend too eager to help you through a rough time with him? In fact, she may want him back too profoundly to be of any real comfort to you. She doesn't bad-mouth the man, she preys on your vulnerability and tells you how he makes you suffer and also tells you exactly how the suffering will escalate in the future. (She either wants him, or wants him hurt.) You become more vulnerable to her as she becomes more generous, giving you the knife from right out of your back.

Living spies are proficient in the way they handle things. These are people whom you know are reliable and can trust to report back to you honestly and frequently. You need to employ living spies when you feel you need all the help you can get.

Barbara is one of those women who needs both organizational genius and living spies. Divorced and in her late thirties, Barbara is a former dancer who had gone into business with three other partners. She has style and charm, discretion and good taste—she was known for it—that is until she met Allen. Ten years older than Barbara, Allen is a golden boy charmer, second in command at a large corporation.

"We met at a Wall Street Christmas party. Allen was a friend of the president of the company, and I was a client of some midlevel broker," Barbara said. "We spotted each other across the room, he walked over and we walked out, arm in arm. We were nearly inseparable for over three weeks."

Every evening for almost a month, Allen stayed over at Barbara's apartment, then each morning he'd return to the apartment the company held for him to change clothes before going off to work. Barbara learned that Allen's marriage was on the rocks and that his wife was in Nevada, getting a divorce. They spent every weekend together and, during this time, they fell in love, both of them believing that there was divine intervention. Their fifth weekend together, Allen proposed marriage.

"I thought we'd conquer the world," she said. "We both had so much going for us and I had this 'it was meant to be' feeling."

One night Allen didn't show up but called saying that the worst had happened—his wife had returned home and discovered she had ovarian cancer. He couldn't leave her side until after her surgery. The divorce, he said, had gone through. Now he was worried about her survival. Barbara said she understood. (She's a compassionate woman but wondered why she was dealt such an obstacle. It seemed that the whole universe had wanted her and Allen to be together. Then she felt guilty for thinking those thoughts.)

Allen called her a few more times, reporting on his distress, how he missed her, and relayed his wife's poor prognosis. When she didn't hear from him for almost a week, she called Allen at his office. He called back, and they continued to have passionate nights, although not overnights. Allen didn't want to abandon his wife while she was ill. After a few weeks of this, Barbara realized she needed the help of spies.

Barbara wanted to be discreet, but she needed to know more about the man and the marriage. She called her friend Jack, the broker, to see what she could learn. (He was the one who took her to the Christmas party where she met Allen.) Did he know how to reach Allen? He did. She thanked God for brokers.

Meanwhile she recalled that Allen mentioned a few of the charities his wife worked for as a volunteer. Barbara immediately called one of those charities and found out where they were having a fund-raiser. She asked her sister Rita to volunteer. Barbara now had two *living spies* on her side, both who gave her access to Allen's guarded battleground.

Although she wanted to do it herself, she enlisted Rita to call Allen's home number; a woman answered. Rita asked if she was Allen's wife and the woman said yes, in what sounded like a robust voice. Rita said she was fund-raising for a woman's health charity, which she was. Calmly, Rita asked if she knew any women who'd suffered from any disease specifically relating to women. During that conversation, Allen's wife revealed that she had a friend with ovarian cancer, but that *she* would not have to worry about it personally since she'd had a hysterectomy after her third child, twenty years ago. (Rita, by the way, fulfilled her obligation to the charity by raising thirty-five hundred dollars and felt good about it.)

Still hurt, Barbara at first wanted to believe that Allen's wife wouldn't want to talk about such a critical illness and might, in fact, lie to a stranger on the phone. However, she finally faced the facts. There was no divorce. There was no illness. There was only a lying man.

No one in an army is treated with more familiarity as are spies, rewards to spies are rich, and no matter is more secret than espionage.

BE GRATEFUL AND GRACIOUS TO THE FRIENDS WHO ARE HELPING YOUR LOVE LIFE

Compensating your spy network means that you give of yourself. At the same time that your spy is helping you, find out how you can help her with some problem she is having. You may think that your intense love situation is so needy that it should be taken care of first. Be selfless enough to know that someone else's problems can be just as important as yours and your attention toward the other person's needs is vital.

Secrecy protects spies and their operations. Do not in any way betray them. Suppose they have helped your love to flourish. Don't ever expose them by feeling so close to your lover that you tell him what your friends have done for you.

One cannot use spies without being wise and knowledgeable about them. One cannot use spies without having humanity and justice oneself, one is not able to receive the truth from spies who are not themselves subtle. The delicateness of this matter must be paid attention to. Spies are useful everywhere.

Choose Carefully Those Who Help You

You cannot use spies who do not have special knowledge of human behavior—a good understanding of motivations, drives, and needs. Spies without heart and a sense of what is right and what is wrong are also useless to you, no matter how eager they may be to help.

If you had to divide your friends into two categories, relating to who would and wouldn't be a good spy, there are probably those who are more careful and charming, and those who are more direct and honest. Forget about using the direct and honest ones. They don't know how to draw information out of somebody without that person knowing it. Also, the character of a spy is very important. If you send in an outrageous-acting friend to get information for you, she is bound to blow her cover or approach the enemy too head-on. Be sure your spy knows your style and what you want, and that he or she has the ability to be subtle. "She says the sex is great" is not something you want broadcasted.

Most importantly, your spy must be someone who can take themselves out of the picture. She should always be able to react casually and get in and out of conversations flawlessly. If you send in a friend who overreacts, you might find that she gets emotionally involved in the situation, and that her spying days should be over. She will make your romance be all about her.

It's very useful to find a spy who is in the business arena with the man you need to know more about. Here are the questions to ask your spy:

• Is he respected for his abilities on the job and as a man? Is he seductive and suggestive, within legal guidelines, with women at work?

• Does he come in mornings looking like he's slept fitfully, the result of too much alcohol, drugs, or partying? (Apologize for keeping him out late.)

• Is he ill-tempered in the mornings? Later in the day? Or is he generally even tempered when there is a major problem? Does he get out of control? (Mention how under control he appears to have things.)

• Is he a manipulator of events, information, and people? Is having control of the flow of work more important to him than the work itself? (Ask if you need to be aware of him staying late at the office.)

• Did he have a meteoric rise to the top and does he feel humble, deserving, or arrogant about it? (Mention how many toys, boats, cars, Range Rovers, he has.)

• Or is he a man who always takes the middle road, a hard worker who knows his limitations and has made peace with staying at some midpoint plateau? (You need to know if you can respect such a man. Mention that you don't have a window in your office either . . . yet.)

• Has he floated from company to company, state to state, telling himself he likes the wide experience in job change? Does he purposely uproot himself and leave one company when his success there—by promotion or salary raise—seems very imminent? (Talk about how stable you are.)

• Is he able to take direction or supervision, if that is the nature of his position now, or does he fight every order? (If it's true, say you never fight.)

• Is pleasure in his work or a job well done important to him, or is he motivated by money or status? (Drop in to the conversation where you think he'd like to live.)

• Does he lie about his credentials? Do others suspect he padded his résumé or is his Ph.D. degree from a school nobody ever heard of? (Brag about him.)

In any event, attack him with *subtlety* in the workplace. Rule out sexual games that involve calling his extension at work or hiring people in costumes who might drop by his office with helium balloons and naked breasts and embarrass him. Don't leave cute or suggestive notes on his car windshield, especially if he parks in a company lot.

Don't engage his secretary in a conversation, then ask if she can tell you *what he's really like with women and how many of them call him at work.* She works for him and needs her job.

❦

Whenever you want to attack an army, besiege a city, or kill a person, first you must know the identities of their defending generals, their associates, their visitors, their gatekeepers, and their chamberlains, so have your spies find out.

KNOW THE PEOPLE AROUND HIM

Whenever you want to make it impossible for a man to live without you, first you must know the identity of his parents, siblings, friends, acquaintances, and co-workers and understand their influences on him. Enlist your spies to uncover what these people mean to him and keep your distance to protect your position.

Who he surrounds himself with tells you a lot about the kind of man he is. (Just as an example, if he hangs out with men who are more successful than he is, and he's the one who always does them favors just so they'll like him, that will be a clue as to who he might marry someday—one of those skinny blondes who has to be catered to.)

If he has close family ties, will you always take second or third place to his relatives? Will his mother always do his laundry? (You can only hope.) Will each holiday season be decided in favor of visiting his family rather than yours? Or does he keep you and his devotion to family in balance? Does he have close friends or is he a loner, more comfortable with casual acquaintances and a girlfriend to take care of his needs? If so, the two of you may not have really close friends together as a couple. Is he popular, good in a crowd, but uneasy with intimacy? (Having friends and family relationships are two different talents.) Does he intend to create his own generation of close family ties—making his wife and children his whole life and resenting his wife having outside interests or friends? Observe his parents' marriage, then find out if he admires it.

At some point in your relationship, most likely early on, he will want to meet the people who surround you. Your parents can be brilliant tacticians in the role of blatant *local spies*, and every man knows it. *Any man presenting himself at the home of a woman he's dating expects a woman's mother or father to grill him on a few basic issues.*

Remember, you have probably asked him many of these questions already. However, he might have slightly different answers for your mother, who should have worked for the CIA, than he had for you. So listen closely and judge carefully.

• Was he married before and what happened? If he was, does he see his ex-wife?

• Does he have any children? Does he want children in the future?

• Does he demand home cooking, or is he happy to live on six-packs of Hungry-Man frozen dinners? (Most men fall in the middle.) Does he want to cook and keep you out of the kitchen? (One man actually said he was grateful because he had finally found a woman who, when it came to food, let him take care of himself.)

• How well is he doing financially? (This doesn't necessarily mean you want a man with money. It is simply one of the factors you should know.)

• Where did he grow up, what did his father do? Did his mother have a career? If so, did he resent her for it when he was a child?

• Is he religious? Is he a bigot? This is uncovered by bringing up the subject of God, worship, racial tensions, or public figures connected to these issues. (Do you think your mother won't bring up religion? Do you think your father won't get into politics? Most likely they will.)

• What does he think of the president? You'll be able to witness in him a range of emotion, how he expresses himself, and a greater sense of where his politics and sense of humor are located.

* * *

Parents may or may not extract satisfactory answers from a man, but you'll learn a lot about him by noticing which questions he avoids, which ones he goes on about, which ones make him squirm (both parents can do that), which ones require his squelching red-faced irritation. If all his discomfort is focused on matters concerning his father and his disadvantaged childhood, you have uncovered useful information.

When you feel you know him, *you* may or may not see yourself as his ideal mate and you may or may not want to compromise to please him. Don't change who you are; it's harder to return to a place where you won't compromise again. If it's his ambition to live on a boat and you loathe water, discuss it at a time when he's hungry for you. Disagree with him when the subject comes up. He won't leave. He also won't be bewildered by your feelings in the future when he wants to take to the sea and you remind him that you'll live only in a house.

CHAPTER 10

FORCE . . .
DETERMINATION TO MAKE THINGS WORK OR LET THEM GO

Governing a large number as though governing a small number is a matter of division into groups. Battling a large number as though battling a small number is a matter of forms and calls.

—Sun Tzu

The theme of this chapter has variously been interpreted not only as force, which is *might*, but also as influence, persuasion, and power—strengths needed to win any battle.

In the process of finding love, you will be dividing men into groups, eliminating those you can't tolerate until you find someone ideal. Women have always followed the rule of divide and conquer.

Sun Tzu talks about "large" and "small," which can refer to the priorities in your life—what is most important to you and what is incidental? These are issues that only you can know. To one woman, it may be important that a man she's with believes in God. To another woman, it may be important that a man doesn't say, "I will *never* wear a tie." (She is not shallow for thinking this way. It means that this man will be unhappy about all occasions where a tie is required. He would rather pass up a great meal at a great birthday party for the sake of his "cause.")

Make sure that you don't brush away the things that you cannot live with. In order to find out what might be on your list, think of the basics: eating, breathing, sleeping, walking, and talking. Is there anything about him concerning these most basic elements that annoys you now? For example: eating—his manners are bad or he grunts his food down. Let's say this bothers you even when the two of you are totally alone and embarrasses you when you are with other people. Can you put that aside?

Some women are interested in men with money and are willing to reject all others. Jennifer's story of finding a man of means is a humorous one. Jennifer, a perfectly sweet woman who happened to have very expensive tastes, knew that she wanted a man who could get her what she wanted. She was hoping to retire at thirty-one.

Filled with plans to find a rich husband, she went to gamblers anonymous, because she felt that men who had enough money to gamble away could get it again. She also pretended she was doing a story for *New York* magazine about the ten most successful bachelors in New York. This one backfired because successful bachelors don't want their finances known. One day, while riding home on the subway and vowing someday that she would be able to take cabs, she came up with the idea of pretending to sell a Mercedes.

Since Jennifer is the type of woman who makes things happen, she went right to work. She made sure she could rent a brand-new Mercedes two-seater for the following weekend. She put an ad in the *New York Times* and the *Wall Street Journal,* saying that she had a brand-new two-seater Mercedes 560 for sale for seventy-two thousand dollars. She wanted the price to be a bargain, but not so low that it would appear made up.

Before she even got home with the car on Friday, there were messages waiting for her. It seemed everyone in the tri-state area wanted this car. She immediately eliminated the messages from women but wrote down all the men's phone numbers. And for the rest of the night, the phone didn't stop ringing. If a woman called, Jennifer said the car was no longer available. If a man was on the phone, she reminded him that it was not a family car. Some of these callers said, "It's just me and my wife." They were instantly eliminated and told the car was sold. Others said something like, "It's just for me, I don't have a family." They were scheduled for a test drive.

Jennifer had it all figured out. A fifteen-minute test drive with a single man who could afford a seventy-thousand-dollar car was worth the effort. In essence, she had scheduled twenty blind dates for the weekend, all men who could afford her.

It worked out well until Sunday, around four. She had met a professor with family money, a broker who was considered a genius, and a dentist who had other dentists working for him, among others. The problem late Sunday was that she had practically all of the twenty men standing around the car, fighting for it. Nobody was paying attention to her. The only body they were interested in was her car's. Checkbooks got waved. They argued about who got there first, and what right they had to the car. Jennifer tried to explain that she could not accept a check on a Sunday, when the banks were closed. But this did nothing to calm any of the men down. They formed a little vigilante group and directed their anger toward her. Within minutes, all her "blind dates" rejected her.

Jennifer hasn't given up. A week from Sunday she's renting a Jaguar coupe. This time, she will make sure only one man at a time gets near the car. (If you're under thirty, choosing a Mustang convertible would probably be the way to go.)

Although Jennifer's tactics have as yet been unsuccessful, there are some real tips to be taken from her endeavors. Jennifer began by singling out only those men who met her qualifications. This strategy is what every woman does naturally when she wants to couple. She may eliminate those who don't have the same idea of what fun is, because sailing is important to her. She may eliminate someone who will live only in a city, because she wants to live in the country. (You can compromise your ideals, but only to a level that will keep your happiness intact.)

Your strategy in choosing a man comes from a set of standards that you have developed throughout your life—ones that you feel you need. (When you were twelve you might have wanted to be with a rock singer. Hopefully, now your standards are more complex and you want to be with with a rock singer who has a neurology practice as a hobby.)

In all species, either the male or the female chooses the mate. In humans, it is the women who are the choosers. This will probably come as a shock because most women feel that they are always waiting to be chosen. But picture yourself standing in front of all the men who have interested you or those you would like to get to know and love. You stroll through the rows of men as if they were Christmas trees. Your job is to pick the best one. Practically every woman would say that this is a fantasy. Whether you see it or not, men gather for you. So let's not argue with the biology and assume that you are the one who is going to select. It will be much easier for you if you consistently weed men out of your life. Basically, you are going to have to choose a man with the genetic makeup and the temperament that you want and need. Organize your thoughts: what qualities are most important to you, least important to you, or of no significance? The truth is that you're not open to everyone, nor should you be. You want the best you can get.

What kind of man do you want? Consider the following:

• Appearance counts, or does it? To some women, the way a man looks is very important. This is especially important when you are young and first dating. You enjoy having a boy beside you who your girlfriends think is handsome. (By the time you are sixty, this feeling should go away.)

Smart, mature women today are usually attracted to the whole man. His nature becomes more important than anything. His face and body will not look so beautiful if his nature is ugly. Usually both the male and female choose someone within there own range of looks and intelligence. (When they don't, one member of the couple always feels superior.)

• Is social standing an important issue? In the early part of this century, women had no money of their own and had to marry a man who could take care of them. Now that there is no stigma attached to a woman who works, status has become less of an issue. There are still people who want their sons and daughters to marry their own "kind," but the world is too big today for them to be able to control who their children will meet.

The best universities are no longer just for the privileged.

• How much does money count? We already know that to Jennifer it counts a lot. The best advice, though, is to treat the giant of industry as well as you treat the handyman. In an economically volatile world where jobs are no longer a lifetime contract, don't consider the work, consider the man and his ambition to do his job well.

The important thing is to be honest to yourself when it comes to the question of money. Is it important to you which one of you is the breadwinner? Is it important to him? Ask if you can live a life where you'll have to be very careful about what you can spend or if you can live with not knowing where money will be coming from. Imagine the future and picture the type of home, car, education, your children will have. Ask him to do the same. Money is an extremely large issue because as we grow older, money replaces the security of your childhood home. Also realize the number one thing married couples fight about is finances.

• Is his ability to conform important? Obviously most of us are conformists. That's the nature of conformity. However, some men aren't. They don't care about what they are wearing, doing, acting, or how they are behaving, for they have committed to not conforming to society's rules. The nonconformer can be a very exciting man. But be sure he wants the same basics as you do. Can you live with a man who can't stand the idea of a regular job or who doesn't want regular sleeping hours and goes to bed at 4 A.M.? Are you perfectly comfortable if the man you're with doesn't follow the traditional rules of your family at Thanksgiving dinner?

• Do heritage and tradition count? When people first

get together, they see the similarities between them. As time passes, their differences are exposed. When you move deeper into his world, you both start to discover things. He subscribes, like his father does, to, say, a new branch of old-world machismo. This machismo may not kick in until he's comfortable with you, then he demands that certain influences become the guiding *force* behind the relationship.

Claudia can tell her story of this experience: she married a Mexican doctor in the Southwest and discovered he was very liberal in certain matters regarding women—he loved creative, dynamic women who made a mark. One of the chief reasons he was attracted to her was because she was a gifted sculptor. But (and don't you hate that there always has to be a *but*) when he was among the men in his family, he became "one of the men" and stopped treating her as his equal. "There were times when we were with other people and Tadeo spoke over my shoulder, as if I were inferior," Claudia said. "He behaves jealously if another man seems too chatty with me and stands too close. But when we're alone, he's a good and loving man." In Tadeo's world, he diminishes Claudia. She had to ask if she could handle the trade-off. She was committed to trying.

Eleven years later, Claudia is still dealing with it. She knows what he is and that she cannot change him, a lesson most people never learn. To Claudia, the relationship is worth it because one-on-one he is a wonderful man, and 90 percent of their free time is spent one-on-one.

• "I can't live that way." Be clear about the issues on which you will be able to compromise. It may be about spending, where he wants to live versus where you don't want to live, how many children he does/doesn't want or whether or not to socialize with his friends every weekend. At least question what you cannot tolerate. Then if it's something you can't live with, take that man out of the running.

There are many issues to consider when choosing a man. It is important to keep your eyes open and to keep making evaluations.

What kind of man don't you want? Besides the obvious—a man who can't or won't love, a man who abuses, or a man who refuses to grow up or have fun. You don't want a man who, if you're late meeting him at a bar or restaurant, already has someone else's telephone number written on his hand. Remember when he wrote yours in the exact same spot, promising never to wash again? Men with roving eyes are ugly.

❧

Making the armies able to take on opponents without being defeated is a matter of unorthodox and orthodox methods.

FOLLOW THE RULES THAT ALREADY EXIST AND MAKE UP YOUR OWN

In the battle of the sexes, the early stages of courtship will incorporate unorthodox and orthodox methods of winning over a man.

Get in your mind the image of a war room where generals plan the strategies, tactics, spy systems, and subtleties of the battle. These subtleties include the small deceptions and illusions meant to get the enemy off guard.

Coyness and deceit were once a given between men and women. Women were taught to tease men, to appear accommodating but to play hard to get, whether they were or not. In your grandmother's time, in order to attract a man, she made your grandfather think he was smarter than she was. And she let him know that he was going to be the boss, not to mention losing at tennis and chess.

To learn more about today's orthodox coupling habits, first look back a few decades. Watch a movie made before the sexual revolution in the 1960s and you can see what society accepted as normal courting behavior. (While not everything in Hollywood movies is historically accurate, of course, the depiction of gender roles was often right on target. In the movies in the 1950s, you see women in high heels in their own kitchens. This actually happened!) In movies and in life, behind the appearance of accommodation, women used *trickery;* they lied, cried, and adjusted their personalities just enough to suit the temperament of the man and the need of the moment. She stroked his ego and held out the promise of sex. Virginity was a woman's gift to a man.

Today a more honest approach is acceptable because women are allowed to be *real*. Men see women without makeup. They see them sweating. They see them winning. They know that women can take care of themselves financially. Coupling has become less of a necessity and more of a natural desire.

What is orthodox today is using *seductive openness*. The goal is to let a man know what you want without sounding demanding, inflexible, or desperate. The immediate goal is to get him interested in the two of you pursuing each other. You don't want to hear this, but chances are that you may have to make the first move. Your move should be a small one. Touch his arm, get him used to your touch. Open your heart while you're waiting for his. Forgive him for not being aggressive. (This is because today's young men have been raised by women who fought for women's rights. They raised their sons to be considerate and to not consider women as sex objects. Their bodies see you as desirable, but their minds are too considerate to let you know this.)

Smile. See to it that the two of you spend time alone, even if it's just a few minutes. Introduce conversations of fantasy. In other words, talk about places and things you want to see, even if it's just the latest box office hit.

If you are interested in a serious relationship with one particular man, don't overdue seductive openness. By the third date, men and women begin to fill in details of their lives. Panic may set in if a woman likes the man and fears he's not as interested in her. She resorts to more attention-grabbing stories to emphasize her desirability. She establishes "proof" that other guys have wanted her, relating graphic tales of her sexual encounters. Telling a man you are a sexual expert doesn't make him hunger for you. He will feel that too many have already conquered you.

Don't try to impress him with sexual tricks because you think that's what everybody else is doing. Don't be too eager to show how limber you are or that you know the most arcane postures from the *Kama-sutra*. To a man, the excitement of having you for the first time is enough. He'll be back, and as you get more familiar with each other, you'll have time to explore fantasies and new things.

Surprise him with your restraint—charm him, entice him, and seduce him by listening to what he says and by being good to him.

What about major deception? Deception works to intrigue a man if you pretend not to be available when you are; to suggest there is another man when there's not; and to withhold sex. You can accomplish the same results in an honest way. Don't be available by continuing to do what you enjoyed doing before the two of you met. You are unavailable because you have not dropped your friends. You can't see him all the time because you have classes to go to and tennis matches to win.

Don't have sex until it feels like you can handle whatever emotion comes with it. Sex tends to bond you too quickly to a man. It causes you to focus on the future rather than the present.

What is seductive is that *you are capable of being happy without him*. Men have a tough time accepting this because they believe it is they who make you happy. They want to be with you as much as possible to prove this.

If you want to go away for a weekend without him, just go. Women want to do this but fear if they're not available, the relationship will fall apart. Trust that it won't. What's more attractive than a woman who enjoys many things in life?

- Establish brighter facets of the interesting life you have. It's healthy for you and confusing to him that you are building your life without him.
- Tell him how great it is to be alone with him. Women forget to compliment. Seduction requires complimenting. Men return to where they feel good, so make them feel good in your presence.
- Be honest. If you had a hard day at work and you're tired and he wants to come over, you're allowed to say no in a nice way. Saying no helps seduction in a case like this. If he arrives and you really don't want him there, you are not going to be in the right mood. When you're tired, what you need is sleep, not him.

* * *

Realize that both men and women use minor deception. He'll hide his temper, you'll color your lips. (No
one has the color of lips that lipstick brings. And lipstick
is just one example. Your eyelashes aren't that thick,
long, or dark. You deceive in a million small ways
whether you want to admit it or not.)

The most seductive thing a woman can do is to tell a
man she loves him when she does. Those are very
powerful words from an honest woman.

• Understand why seduction is necessary: there's a
saying that when a couple gets married, a woman gets
her dream and a man loses his. Her dream is to be
coupled; his dream is to have every woman on earth
want to couple with him, even if it's just for a night.
Men need and depend on women, but that's not how
they perceive it. Women need to seduce them into the
joy love brings.

Boys don't grow up playing with groom dolls like
girls grow up playing with bride dolls. Men plan their
lives around conquering other men. Mother/daughter
talks center on choosing a career and a mate.
Father/son talks focus on becoming skilled, achieving
success in business, and understanding family obliga-
tions. Marriage is usually a given for men, but not
something they fantasize about.

Therefore, you need to remind him what you can
offer each other. Don't do this with words; make his life
better, not just in bed but by doing things for him and
giving him things he needs. (If he does this for you in
equal amounts, you have a match.)

• What is unorthodox is telling a man what you want
on the first date. Let's say that it has always been your

229

intention to get married. Let him know in a light, unemotional way that you want to get married some-day. Make it clear that you are speaking in the abstract and not proposing. If you do this, he'll know from the start what you want out of life. If your desires come up after the two of you have been together for five months, it will be much more difficult, and there will be much more anxiety when you have to bring up the subject of marriage or living together. It's much smarter if you are honest over your first glass of wine. Be unorthodox at the right time.

The reason the above strategy works is because, in the very beginning, it should be easy to talk about long-term commitment. At that time you are talking to a stranger and have no emotional investment in him. And you're only mentioning it. There shouldn't even be a prolonged conversation about it. The most he'll say, at this point, is that's what he wants or doesn't want. If at the end of dinner, he asks for the check and shakes your hand good-bye, you know you don't want to pursue him.

If you don't hear from him, the rejection is less hurtful because it isn't about you—so far, your rela-tionship is only hours old. If he does call you, he knows your plans and does not fear them.

You can easily recognize whether what you're doing is orthodox or unorthodox. The things that your genera-tion has brought to relationships are unorthodox. (Such as letting a man know what you want in life and not disrupting your life because of him.) Orthodox methods are those that have been used since the beginning of time. Both work.

For the impact of armed forces to be like stones thrown on eggs is a matter of emptiness and fullness.

DON'T BE TOO HARD OR TOO SOFT

In matters of love, you don't want to be so hardened you destroy a man; nor do you want to be so impossibly fragile that you make a man feel that love can crush you.

Sun Tzu's reference to fullness and emptiness says that a stone can never be emptied—it is only itself and it is full of itself. When a stone breaks an egg, it exerts the force of its nature and its will. That's no fair fight, just a massacre.

There is always one person who considers the relationship more fragile than the other. They think that what they have with this person is easily vacated and crushed with little effort. That person, metaphorically, is the egg, and it's usually the woman. She may not be aware how easily she can get hurt until the first stone is thrown. If this has happened to you, your strategy should be this:

• Do not stay away from someone stronger, but get stronger yourself. Everyone needs an egg. We all have ideas, but we need someone to help bring those ideas to fruition. Nothing succeeds without an egg to nurture the plan.

If you are the stone and he is the egg, let him get stronger. Stones have a way of toppling and rolling; unless they meet a greater natural force, there is no match.

In battle, confrontation is done directly, victory is gained by surprise.

COMMUNICATION AND MYSTERY ARE BOTH IMPORTANT

Thus, in the battle of the sexes, use confrontation to settle issues and unexpected acts to make your love more interesting. Interesting, unpredictable love is what a man wants.

Each person brings to a union a concept of how the relationship should work; since two people rarely think completely alike, expect disagreement. Disagreements never doom a relationship—silence and silent suffering do.

Disagreements require confrontation, if you are to solve them. Direct confrontation means you face your opponent in a fair fight in which each of you expresses an opinion and listens to what the other has to say. Confrontation is a healthy part of emotional "warfare." It's important to exchange ideas and let someone you care about know what you feel. *Never forget that his feelings are also valid.*

It would be wonderful if couples used a variation of the rules the Supreme Court does. You would get to tell your argument for fifteen minutes with no interruptions, then he gets to do the same. You each get a five-minute rebuttal. The ruling should be voted on by both of you, but hours later.

Confrontation should not imply failure. Rather it should set up an opportunity to discover why the relationship isn't meeting needs. Confronting your partner on the issues, without fighting, is one of the most difficult things to do.

Penny, now in her midthirties, has never wanted a child. Mark, her husband, wants children and is pressing the issue. Mark refuses to accept what is for him the bitter truth that Penny prefers to go childless. The sight of a small child perched on its father's shoulders makes Mark feel jealous, cheated, and deprived of his right to procreate.

When Penny got married at twenty-six, she was honest with Mark and told him she had no interest in children. He believed that over the years her maternal instinct might ignite. It didn't. Mark began using the childless issue as a weapon. Once Penny accidentally threw away some papers Mark needed. Mark's irritation turned on a dime from "You never look at what's in front of you, you just toss stuff away" to "You have no regard for my stuff" to "Once in a while I'm happy we don't have a kid. If the child were sitting in the wrong place, you'd toss it out!"

Penny had to make a decision. She wanted to save her marriage but end the issue of parenthood. She had to confront him the right way, without fighting and with the *force* of her commitment to her decision. She told Mark that the issue of childlessness is no longer open for debate, nor would she bear his jabbing her over it. The subject had been a source of *painful* emotional manipulation, and she wanted that stopped.

"I told Mark I loved him and valued the relationship," Penny said, "and then I had to say something I didn't think I had in me. I said I won't have children but that I respected his need to be a father. There's nothing I can do to make that happen for him. If he wants fatherhood and a family more than me, he should tell me now."

Penny's news that she didn't want a child did not

come as a surprise to Mark. However, he was shocked to hear her say that his mocking her about motherhood was unacceptable and, secondly, that she was giving him an option to end their marriage. He never thought he would hear those words. With this new reality brought to light, he knew he wanted to stay with his wife. In order to let Mark fulfill his need to nurture a child, Penny gave up being with him on Saturdays so he could become a big brother.

Surprise is a very powerful weapon for a woman. There is *benevolent* surprise and *threatening* surprise, and both may bring victory. (Choose benevolent surprises if you want the relationship to survive.)

For the sake of the relationship, choose your surprises wisely. It has already been said that you should not surprise him at the office. One woman did. She snuck past the receptionist, heard someone coming, and ducked in a closet door. Unfortunately, it was a door that led to a staircase that connected the ninth and tenth floors. Unfortunately, the door locked behind her. Unfortunately, it was a Friday and she panicked about being locked in all weekend. She started screaming and pounding on the door. That's how the man she was surprising and a dozen other company employees found her. She fled. So did he.

• *Stirring up jealousy:* The sudden shock of fearing competition is a *threatening* surprise; it works and shouldn't be used if you love someone. Jealousy, after all, is a greedy, sly, and volatile emotion. Despite its connection to romantic notions, jealousy is really a barometer of insecurity, not passion.

Surprise when it leads to pleasure excites any relationship—people may split up because they're entrenched in a monotonous groove they cannot climb out of.

A woman who gives the gift of surprise is always victorious. Tell the waiter that it's his birthday when it's not. There's nothing that surprises more than a cake with a candle on it when a birthday is nowhere near. Get him two tickets for a hockey or basketball game. It'll be a surprise if it's for him and a buddy. It shows you are embracing *his* idea of fun. Buy him the tennis racket he wants, even if you just met him recently. Since women usually don't give gifts to men at the beginning of a relationship, this gives them the benefit of surprise. It will stir him. You'll represent the unselfish, giving woman he wants. These generous acts work to influence him and get him moving toward you.

• Don't surprise him by inadvertently humiliating him. Don't surprise your husband, or any man you have had a long relationship with, by wearing only a Victoria's Secret thong lace panty and a Saran Wrap bra of your own making when he comes home from work. This is pressure to him. Your outfit demands him to perform. Do surprise him by initiating lovemaking. This is every man's fantasy.

• Don't throw him a surprise party—it's a big joke on him. It means he has to stand there looking pleased at all the attention while he's secretly embarrassed, if not horrified and angry at you for thinking he'd like such a display. Surprise him by being very nice and warm after a fight. Being removed or bitchy indicates that you are still trying to win, and most of the women he's experienced before you have done just that. If you really want to shock him, admit that it's your fault before the fight begins.

• Never forget that surprises should be for his benefit. If he loves you, he will surprise you, too. And men's surprises can be bigger and flashier. When they're in love, they do things like taking you away for the weekend. They spend their last dime on a ring. This has nothing to do with materialism. He wants to give, and adorning the woman he loves is the way he does it. He also wants to signal to the world that you're taken.

❦

Therefore those skilled at the unorthodox are infinite as heaven and earth, inexhaustible as the great rivers. When they come to an end they begin again, like the days and months; they die and are reborn, like the four seasons.

LOVE GOES THROUGH CYCLES AND SOMETIMES DIES

We must accept the fact that life goes through fated cycles. Out of cyclical change or unpredictable loss there is growth and strength.

A relationship, like nature, goes through phases. It can have deaths and rebirths. In long-term marriages, you can fall in and out of love with the same man many times. The basic love is always there, but the excitement of having him can come and go. If a person is tenacious enough, they can possibly revive a lost love. This takes a lot of effort. It requires you both to go back to being the people you were when you fell in love. Sometimes this is impossible.

When love dies and a split is inevitable, consider the following to get through the stages of separation with fewer tears:

- *Keep the momentum of your life going.* Don't stop the flow of your interests and schedules and obsess over why he loved you once and doesn't now. Or worse, don't be obsessed over being a failure in making relationships work. *All relationships fail until the one that doesn't.*

• Don't make your ex the villain. When you're hurt you want allies—and you want others to shun the man who is shunning you. In the war between the sexes, this is done by making an "ex" mean and you his victim. It doesn't matter who leaves who. The misstated truth about him can paint him as unredeemably evil and raises the obvious question: what were you doing with such a man?

If he was a monster, an abuser, or a humiliator, give yourself a limited amount of time to rage against him. Get it over with and out of your system as quickly as possible so your anger does not consume you. He's already taken too much of your life and energy—give him up, give up thoughts of him and how he inflicted pain, and give up the rage, now. Put him in a garbage bag and leave him at the curb. You don't want to give him more time than you already have. Don't make elaborate plans of revenge. Don't try to convince him that he's wrong and that he's made a huge mistake. (No one has ever been convinced of this by speeches. What might bring him back is his need for you.) Renew yourself and promise to start a new cycle free of him! *Will* yourself to be a person who can change for the better and get through the crisis. What helps is to indulge yourself as much as possible. Take long baths, buy yourself flowers. Especially take advantage of things you couldn't do with him, like having girlfriends sleep over or see all the movies that he wouldn't see with you. Get the fun of your past back. Wear a rubber band on your wrist and snap it every time you think of him. Soon you will realize that he is the source of your pain.

- Build your army. Just as a general must rely on his foot soldiers, it is important for you to create a reliable support system that will be there when you need it. If you require guidance to sort it all out, talk to a sympathetic but astute friend. She will help you clarify the dynamics of the relationship. After all, she's probably been there herself. Don't forget, though, talking about details over and over again will annoy anyone eventually.
- Behave as you wish you felt. Women ask, "Will I ever be happy again?" Assure yourself that you are okay fifty times a day. It's a matter of science: when you reinforce a thought, you toughen the brain cell connectives that make habits and other types of behavior automatic. (The brain doesn't understand sarcasm, so if you say, "I was stupid" sarcastically, the only groove the brain makes is "I am stupid." Don't say things like "nobody will ever love me" because that is what your brain is going to feed back to you someday.) Remind yourself that you are lovable, and that you will love again. Why should you think the last person you were with will be the last person you will ever be with? It's never happened before.

One second can change your life again.

CHAPTER 11

NINE GROUNDS . . .
STAGES OF A RELATIONSHIP

According to the rules for military operations, there are nine kinds of ground. They are: Dispersive Ground, Light Ground, Trafficked Ground, Intersecting Ground, Ground of Contention, Heavy Ground, Difficult Ground, Surrounded Ground, and Dying Ground.

— Sun Tzu

This chapter is about strategies on *terrain,* or *grounds.* Let's say the grounds can either be physical "territories," such as places where we live, or those within a psychological landscape.

Dispersive ground, according to *The Art of War,* refers to a time when the troops wanted to return home because they thought the battle wasn't worth it. Returning home in love relationships is realizing early on that this is not the person you are going to spend your life with. You may not be attracted. You may not like the way he kisses. You've had a few dates, but there's nothing there. The two of you "disperse."

Consider Barry and Alicia. They met at Starbucks when the man behind the counter gave them each other's order. (Alicia, being a very emotional woman, felt it was divine intervention and didn't mind consuming the whipped cream she would never have ordered.) They have been dating twice a week for the last two months and have been spending weekends from Friday nights to Sunday after brunch together. Barry is gregarious and charming, but he's always vague and oblique about his past and about his job as a law associate. Alicia accepts this remoteness and believes in time he will open up to her. (Never count on a man changing.) Since she likes him, she wants to move the relationship forward. She wants to be able to contact him and talk to him during the day. He will not allow this.

Instead of accepting this and realizing it won't work, Alicia decided to penetrate his private territory. In this case, Barry's office phone. (You've already learned not to invade on this front.)

Annoyed, Barry told Alicia that she is intrusive and prying and said, "What difference does it make if I can't be reached when you want to reach me? *I'm busy during the day.* I'll call you when I have time." And then the line that no woman wants to hear: "We see each other enough, don't we?"

Then he began cutting back on their midweek dates. "Work is hectic," he said. This was the time for Alicia to disperse. When women are in love they want to see the object of that love more and more. Men do, too, unless they have a lot of anger they want to hide and can't tolerate being around anyone for too long.

Now Alicia worries that Barry is going to disappear. She assures him that she isn't calling to have a cozy chat with him at the office but to confirm a date or change a time, or to just say hello briefly. Why is this intrusive? What is he hiding? Or, worse, does she mean this little to him? She immediately wants to call back to discuss the first unsuccessful call, which would have been instant death.

The confrontation suddenly clarifies the relationship for Barry. He hurt Alicia's feelings, and it doesn't matter to him. Nor does he care to work through the issue of her calling. He doesn't want to go through offering a reasonable explanation for being incommunicado. He especially doesn't want to go to therapy to "work out the problem." She obviously wants more from him than he can provide. He offers his solution. "It's not worth the fight," Barry tells Alicia. "I want things to be comfortable for me, or not at all."

Alicia is hurt because Barry has kept her at arm's length, the place that is most comfortable for him. Her simple demand to speak with him during the day was the deciding factor for Barry; he wanted out of the relationship. The petty fight was justification enough for him. If a man wants out, he can start a fight over anything.

Dispersive ground brought Alicia to earth in a number of revelatory ways: men, more than women, use a fight to get out of a relationship. If the first fight brings dissolution, that is proof that the relationship is simply not worth fighting for.

• Dispersive ground is an unavoidable aspect of relationships. There will be times when you'll think the man you are seeing is perfect, then impossible, then vulnerable, then perfect again. However, if you're seeing him as more impossible than anything else, you will never achieve the right balance.

* * *

Sun Tzu's strategy for getting through dispersive ground is to remember that it is a *testing period*. Too few women give the test. They only take it.

❧❧

When you enter others' land, but not deeply, this is called light ground.

NOT RUSHING IN

When you begin a relationship and start to explore each other's world, you enter *light ground*.

Light ground allows each of you to introduce the other to landmarks in your territory. You want him to see where you live. You want to take him to places you know and think he will like. A man brings you into his world, too, showing you off a bit. He watches how his friends react, takes you to hear his favorite band, and decides if you could fit into his life. At the ground-floor stage, it's flattering to take these brief excursions into a foreign land. You are both considering getting closer.

But be aware. Men tend not to introduce "playmates-for-sex-only" into light ground because they're not interested in connections and continuity. A dark restaurant, your place or his, is the typical range of travel for lovers they don't want to flaunt. They can be interested in keeping you around, although under cover.

If you like each other, light ground is about a tentative, but not yet exclusive, relationship. Some women find this unnerving because they need to know where they stand. Instead of worrying, keep your options open. Don't be exclusive to him if he's not being exclusive to you. Having tunnel vision is one of the biggest mistakes women make. They are so anxious to get onto steady ground that they fool themselves into thinking they're there. You should be on light ground with more than one man at a time, but let's face it, it's hard to do.

⋯⋯

Land where you and others can come and go is called a trafficked ground.

SAFETY IN NUMBERS

In the war between the sexes it is important to identify the territory you're on. When a man and woman meet on *trafficked ground,* meaning public places, a woman is protected and a man knows he must be in control of himself.

• Start a relationship in a public place before you end up alone with him. The first physical contact should occur on trafficked ground—holding hands, your head on his shoulder at the beach. Society has provided certain ground rules, and one of them is to not have sex while others are around. So keeping your relationship public until you know a man gives you protection. (Animals have sex in public, and we always point them out when they do.)

Also concerning trafficked ground, if you're willing to let him into your heart, into your mind, and into your body, remember he could just be at a stop sign. Things can go well on trafficked ground. It's the time to enjoy life. Eventually you may enjoy each other, but you have not isolated each other yet.

⋯⋯

Land that is surrounded on three sides by competitors is called intersecting ground. He who first gets access to the land gains the support of all the people.

WINNING OVER THE COMPETITION

A man with many women in his life is surrounded. It's possible that your competitors are on three sides of him, or maybe even more. To win him over, figure out a strategy that insinuates you into as many "intersections" of his life as possible. When you make such an effort for the right man, you can eliminate the competition.

No matter which route he takes, you want to be at the crossroads so that he notices you.

• Have courage. Take a chance on yourself and assume you're going to win. Women who hide in the bushes or stand at the side of the road and watch the traffic go by don't get what they want.

Don't give up because he is seeing other women. Dating is a process of elimination. Instead of being sarcastic or critical about the others, make him feel that he is at home when he is with you. One of the best things you can do is to make space for him in your life and allow him to pursue his own interests. He should not have to be focused on you every minute that he spends with you. When the relationship is really good, you won't speak to each other for hours at a time. You'll just feel each other's presence.

• Have knowledge: listen to what a man is telling you. Do something that shows you put him first. (According to him, his last relationship failed because the woman demanded too much time or didn't pay enough attention to him.) Tell him you'll reschedule dinner with a girlfriend to go with him to his company dinner. This is putting him first, which your competitors are not doing.

• Be prepared—plan your moves. The best way to make a man feel comfortable is to re-create the fun and relaxing moments that you had when you first met. Keep on laughing. Continuously reinforce that he's going to have a good time with you.

Sometimes a man will have one woman for sex, one he can really talk to, one he doesn't have to hold his stomach in for, and one who is his teacher. Be all those women to him so that at every turn he's facing you.

Laura is a thirty-two-year-old sales rep for a cosmetics company who has been dating Scott, a thirty-seven-year-old mining engineer. They met in an emergency room while waiting for friends, when they were both worried and preoccupied. They considered it great that they met under nightmare circumstances. He asked her out but told her he would still be seeing other women. She decided to see him and win his exclusivity. He dated Jackie and continued to see Melissa. This truly made Laura very nervous, but she hung in and didn't mope about the situation. Her girlfriends heard her frustration and advised her to break it off.

It may seem that Scott is having a good time, but he's not. He's not enjoying the secrecy that he needs for Jackie and Melissa, and doesn't want to hurt anyone. He wants to make sure his affection for one woman will signal him to stop seeing the others. Laura wants to eliminate her rivals. How? She did it by revealing her love. She didn't talk about it. She continued to live by the rules of the relationship. By doing that, she presented the peace that the others didn't.

It doesn't matter if the other women, on the surface, appear to have more than you in one area—supermodels (beauty), heiresses (money and social access), or celebrities (fame and access to power). If he wanted a commitment with any of them, he would not still be dating you.

Laura decided not to show much interest in asking about the others. (That would have injected them into her relationship with Scott.) Her best strategy under the circumstances is that she *need only be the woman that Scott feels most comfortable with*, the one Scott meets at any intersection. The other women in his life might be creating excitement by making him feel insecure. You substitute that with mystery and excitement that doesn't have to do with threats. You let him sample what life with you would be like . . . very interesting, but not scary. If he's mature, he will not be attracted to women who are drama queens.

Scott wasn't mature enough. Laura thought he was worth putting up with for about four months, at which time she left him, knowing she had tried her best. And her experience with Scott taught her how to deal with men at intersections. When she started dating Ken, a man who was also seeing other women, she bought a very distinctive perfume and she bought him a distinctive key ring—something he always has with him. When he puts his key into the ignition or opens his apartment door—even to bring another woman in—he thinks of Laura. Ken is a nice guy. It took five months, but Laura won his exclusivity. Let's hope it lasts.

⚞⚟

Land equally accessible to both the enemy and to your army is called ground of contention.

SEEING HIM CLEARLY

A relationship is on *ground of contention* when you get close and reality strikes. There are problems to solve and stresses to calm. This is when you begin to see each other's faults. A man can get paralyzed on ground of contention, not wanting you to know about him or to discover anything about you. And even though contention leads to arguments and fights, he prefers staying there. Men don't want to move backward or forward. Chances are he will only move forward if he's scared he'll lose you. Don't threaten a man you love. Spend more time alone or with friends. You will create an emptiness that he'll want you to fill. Also it gives his possessive nature a chance to come out. When you're not with him, even though you assure him you're faithful, that nature will inevitably gnaw at him. This retreat should not be done to hurt him. It should be done to protect you.

There is a way through the ground of contention: Sun Tzu advises generals to block the exits and face the issues. Couples must do that also. The intensity of the emotion you are feeling strengthens his hold on you.

• Remember this: when a good man is bad once in a while, hang on to the good things he's done.

• You can be on ground of contention with the same person, many times.

❧

When you enter deeply into others' land, past many cities and towns, this is called heavy ground.

247

HEAVY RELATIONSHIPS

When you enter into a relationship that's deeper than all others before it and you reject all other men, you are on *heavy ground*. (It is even said that you are in a "heavy" relationship.)

• On heavy ground, you are no longer dating a man casually but *exclusively*. On the other hand, heavy ground does not necessarily mean that the two of you will marry. It means that the two of you have committed to each other *for now*.

• Passion rules—sexual attraction overwhelms the both of you. If the sex is dizzying, then you want to live with this kind of vertigo forever.

• Since exclusivity keeps the relationship intimate and on heavy ground, be aware, clear your head, and try to confront serious issues. You'll have a very hard time doing this because heavy ground is the only time a woman's mind and body separate. You want and need to be touched and are not thinking. You crave to be held and are becoming addicted to his body.

• The measure of emotion is more intense with this man. Separation makes you scared. You worry when he is out of your sight and fear he may not return. Daily separation feels like abandonment. There is a dependency that you feel. This is the time you should retain your independence, but it's hard for many women to do because they lack the confidence in themselves.

• The relationship consumes both people and neither of you has time for anyone else. Perhaps a lesson can be learned from this tale of popular folklore: There once was a young couple who thought they were the only two people in the world. The young girl's parents went away for the weekend, and the girl, seizing the opportunity, invited her boyfriend to stay with her. On Saturday morning the young couple decided to do some laundry and put their clothes in the washing machine. They spent the rest of the morning naked, in bed, doing what crazy college kids do naked in bed every chance they get. After a couple of hours, they decided to take the clothes from the washer and put them in the dryer, but, get this, they didn't have a stitch of clothing on and he carried her downstairs piggyback. When they got to the bottom of the stairs, a large group of people, including the girl's parents, yelled, "Surprise!" The parents hadn't gone away for the weekend. They just told their daughter they were going away so that they could give her a surprise party. The point of this tale, and maybe it's not a tale (many people swear it really happened to a good friend of theirs) is that you should never think that only the two of you exist. It's a great feeling, but it's not realistic and can often lead to trauma.

• A relationship on heavy ground may be short-lived but meteoric. It will be hot, volatile, a dazzling show, but it may burn itself out quickly or pass through your life in a flash. Or it may last forever. People who have been mostly happy with each other for fifty years have a heavy relationship.

The strategy that gets the troops through heavy ground with the fewest casualties is not to retreat, deplete, or plunder the terrain but to *provide*. Women are more willing to do this than men are. Since you have the man's full attention while on heavy ground, make it a time when you can start to communicate on a deeper level. You do this by making sure that the relationship isn't just all about sex. You want your partner to care about you emotionally as well as physically, so make important changes while things are on heavy ground and he's totally yours. Men listen at this time because they are totally involved.

If he doesn't feel well one night, make sure you let him know you are willing to be with him without having sex. He will appreciate you bringing over mushroom-barley soup. (You don't have to make it, just carry it from the store to him.) As for his part, a real test of the relationship is if you don't feel well. He may not bring over soup, but he should be there for you, not just for the passion. If he doesn't offer his help or time, consider what he really wants you for.

To take a relationship from "hot and heavy" to "hot and with a future," you must cross heavy ground and offer support to each other. Give the basics. Food is enticing. So is a massage. So is his comfort, so is your help. On heavy ground, let him see that being with you is helpful to him. (Don't forget to examine whether he is helpful to you and whether he gives you comfort or takes it away.) You don't have to do his laundry or cook and clean, but you do have to add to his life. Treat him to life. Buy him new sheets. Go with him to pick out clothes if shopping bewilders him. Share responsibility and let him see how much easier life is when he couples with you. If he hates doing his taxes, help fill out the forms. If he loves his nieces and nephews, share them with him. Harder still, let him take over some of your responsibilities. Don't feel guilty that he's carrying the chest you bought at the flea market all the way back to the car. He's supposed to give.

Small things will let him know what you're like. He knows your body; let him know your heart.

The best thing you can do for a man is to let him know you're having a good time. Too many women complain about the new things they're seeing and forget to weigh them against the good they've already seen. Too much complaining and overanalyzing will make him wonder why you're with him. He'll leave if he thinks he's making you unhappy. Heavy ground is confusing. You didn't have to make much of an effort before this, you just had to exist and show up.

When you traverse mountain forests, steep defiles, marshes, or any route that is arduous to travel, this is called difficult ground.

LOVE CAN BE DIFFICULT

When you face obstacles and unexpected problems and the relationship is threatened, you're on *difficult ground. The Art of War* suggests that armies avoid harsh land that's too hard to cross. Ho Yanxi, one of Sun Tzu's interpreters, added that since difficult ground is hard to chart, one would not know where to build forts or dig trenches. So, if you see too many obstacles to laying foundations or find yourself having to build defenses, remember that harmonious love requires some effort but should never be so stressful that it saps your strength.

The same is true in the battle of the sexes. If you are having problems, you need to determine which problems are impassable and which only appear that way. If the problems are too difficult, and you stay, you will be fighting an uphill battle and getting weaker and weaker as long as the two of you are together.

No good relationship comes ready-made and fracture free. As there are tender moments, cherished memories, shared history, so are there periods of distress, compromising secrets, bad luck, accidents, outbursts of anger and frustration.

• You first reach difficult ground with a man when unresolved complaints, disappointments, and shattered expectations begin to grow. When you get to know him, there will be things you don't like about him. Tell him. Tell him kindly, but tell him and then let it go. The fewer words you use the better. Let's say you tell him that it's frustrating to you when he promises to call at certain times and doesn't. And let's also say weeks later, you see no change. You have two choices: leave if you feel he's really inconsiderate or stay and realize he's the type of person who loses track of time. Couples part over small things that are big issues. On difficult ground, things are taken symbolically. For example, if he doesn't call on time, you believe he doesn't love you enough. This may be true or you may look for signs of love in other things he does and says.

• He has complaints about you. He doesn't want you talking about how fat you feel, and weeks later, you're not sure why you should compromise to please him. To save the relationship and move it out of difficult ground, act on his complaints one at a time. Don't worry that he is not yet making an effort for you. Many couples go down the drain because they wait for each other to make the first move. Adjusting and changing is considered proof of love. Prove yours by not waiting.

It's not unusual to feel self-conscious about doing what a man asks you to do, especially when he asks for change.

What you must consider on difficult ground is this:

• *Difficult ground* breaks the spell of romance—reality enters and destroys the idyll you've created. Be prepared to clean up the mess. If a particular man in question is important to you, he's going to see you at your best, your worst, your most natural if not visceral—from seeing you standing naked in broad daylight to holding your hand while you're giving birth. And so will you see him, in all his range of normal living. Sometimes you'll hear more about his bowels than you need to know.

• At times ground gets too difficult. You're trekking through minefields with a man who, you discover, wants to control your mind. He reminds you of your weaknesses to keep you more insecure. He invites you away for the weekend then doesn't mention it again. He disapproves of what you order in restaurants, saying things like, "Are you sure you want to eat something that rich?"

Controllers like these are abusers, too—although the abuse is verbal and his need is to humiliate you. If he's this rough, *move on.*

Other types of controlling men can become obsessive about you and the relationship. Although it's fun at first when someone is crazed for you, watch out when it goes too far. One young woman living abroad was at first smitten by a very glib British man she met in London. The first stages of the relationship were exciting, and he was far more flattering than any American man she had dated. But when she returned from a week's vacation in Spain, his flattery became scary. A photo album of hers was now, suddenly, missing. When she went to his house to question him about it, posted up on his bedroom wall was a life-size, color photocopy of one of the missing pictures of herself. When confronted, his only comment was, "I don't care if you rip it down, I made extra copies."

Difficult ground sets up challenges and a test of character, endurance, and heart, some of which this man may fail. As your best friend would say, "You deserve better."

When you're not sure if you should leave a man due to the trials of difficult ground, ask yourself:

- What is his idea of love? (He should consider your feelings as often as he does his, if not more. Some men feel they can be inconsiderate because they're in a bad mood. You don't do that to him. Why should he?)
- How does he handle the problems you should share—does he make light of what hurts you or does he offer comfort? "Why are you making such a big deal out of this?" shouldn't be a question you hear.
- Are the difficulties you're experiencing with him related to something that's current in his life—or is it pathological?
- Relationships shouldn't be impossible or an emotionally exhausting hardship. If you can't get over the rough spots without getting hurt, give up the battle. You're not surrendering, you're stopping the blood flow and ending the war.

❧

When the way in is narrow and the way out circuitous, so a small enemy force can strike you even though your numbers are greater, this is called surrounded ground.

WHEN OTHERS INTRUDE

When a relationship suffers because of outside events, this is *surrounded ground*. This is also a time when outside influences may overwhelm his affection for you. When your relationship is at the mercy of such influences, you must strategize through the frustrations and find your way to securer ground.

There's a wonderful Norman Rockwell illustration that tells this story: a boss yells at a man on the job, the man comes home and yells at his wife, she yells at the kids, who yell at the dog, and so on. Frustration rolls over down the line. The message is, you are blamed for events and feelings that have nothing to do with you. (One Columbia University teaching assistant was going out with a student who his mother couldn't stand because of her nationality. He couldn't face telling her, so he flunked her in an anthropology course. Nice guy.)

What "surrounds" him? The guy has alimony payments, a kid who is failing fourth grade, his business is on a roller-coaster ride, his mother is pestering him, his best friend was just in an accident. He is encircled by life's problems, which make their way into the relationship. He's edgy, impatient, short-tempered, uninterested in sex, and perhaps overindulging in alcohol or drugs to calm himself down.

Unless you live a charmed life, the universe will deal you periods of surrounded ground. It is unavoidable. Where there is change, there is pressure and stress. Things get accomplished under pressure; time limits and personal crises demand immediate decisions.

Solving problems may be pleasurable to one man because it means he's capable and needed, called upon by many people, working and busy, facing challenges. To another man, pressure forces his low-gear personality into high gear, and he can't cope. A clogged drain gets him angry out of proportion, the cleaners closing before he can pick up his shirts makes him feel victimized by industry, and his associate backing out of playing third base in the company softball game makes him feel betrayed.

- Evaluate the nature of the relationship, your history with him, and if being on surrounded ground is normal for him. Some men manage to accumulate problems that need solving and do so around the clock. Some are workaholics and are at the office twelve hours a day. They feel they are the one who has to save the company. Some are the family "therapist," so everyone comes to him for help. Some are wheeler-dealers, so even a spare half hour at the gym is about giving and getting information from the guy on the next Stair-Master. Having a relationship may be part of the total package for such men, but your purpose in their lives is little more than filling a gap.

- If he is going through an atypical period of extremes, let him know that you are there for him. No one likes to appear weak and ask for help. Be sympathetic. When he is sympathetic, it's something you remember for a long time.

- Don't expect men to always consider you their top priority. In the earlier stages of a relationship, most women can be with the man she loves twenty-four hours a day. Many men aren't capable of such familiarity. They prefer a different balance—work, play, love, and other people and events. They don't like to feel you are becoming one of the obstacles to freedom on surrounded ground.

- Focus on what can lead you to greater peace and comfort in the relationship, not on what is keeping you enclosed in your sense of neglect. Surrounded ground presents a situation in which your affection for a man can help him through his difficulties.

- If he is in a tense worried state every day of his life, your kindness is a waste of time.

When you will survive if you fight quickly and perish if you do not, this is called dying ground.

THE END

Love will survive if both of you fight *for* it and will perish if you do not. Your choices are two: fight or flight. You may flee from an abusive relationship or fight for the relationship if there's enough good in it. These are the conditions of *dying ground.*

Dying ground is an unpleasant place to be emotionally or physically. We even use expressions that are symbolic of it. For example, "He's killing me . . ." Whatever the analogy, the scared feeling could not be any clearer: faced with a dying relationship, you fight with the courage that comes out of desperation. If you don't fight for it, the relationship will be dead— something you'll regret. And if it's hell on earth, you need it to be over. An abusive relationship can destroy both your body and soul.

Even solid relationships can stagger through dying ground once in a while. On this type of ground you have no choice *but* to face the "enemy" and hear his demands. If you have the fight in you, he must also hear yours. The distinction is not to fight with your partner to the death, but to fight for the *survival of the relationship.* You fight on dying ground as a last resort.

There are good reasons for flight from dying ground. Verbal or physical abuse must not be tolerated. If he's violent, indecent, or immoral, leave him. Run for your life.

257

Many women would rather face the devil than break off a hellish relationship because they are willing to endure pain in exchange for the "security" of having a man. But a man who disrespects you has nothing to do with security, and even less to do with love.

Consider Marcia and Roy's trek into dying ground: Roy is an engineer who lost his job. He started his own company in his garage, doing freelance work—and also earning extra cash by tooling machine parts for industrial equipment, a skill his late father taught him.

After a month of dating, Marcia began spending Friday to Sunday with Roy at his house. Marcia saw, she said, a "grown-up who could take care of himself, his kids who he saw regularly, and the madnesses of life."

Too good to be true? After a few months of dating, his wife demanded more child support and his son decided Roy was the enemy and wouldn't speak to him. Roy began arguing with Marcia. Although she couldn't influence any of the unpleasant family-related events in Roy's life, she tried to understand how he felt about money—the biggest source of contention. Roy argued that Marcia talked too often about "how much" and "how impressive" things were and forced him to spend money on their dates.

They hit difficult ground one night when they were out at the movies with another couple, and they decided to chip in and buy food at a deli and eat it at Roy's. Marcia added a couple of small tomatoes to Roy's basket, bringing their share about half a dollar over his chip-in limit. Roy made a crack that he wouldn't pay the difference in a way that embarrassed Marcia in front of the others. She paid their whole share.

When a man starts dragging you into hell, beware. For

Marcia it occurred this way: later that night, Roy called her a bitch for making him look cheap.

As she tried to explain herself and clarify what was happening between them, Roy exploded and told her to shut up and get out. When Marcia asked if he was leaving her, he punched her, hitting her high on the cheekbone, part of his fist tipping into her eye. In tears, she fled and went to a friend's house, where she sat up the whole night with ice packs on her face.

Roy called her at work a few days later to apologize and swear such violence would never happen again. She said, "You're right, because I won't be there the next time you take a swing." He told her it was the alcohol that got him out of control—which is why he rarely drank. On top of that, he begged her to understand the monumental pressures that all at once were on him. How could she leave him now, when he's down? He loved her. Would she come back if he promised never to have more than one beer in her presence? Marcia moved in with him. (She might have been out of her mind, but many women lose all sense when they hear the word *love*.)

Two months later he lost an account and began drinking every night. Marcia heard him tossing tools around the garage, then he stomped into the living room, putting on his coat, announcing that he was going for a drive. "I calmly asked him to stay home with me, to sit down and talk out what was bothering him and what to do next about that lost account," she said. "The next thing I knew, he'd grabbed my hair, punched me in the face a few times, and flung me into the wall. He said, 'Never tell me what to do' and slammed out. While he was gone, I called my sister and had her come get me, to help me pack. I spent two days in the hospital because of that attack. I was so embarrassed I used the typical 'I fell down the stairs.' I could see the male nurse who was helping me out of bed didn't believe me."

Roy called her at the hospital, crying, again begging forgiveness. Marcia was sick at heart and had no pity for him. To her, violence was repulsive. She never went back.

Consider this about dying ground:

• If you're involved with a man for whom violence fulfills an emotional need, tell yourself the truth about why you're with him. Do you have a need to take it? Or are you so desperate that you'll take anything?

If you believe you are the one who is provoking a man by picking on a sore point, manipulating him into situations where he feels inadequate or threatened and that is why you are his "whipping girl," jump out of his life first, then think it through. Even if you do provoke him, he has no right to take it out on you.

• Don't confuse love with punishment. A man who punishes by violence or even by ignoring you doesn't love you.

• It's natural to be afraid to leave dying ground because the familiar is more of a comfort than the unknown. You must convince yourself that in an abusive circumstance, the unknown is preferable to what you've been familiar with. Leave your things behind if you must. Clothes, dishes, and jewelry are not as valuable as freedom and life.

Ask yourself these questions: "Do I want to live?" and "Do I want this to be my life?"

• What if he's not a cruel man or an abuser like Roy but a nice, giving man who wants the relationship to end and won't fight for it? Perhaps he thinks he's grown away from you, that he's no longer attracted to you, that you don't make him feel good? He is fleeing because flight will stop his stress, anger, or annoyance with you. What if he's encouraging conflict to get the inspiration to leave you? How do you win him back?

A man who feels he's "fallen out of love" is not going to respond to the most brilliant of speeches about what he means to you. (Begging also doesn't work.) He's not going to respond to threats. He's not going to respond to accusations that he's walking away from a responsibility. And he certainly won't respond when you call, crying and reminiscing about the good times you had together.

• The best thing you can do at the end of a relationship is to be nice. It's almost impossible to do when you are devastated. However, don't have endless conversations of blame. Don't scream. Don't show your ugliest side. Why should you give him the convenience of thinking he was right? Being faced with an enraged woman can further convince him that he should have left you. Leave as the person he once loved, and there's a good chance you can annoy him forever. You can at least make him question his decision even if you never want to see him again.

Being nice at the end is a brilliant strategy. You are not doing this for his benefit. In practically all movies about romance, the writer writes three different parts: boy meets girl, boy loses girl, boy gets girl back. It's possible that he will want to return to you. You may not want him back or you may be happy with his return. (His chances will be better if he left kindly, not screaming and blaming you.)

Even if you don't get back together, if you leave with

dignity, there will be times when he will be hurt when he thinks he shouldn't have let you go. Everyone enjoys revenge: showing your best at the end is the way to get it.

If you leave him, do it as nicely as possible. It's almost as hard for a woman to leave somebody as it is to be left. Break up as quickly and briefly as possible. (The choice of fight or flight is simple. If you chose neither it causes unimaginable stress because it is a position that your mind and body fight against.) You will hurt him, but you will hurt him more by staying or letting him stay. When it's time to say good-bye, tell him the truth. Even if it is that there's no love coming from your heart, tell him. It will be easier than having him imagine what went wrong. If you feel you won't be able to live with him because of personality problems or different opinions about life, tell him. Don't have long discussions into the night or those that go on for days and days, but be kind enough to let him present his side, which will be "why the two of us should be together." You know the two of you must part, but he'll want to give it a last try, just as you would. The one last try needs two things: a time limit such as "We'll give it two more weeks" or "We'll have two appointments with a counselor." The second thing it needs is your will to try. If you don't have that, give it up. Beginnings are easy. Middles are difficult. Endings are tragically sad, but look forward to a time when there will be no ending.

Chapter 12

Fire Attack . . .
Sex

There are five kinds of fire attack: burning people, burning supplies, burning equipment, burning storehouses, and burning weapons.

— Sun Tzu

Sex Creates Burning Desire

There are five kinds of heat in a relationship: thinking someone is hot, warming up to him, getting fired up, having sex, and getting burned. Since sex can be a firetrap, be aware of the five kinds of fire and master each:

• Thinking a man is hot: a man and a woman meet, lock gazes, and sometimes there's a spark that propels the two of you toward each other. In the courtship dance between men and women, this is where the sexual motor is started. During this phase women do innocent things like smiling when they are remembering him. This is also the time that an unrequited love can begin. Be careful if the spark is only in your eyes.

Because of traditions in our society, despite the sexual revolution, it is considered the man's job to do something about the spark. He's supposed to follow up on it by making contact, getting your phone number, and asking you out. It's not easy to wait for him to make his move. It's also difficult for him to risk rejection. It would be nice if the first spark carried you to the next step magically, with no words needed. That only happens in movies. However, feel comforted by the fact that sparks can't be avoided.

Those of you in your twenties will automatically create the spark. It's a mating call. However, the call is not necessarily being taken care of. Both of you are giving signals, but you're still going out in groups and having drinks after work. Moving this from friendship to relationship takes some skill. It will be your job to create a romantic situation. Lock eyes. Don't just stare at your half-empty glass. Talk about movies you love. When you find one in common, rent it, tell him you're going to watch it, and then invite him to join you. Isolate him.

Your objective is to get the two of you alone. Play one-on-one tennis. Send him an article you think is funny. He'll call you. Hopefully, he'll call you. If he E-mails, at least you'll have notes going back and forth, which is very romantic.

• Warming up to a man: this state is a romantic celebration, a pageant of romance. You are one degree of separation from the first sexual contact. (Not going to bed, but feeling his touch.) Instead of jumping into the fire, consider what you may want from him. Just sex? All right, jump, but remember fire can burn. The following day it's possible that you'll be planning to go to breakfast and he'll be using his speed dial to call other women.

All men have a personality, drives, goals, and ideas on how they want to spend the night with you. This is the time for you to decide whether you are looking for immediate gratification or a long-lasting love. It's sad to realize that other animals take more time to get to know each other than humans do.

Female swans start seeking a mate when they are adolescents. Since the female mates for life, she will give the male one year to meet her standards of compatibility. Swans are a lot more discriminating than we are.

You can't lose a man by not having sex. You might think that another woman will go to bed with him if you don't. That could happen, but then you know he was interested in a body and not the whole woman.

• Being fired up: perhaps he's pressuring you to have sex with him. He's in a high hormonal haze and you may be, too. At first the two of you are in a very early stage of sexual exploration—clothed but touching, a bit knowledgeable about each other's bodies. At this stage, he may become adoring of you; you may become adoring of him. Some fantasies are still active, and you passionately overevaluate him—that is, that he's "the one." Don't forget, getting "fired up" happens in the beginning stages of a relationship. You know a little of his history and what he does. You even welcome his shortcomings, so sure are you that he's right for you. In today's culture, there is a lot of talk about sex; it is always verbalized before it's done. (There are also other signals such as showing palms. Human beings unconsciously open their palms to each other as a signal that they are open to each other.) Don't forget you are still at the discussion stage. Realize what you want and be sure. No woman has said, "I met the greatest guy last night. What I want is to sleep with him, get close to him, and then get him to walk away from me as if nothing happened."

• Having sex: you'll learn more about the complete man—not only his sexual technique and preferences. You'll learn from sex how considerate he is. Some men are loving after lovemaking and want you close. Some men have too much energy to stay in bed after sex. Others feel melancholy. Some have other appetites stirred and need food. Some men are cool and detached. Some cuddle because they know the woman wants them to. Some fall asleep, which is almost always insulting to a woman. Some women can't sleep and want to relive the whole experience but with words this time around. Women usually want this moment to last for another twenty-four hours, unless her lover didn't give her pleasure and the sex was very disappointing.

A woman needs to understand how differently men and women think about sex. Women want to linger, but men prefer to continue life. Don't forget both men and women want to provide. It's easier for him to put his feelings aside and get on with his life. In today's world, both men and women have a desire to nurture, but you can live out this desire longer than he can. Men and women have differences whether you want to admit them or not. Fathers are able to leave their newborns and continue their life much more easily than mothers.

• Getting burned: the relationship has peaked and neither warmth, intimacy, nor passion can keep it together. A man begins to distance himself, neglecting you and eventually leaving you, many times without warning. It is normal to mourn and feel that a great tragedy has occurred. Women do this because the possibility of coupling and having a family with this man is gone. (Interestingly, it is not that different from the feelings that women suffer from severe PMS, when their bodies unkindly remind them that they will not be having children this month.) Depression may set in as you think about having to begin the search again.

This is why you don't want any of the five kinds of sexual behaviors to get out of your control and become an obsession. There are appropriate times to use your body seductively and times to protect your impulses. Protect yourself when he can't answer questions such as, "Are you sleeping with another woman?"

Passion can cloud reason, pushing you to be sexually aggressive with a man who is happy to take you to bed, but forgets your name an hour later. Don't blame him. It took the two of you to set the fire. Just remember, though both of you may ignite passion, he might only be interested in his orgasm. There is an excitement about sleeping with an attractive stranger, although it's slightly different for men than for women. A woman's sexual gratification gets better the longer the relationship lasts. She becomes more comfortable and less self-conscious.

Laurie was literally chased by a man. They were both on Rollerblades at the time. When they ran out of breath and were sitting on a bench, he told her to consider herself pursued. She melted, since most of the other men she'd dated considered themselves the prize.

Then the one perfect rose arrived. Then the special Italian dinner. Then a night of sex that turned into a weekend of rapture. Before you get entirely jealous, realize that this was too much too soon. Her body had never been ravaged like that before. He said he couldn't get enough of her, and on Sunday night, after having sex with her for the seventh time, he told her he loved her and gave her an antique-looking pin that he had in his underwear drawer. She didn't question why he had it.

She did question his love. "Do you tell everyone you love them?" Laurie asked. He said, "Not in the same way," whatever that meant. When he told her he talked about her to his psychiatrist, Laurie was hooked. That and the sex became a lethal combination.

He loved her and made love to her for four weeks. She loved him for the next four years. When he started to pull away after that intense first month, Laurie got scared.

At first she sent him those cute cards with couples running down the beach at sunset. Then she sent gifts. She tried to remember everything he wanted, everything he touched in a store. Then came her constant calls to him. Then she helped him get a job he wanted, which was as effective as the cards. Then she cried and tried to get his friends to convince him to marry her, then she hired a detective, then she spied herself. Laurie was finally convinced of her addiction. Would it have happened if they hadn't saturated the early days of their relationship with sex? Probably not.

She was finally convinced not to see or speak to him. Laurie treated him as if he were alcohol and she the alcoholic. She took it one day at a time, and it took a total of three years to get him out of her system.

On the other hand, her friend Katherine slept with a

man on her first date, lived with him for five years, got married, and lived happily ever after. In the scientific world, this is technically referred to as incredible luck.

There are suitable times and appropriate days in which to use fire, thus equipment for fire must always be at hand. "Times" are when the weather is scorching hot, "days" are when the winds are rising.

SEDUCE WHEN THE TIMING IS RIGHT

Fortunately for both men and women, the equipment for fire is always at hand. (It is conveniently located on your body.) A smart woman learns how to use a man's desire for her to establish rhythms that keep drawing him back to her. Sex uses certain ground rules. Don't use your body as a gift or punishment. There are suitable and appropriate times for being seductive. Use seduction when the atmosphere is free of interruptions, problems, and rivals, and you will have established rhythms and patterns with a man you feel won't disappear, until you want him to.

As with an army moving with a purpose, love perishes if it has no provisions. (Your equipment is perfect. How clever it was to design the human body so that it gave you pleasure when you're with the opposite sex.) Equipment may further be defined as the basic needs for love to grow in—comfort, intensity, and privacy. (Novelty underwear is optional.)

If you have feelings for someone, you'll want to make a man feel comfortable both physically and emotionally. Being physically comfortable means finding an alluring spot that both your bodies will enjoy. It may be an exciting notion to make love on the beach, but lovers never factor in that sand, water, small rocks, and private body parts are not always a good combination. Young boys who are just interested in sex don't care where they perform the act. You'll probably want to be in a situation that's more satisfying. Don't decorate for anyone who isn't going to be in your life, but when considering a physical relationship, do factor his comfort in. Men don't like lying down on a bed with fifty teddy bears.

When fire can be set out in the open, do not wait until it can be set inside a camp — set it when the time is right.

THE RIGHT TIME FOR SEX

The time is right when you trust this man, with your body and your heart. If you don't completely feel safe with him, move away from the fire. When you feel right and can be open with him about your passion, do not hesitate. Don't withhold sex for the game of it. This doesn't give you control. It makes you bitchy. If the intimacy is right between the two of you, do not use sex as a weapon or as a way to get what you want. Hookers get paid for sex. You do, too, if you use it as a manipulation.

When fire is set upwind, do not attack downwind.

IT FEELS GOOD TO BE FAITHFUL

When you light his fire, don't look for passion with another man. If you are interested in a long-term relationship, make sure the man in your bed knows you don't have any sexual partners other than him, or he will never take you seriously. Men and women want to feel that they are each other's only sexual partner. The man fights for your exclusivity out of pride. The woman requires it out of necessity. (At one time she had to know who the father of her child was so that he could provide for them. Even though times have changed and women can provide, there are still residual feelings in this area. The identity of the mother is always known.)

If you are interested in a long-term relationship, don't behave as if sexual encounters will amount to one-night stands. It can even be insulting to a man.

- Remember that men must be able to maintain the illusion of pursuit to be potent. Overly sexually aggressive women pretty often attract passive men who enjoy being pursued. While this may be fun for a while, you will lose interest or feel badly about always having to be the aggressive one. He, too, can lose interest if aggression is important. Men do like women who initiate sex, and you *should* when the mood is right. Remember, though, that variety is the spice of life, and alternating the role of initiator can only add to your sex life.
- Don't have sex to prove you're trendy, uninhibited, cool, or whatever social pressure is affecting you and directing you to give in. Surrendering to outside pressures indicates to a man that you undervalue your body and are weak. They'll figure out that you will end up in bed with anyone to prove you're cool.
- Remember that casual sex leads you to being treated casually.
- Forget about competing with other women, thereby trying to be the sexiest woman out there. On some deeper level, men are looking for permanent relationships with a woman. They want someone they can love as well as someone who will have their children.
- It shouldn't feel good to put yourself on exhibit for

271

him. Beware of the man who wants you only for show, not for intimacy. If he always says something like, "We're meeting my friends for dinner . . . why don't you put on that little spandex dress that shows off your boobs," think twice.

• "Setting the fire" is legally in a woman's control. She has the right to say *no* up to the second of penetration, even if she's naked and in his hotel room at two in the morning. Even if a woman is anticipating sex, a man can't force her if she's changed her mind and is unwilling. The law is on your side for a reason.

• Don't forget that you are both on fire. Be kind to him after sex. If you want this man in your life and want him to feel good, compliment him on his lovemaking, if the compliment is due.

❦

If it is windy during the day, the wind will stop at night.

MOODS CHANGE

If the relationship is stormy during the day, it can be calm that night. Never count on a mood staying put. That's the definition of a mood.

Either one or both of you could be creating a lot of chaos because you think it's more fiery and interesting. It creates a pattern of go away, come back. If you enjoy being on a roller coaster your whole life, this type of relationship will keep you there.

Also, people create fights because having sex after making up feels good to them. (You learn about closeness after fighting as a child if your parents yelled or hit you and then right away hugged you and reassured you of their love.) Sex after fighting feels good but isn't powerful. Many lovers feel sex won't be powerful if things are calm. Sex is powerful when both of you are very much in love and can't keep your hands off each other.

◄►

Armies must know there are adaptations of the five kinds of fire attack and adhere to them scientifically.

REMEMBER YOU HAVE POWER

For women, the strategies necessary for successful fire attack (warmth, sex, and love) rely more on attitude than anything else.

• *Be confident that you can win the battle of the sexes.* Since everyone on earth was meant to pair up, there's no reason why you shouldn't.

To be confident, know where your power lies. Go out into the world of dating at your personal best. This refers to mind and body. A champion would not go into the ring unless he was in prime condition. Nor should you.

When women are honest with one another, they will admit that a Saturday night date really starts on Friday and ends on Sunday. Friday is the day of preparation, getting your nails done, picking up the right shade of panty hose, etc. The day of the date consists of trying on ten different outfits until you find the perfect one. Sunday is spent telling your girlfriends about the night before and praying that he calls (or that he moves to China, depending on how the night went.)

• Be willing to risk your heart.

It is worth repeating: all relationships are failures until the one that isn't.

- Possess a nature that would make a good lover.

Once you are in a committed relationship and are starting to see him clearly, put your inhibitions aside and be willing to explore your sexuality. If your sexual relationship is lacking, make it better. Be more naked, more aggressive, don't always do it the same way at the same time in the same place. (What do you think the dining room table is really for? Be the centerpiece of a big feast.) Try positions you never thought you would. Heighten the passion before you get into bed by flirting, not teasing. Reveal your nakedness. Show him you love your own body. Don't have endless discussions about it. Just do it.

If the sex is great, make it greater. Get a catalog on pleasure toys. Don't buy them, you're a better toy than they are. Laugh with him about what's available.

- By the time you've coupled, you should know who the man is and what you can expect from him as a lover. But you want . . . more. You dream about what sex in all its variations will be. Maybe the guy needs guidance.

There is the story of Frannie and Don, for example, who were living together for two years and planned to get married. They loved each other, but Frannie, it seemed, had never had an orgasm in the two years she and Don had been having sex. One day, Don talked to a therapist about sexual abandonment, and he revealed an astonishing fact about his sex life with Frannie.

Frannie was a seductive and sensuous woman, and he couldn't understand why she'd hold back. "Every night, before I'd get into bed I'd always say, 'Maybe tonight you'll have an orgasm.' Sometimes we'd make love on and off for three hours, and still she wouldn't have one. She says she'll get there. What's wrong with her?"

What Don did not consciously acknowledge was how he was setting Frannie up for disappointment—by suggesting her past "failures," he was implying, in a rather threatening manner, that she'd disappoint both of them again. And he was willing to try to please her for hours on end, so how could it be his fault? Sex was Don's way of controlling Frannie, and she went along with it. Until both of them changed.

Once Don started talking differently to Frannie before touching her, their sex life changed. Nothing was expected, so there was nothing to lose. Once Frannie understood that she could abandon herself, she did, over and over again.

It should not be an embarrassment to tell a man what you want. He wants to make you happy and doesn't want you to fail to make him happy.

If you have something to teach a man about pleasing you sexually—whether it's in his approach or in his technique—educate him, don't criticize him. Guide him. Let him know you can have an orgasm; communicate the information either verbally or by guiding him physically. Gently place his hand where you want him to touch you. Know and let him know that there are a lot of women in the world who don't have an orgasm just from intercourse. He has fingers for a reason. Don't let oral sex be one-sided—indicate that he should do it to you, too. Put your hands on either side of his head and gently guide him. That's the way men do it. You're not in his bed solely for his pleasure. You're there for your own satisfaction, too. Men learn this as they mature.

275

Where there's seduction, there's passion—and it may not be dainty. Sex following a successful seduction is raw and can include odors, perspiration, and noise—and it's just such carnality you're looking for. What you want is the masculinity of it all and how it can make you feel good. Here's how you get there.

Sex begins the second he walks into the room, not when you decide to have sex and start to undress. And that's because much of sex is in the brain: men don't plan their actions while having sex—they begin in a vague hormonal haze. Women are also hazy but get out of it more quickly. Since you're the more aware of the two sexes, be seductive with lusty determination and allow him to seduce you. Tell him why he's desirable. Find something about his body you adore.

The seduction game gets the hormones pumping—his and yours. And biology is often reliable. The neural circuits that mediate sexual intercourse lie in the spinal cord. Stroke his back. Give him a massage. Place tiny purple grapes down his spine and eat them off, one by one. (If grapes are not in season, Cheerios will do, they're always in season.)

• There are traits that a man doesn't have that he wants near him; use them in your seduction. He wants to look, see, and hear your femininity. Have you ever sat on the edge of the sink just to enjoy watching him shave? You want his masculinity around you, don't you? He likes to see you arranging flowers and is fascinated by your ability to smell so good. This has nothing to do with being liberated. The liberated woman is proud to do things men can't.

Lastly, how do you become a great lover? By spoiling the man in bed.

A government should not mobilize an army out of anger, military leaders should not provoke war out of wrath. Act when it is beneficial, desist if it is not. Anger can revert to joy, wrath can revert to delight, but a nation destroyed cannot be restored to existence and the dead cannot be restored to life. Therefore, an enlightened government is careful about this, a good military leadership is alert to this. This is the way to secure a nation and keep the armed forces whole.

ANGER IS NOT SEXUAL

A woman should not act out of anger, nor should she provoke war out of wrath. Angry women are not attractive, and angry men are totally undesirable. There are some couples who enjoy sex more after a battle and actually need one to get started. Eventually, there will be scars.

Sun Tzu tells us to be prepared for battle but to avoid war. War is the result of uncontrolled anger, and for most men and women uncontrolled anger does not lead to sensuality or sexuality.

CHAPTER 13

ARMED STRUGGLE . . .
FACE-TO-FACE

The ordinary rule for use of military force is for the military command to receive the orders from the civilian authorities, then to gather and mass the troops, quartering them together. Nothing is harder than armed struggle.

—Sun Tzu

LOVE ISN'T ALWAYS EASY

The ordinary rule regarding love is for a woman to understand the traditions and rules of the society she lives in (those are the civilian authorities). Nothing is more frustrating for a woman than winning at love, because it can be such a struggle. (Very rarely does a relationship run completely smoothly with no hurt feelings and no anxiety.)

Just a few decades ago, young women observed and gathered information about coupling by following traditions. Even if those traditions were too strict, at least there were rules. Now there are few rules and many options, and women must therefore figure out on their own what is right for them.

Therefore you make their route a long one, luring them on in hopes of gain. When you set out after others and arrive before them, you know the strategy of making the distant near.

Women should make the route to an important relationship a long one, not only to learn about men in general, but also to learn why men are satisfied with certain women. When you study them as a group, you will be able to go on to graduate school, which is the study of one man in particular.

DON'T JUMP IN

Women should appeal to a man's instincts in hopes of gaining love. (His instinct is usually to go quickly toward you at first, and then to slow down and move away. A woman's pace is to move slowly at first and to get closer as time goes by. If you realize this, you won't be as upset when he moves back to catch his breath. This is a dance that can be controlled by a very enlightened woman.)

Lure a man with gentle and happy rewards. Make his time with you fun. Give what he doesn't have—the joy of you and the feminine side of you. Make sure he gives generously of his masculine side. It's wonderful to lie in the arms of a man. Let him rest on the shoulders of a woman.

Once you've been seeing and studying a man for a year, don't let him make the road longer. A man who remains distant and remote, no matter what you do for him, may be building a longer road while you are hoping to build a nest. Let him be the only one on the road he's building away from you. He'll get lonely.

Women have to open their eyes and assess the man and the boundaries he sets. You have to figure out how to shorten the distance between you and the man you like.

• The good news is that it is often possible to draw men closer. Most men have intense feelings for women. They need women, appreciate them, and want to make them happy. However, some men are resistant to love. Handling a man as you would a bird is not a new idea, but it is a good one. Think of him as a small bird in your hand. If you hold it too tightly and squeeze it, the bird will get crushed; if you stroke it and let it fly free, it always returns. Don't squeeze him. His mother did that. Let him leave if he wants to. By doing that, you are actually shortening the distance between you. Yes, easier said than done, but it's more important to be in a man's mind than in his bed.

• A man is emotionally and materially remote when he insists on keeping his possessions, including his mind and body, separate from yours. He is preventing commingling. A smart woman lures such a man into accepting her and her possessions. Don't leave your things all over his place. Astute men understand what you're doing. Buy him or lend him a book that you think he'll want to read, with the intention of getting it back. He'll have a couple of hundred pages of "you" with him.

Don't be rigid about your possessions. There shouldn't be places where he can't sit or linger. Allow him to feel at home. Try and see to it that he spends more time at your place than you do at his so that you have more control of the atmosphere. Keep your home warm and inviting.

• Make the road between you shorter by telling him truthfully where you spend your time. Don't demand at first that he do the same. If he doesn't get the signal fairly quickly, it means he doesn't want to meld his life with yours at this time. When he gets very close, he won't take a vacation without you or even consider going to a family dinner if you are not included. You can become a serious part of what makes life fun if you keep creating relaxing situations.

• Encourage him to share memories of your experiences together. Talk about the good times the two of you have had together, take pictures. What you are doing is reconfirming your life together.

• Remember to accept him as he is. Be content or leave him. Definitely leave if the love doesn't grow.

Therefore, armed struggle is considered profitable, and armed struggle is considered dangerous.

LOVE IS COMFORTING AND EXCITING

Therefore, love is considered profitable and love is considered dangerous.

What you gain from love is a feeling that you are in tune with the universe. It brings with it a wonderful feeling of safety and happiness. You have someone to laugh with and smile about.

When you are in a relationship, there is danger everywhere, the biggest one being that the love will end. It is part of the fun and the passion. Without danger there would be no excitement.

However, some men are so dangerous and irresponsible, the danger leads to nothing but pain. You can want so badly to be loved that you overlook the signs of danger. Here's what to try and avoid:

- Don't leave your home to move into his place until you are sure the relationship has a solid foundation and a future. Jacqueline's experience is a good example of why this is so important.

Her husband of one year left her, taking with him all their money and the new car that they were making payments on together. Gary never said good-bye. He just didn't come home one night. A month later, a private detective that Jackie hired located him, living on the Florida Gulf Coast, where he'd started his own business and was happily cohabiting with another woman.

What went wrong? Jacqueline said, "I met Gary after breaking up with a man I was engaged to for two years. Gary seemed electric, interesting, sexy, and devoted.

"I dated Gary for six weeks, and he never forced sex—we'd neck in his car, like kids. He seemed too good to be true. After two months, he said he loved me and that he wanted us to live together. My apartment reeked with rotten memories of my ex, so I agreed to move to his place. I thought I had found paradise. We pooled everything. I made more money than he did, but I didn't care because I had faith that Gary would do okay. He had such energy. Less than three months after my pots were in his kitchen, we got married.

"A year after that, the day of our anniversary, he didn't come home. He said he was at a meeting and would be home late. I never saw him again. The next day I went to the bank and found that he had taken all but a hundred dollars out of our joint account. There was forty-two hundred dollars in there. He also took the car that belonged to both of us."

Jacqueline was fooled and hurt by a dangerous and reckless man. Obviously, Gary knew what he wanted from the beginning.

Most men don't premeditate. They are as sure as you are that this is right. They just have a woman move in with them, and when they see problems and suspect you're not as perfect as the woman they want, they purposely get impossible to live with so that the relationship fails. Since you've been living in his home, you're the one who has to leave. If you want to create a living space with a man, do it at your house or find common territory.

- Believe him. This advice may sound strange, but men usually tell the truth about what they want. If he says he's not interested in marriage, he's not.
- The greatest danger a woman can find herself in is being with a man who keeps changing his mind, promising love and then denying and brutalizing it. This game can go on for as many times as he is allowed to toy with you. Only the woman who thinks nothing of herself welcomes this kind of torment into her life.

Behavioral scientists conducted a lab experiment in which they studied a "now I love you–now I don't" syndrome. They wanted to see the results of what happens when love is given and then taken away. Fortunately, they used mice instead of humans. Male and female mice felt a small, instinctive pain when a mouse of the opposite sex who they had gotten used to was taken from them. They then were calmed when their mates were restored. The mates were taken away

283

again, then brought back. The scientists kept repeating the process, frustrating the mice to a point that could be compared to a human's nervous breakdown.

If a man leaves once and returns, that's reasonable and normal. But beware the habitual wanderer and heartbreaker. He'll come and go. That behavior will drive you insane.

* Don't fool around with your heart. Take good care of it. If you start to feel danger, the best thing to do is to go to someplace safe. If you get hurt, the easiest way to heal is to have no connection with the man. Don't see him and don't speak to him. That's the only way to break an addiction to another person. Give yourself a two-week mourning period and that's all. It's hard to separate because such an experience leaves you insecure and, as said before, your mind and body were involved in the possibility that his love would last. You didn't lose a possibility, you lost someone who is incapable of loving you.

❧❧

To mobilize the whole army to struggle for advantage would take too long, yet to struggle for advantage with a stripped-down army results in a lack of equipment. So if you travel light, not stopping day or night, doubling your usual pace, struggling for advantage a hundred miles away, your military leaders will be captured. Strong soldiers will get there first, the weary later on — as a rule, one in ten make it.

DON'T CHANGE

* Don't weaken your goals and keep in top emotional and physical shape. Don't double your pace to match his if he wants too much too soon, or wear yourself out

by looking for a new man. If someone leaves, don't feel you have to be out every night of the week. Future lovers meet accidentally, even in line at supermarkets.

Lines, in general, are good places to meet. People have met in movie lines, bakery lines, and in line at the video store. There is a great advantage in meeting someone in these situations. Take the video store for example. You get to see his taste in movies. A man may be renting a video just for relaxation, and there's likely to be an adventure film in his hands. (Men don't rent *An Affair to Remember* over and over again.)

• If it feels as if you are struggling to get a man who is consistently a hundred miles away, it will feel as if your heart were captured by the wrong person. Strong women will be the first in line to try again, simply because it takes strength to try. Some women get weary from having too many bad relationships. Understand that you are eliminating men. It's not an easy process, but those who understand this concept persevere.

Strong women—those who are willing to take risks—understand their chances. Those who are scared of rejection sometimes wait too long. Sun Tzu says one in ten make it. Can this figure apply to love? It would not be unusual for a woman to have ten "serious" relationships before finding the man she wants in her life. It is said that a woman kisses many frogs before she finds her prince.

❧

Struggling for an advantage fifty miles away will thwart the forward leadership, and as a rule only 50 percent of the soldiers make it.

CLOSENESS

When lovers live in different cities, personal impact becomes a matter of ongoing logistics, schedule changes, and added costs. This puts a strain on love. (When you live in the same city but in different "worlds," life is even harder.)

Physical distance between you and the man you love may sound romantic—flying to be in each other's arms as often as possible—but it's not. The separation becomes a third entity in the relationship, and solving the problems of distance become what the relationship is about. You hear yourself arguing about who is doing more of the traveling and making more of the effort to keep the love and the bond alive. Sometimes, for the person who has moved to a new city, the unfamiliarity of the place and the added responsibility of the work makes them overly anxious. There is the problem of fitting in and doing well on a job. Then the mate who's left behind also needs reassurance that the move is not about abandonment or the first step toward a real separation.

In the case of Terri and Jim, the move brought up insecurities and fears.

"What if Jim took the job because he's really thinking this is the way to get away from me—and with a great excuse?" Terri asked. Jim denied her concerns but brought up his own. "There are times Terri forgets that I moved to a city I don't even like only because it was a great opportunity. It's Terri who won't move to Tampa. She's got her job in Washington and won't give it up. She turns the facts around, accuses me of leaving and worries that I'll meet another woman and dump her. I feel she's leaving me by staying." What he doesn't mention is that Terri had a very important government position in Washington, and nobody was willing to move the White House.

If you are separated from your man, there are truths and hormones to consider, in the form of loneliness and sex. Men, like women, don't really enjoy the process of dating. They're creatures of habit, and at a certain time in their lives, they want to settle in, not conquer. If you're there for him in person, you have a better chance to guarantee your place in his heart. Or if you're the one who moves, you'll want him there. Women may be able to deal with separation with inner fortitude for a while, but then they reach a limit. If waiting, traveling, and more days away from the man you love than with him become too impossible, you will soon be living in a phantom relationship.

(Remember that men and women come to love slightly differently. Men decide that the timing is right for them and then find someone to be with. Women, on the other hand, are more likely to be ready for love and respond to the man they're interested in without thinking about whether or not the time is right.) Your grandmother would have said, "You have to live where your husband wants you to." She was right, in her time and age. Now women are financially independent. They don't have to live where he wants to. The decision is for both of you to make.

In today's world, you must decide for yourself what's more important: a new life with a man you love, or staying where you are. If you like your job, your friends, and the home you've created more than him, the choice is easy.

• If you can't be with him physically at any given moment, a terrific photograph of the two of you is a necessity. Let your presence be known. It's a fact that reporters who travel a lot, salesmen on the road, filmmakers who are away from home in odd parts of the world, and other people whose career pulls them from the foundation of home, need something to connect them to home. Soldiers march off to war and don't get to see their loved ones for years at a time. If your lover can't be with you, write letters, send pictures, and stay attached. During wartime, many men have said that it was the love of a woman back home that kept them alive. (It was her picture that made him feel lucky.)

• Make your best efforts to be with him and don't create an atmosphere of guilt. Saying things like "This separation is killing me" just makes it harder for him. And since he doesn't want to kill you, he might want you to find happiness with someone else. When you argue on the phone because you feel he doesn't call enough, it makes him not want to call because he expects you will be angry.

❦

So an army perishes if it has no equipment, it perishes if it has no food, and it perishes if it has no money.

LOVE AND THE BASICS

Without resources to take care of the essentials, no campaign in any battle, no matter how truthful, spiritual, humanitarian, or altruistic it is can work. Having the means to buy the basics you need to survive is essential. As you get older, you realize there is some nourishment and comfort in being able to afford the things you need. When people meet, they don't want to think about money. It doesn't seem to fit with romance. You need to be practical. In real life money sustains you.

In the order of importance of the basics for survival, nourishment matters more than sex. A hungry animal wants to eat and will attack if another animal threatens to take his food. No enticement of sexual pleasure, play, or the offer of a better spot of grass to lay in after dining will stop him from satiating himself. In terms of the male-female relationship, if you are scrambling for food, the rent money, putting off the IRS, and making deals to pay off your charge account debts, all of this will cause anxiety so high that it will take an unusual amount of understanding to keep the relationship together. When people are hungry, they don't have patience.

Parents want you to prefer men who choose stable occupations. Until the last part of this century, before a man was allowed to marry, he needed to prove to a girl's parents that he was capable of taking care of himself *and* taking care of her. This kind of thinking is not viable today because most families have two incomes. However, keep in mind that when you have a child you have a built-in instinct to want to be near it. You can be the breadwinner, but babies are great seducers.

A certain display of money has always been one of the first attributes that men present to women. Most women don't mind knowing a man's ideas about making money, having money, spending money, and saving money. But they don't like men flaunting it or trying to buy women with it. "The Porsche is paid for" is one of the big lies men tell women.

Is a woman's having money a threat to a man? Only if he is insecure about his earning power or he has no faith in himself. (These feelings have been in place since before you came on the scene.) Betty Friedan, author of *The Feminine Mystique* and the first feminist voice heard from in the 1960s, told an interesting story about marriage and money. She said that when she was first married, she earned more than her husband, and it was uncomfortable for both of them. She suddenly found that she was "losing" her wallet or her handbag on the day she got paid. Going home with nothing, said her unconscious mind, was better than coming home with too much and threatening her husband.

Know this:

• By showing you can provide as well as, or more than, the man in your life, you are not emasculating him. (If he feels emasculated, he is creating the feelings himself.)

• Money is a concern for everyone. Even two people, backed by high-paying jobs or enormous trust funds, can have trouble agreeing on how to spend, how to save, and how to give to charity.

• If you fear there will be a power struggle over money, don't take this man into your life until every detail is resolved. If he has a high earning power and you don't, make sure that the person who makes the most is not the person who makes all the decisions.

• Understand what money means to you and what it means to him. Do not jeopardize your future by underestimating its cost to your relationship.

• While they are totally unromantic, prenuptial agreements for people who own property and have bank accounts are protection for both of you.

❧

So if you do not know the plans of your competition you cannot make informed alliances.

KNOW YOUR MAN

If you do not know the plans of the man you're interested in, and what mobilizes him to action, you cannot make a smart decision about whether or not to bond with him and work out the problems of the union.

The plan you want to know, as fast as possible, is if he wants to have a future with one woman.

❧

So a military force is established by deception, mobilized by gain, and adapted by division and combination.

DECEPTION?

Deception is a dirty word, and yet all men and women deceive without even thinking about it. There's physical deception. Take hair for example. Both sexes arrange it, add extensions, color it, straighten it, replant it, and give it curls. Plastic surgery is so common that when a couple has a child, the origin of the baby's nose is a mystery to both of them.

Some men naturally deceive. They'll say "I love you" if they think it will get you into bed. They make themselves look more important by borrowing or renting cars that make it appear that they are in a higher income bracket, because they think it will impress you. They will present themselves as the men they want to be rather than the men they are.

❧

Therefore, when it moves swiftly it is like the wind, when it goes slowly it is like a forest; it is as rapacious as fire, immovable as mountains.

291

LOVE HAS A LIFE OF ITS OWN

When loves moves swiftly, it is like the wind. There is no way that we can stop the wind from carrying us along. When love moves slowly, it is as immovable as mountains. There is nothing you can do to send it away.

It is as difficult to know as the dark; it moves like peeling thunder.

BEGINNINGS ARE IN THE DARK

Lovers are always in the dark at first. The light comes with understanding. Love's movement is uncontrollable, yet it envelopes you and resonates in you like the sound of peeling thunder.

"Peeling thunder" is a romantic but mysterious image. Thunder cannot exist without the radiant heat and electricity that lightening shoots through the sky—thunder is not random; it depends on lightening to exist. It is the mix of mystery, electricity, and unpredictability that makes new love exciting.

To plunder a locality, divide up your troops. To expand your territory, divide the spoils.

LEARNING TO SHARE

When two people meet and want to be with each other, they both expand their territories, and it becomes a win-win situation. Be generous in every way and share the benefits. You do this by giving him the advantages of your life.

Cymbals, drums, banners, and flags are used to focus and unify people's ears and eyes. Once people are unified, the brave cannot proceed alone, the timid cannot retreat alone — this is the rule for employing a group.

SHOWING YOUR ALLEGIANCE

There are markers and symbols that tell others you are part of a couple. When armies march, they show their colors, their allegiances by the banners and flags they carry. The drummer's rhythms lead the men to walk in unison. When you couple, display your allegiance to each other. Couples do not carry flags, but they exchange things or share property and perform ceremonies that unite them. The purpose is to keep rivals and other suitors away as you bond.

When you are ready to unite, the man usually gives the woman something of worth, like a diamond ring. (Giving him an engagement gift should also become a tradition.) This is your banner. When you show unification with your lover, the community of people around you must acknowledge the two of you as a couple. You get invitations together. You will get and send Christmas cards together. All of these signs indicate the real event of coupling. As things progress, you may sign a lease on an apartment or home together. Bank accounts will start to intermingle. If you are both lucky enough to find true and lasting love, you will be displaying your unification to each other forever.

Once people are unified, the brave cannot proceed alone.

TAKE HIM ALONG

Once a couple is unified, the strongest of the two would not want to go on without the other.

CONCLUSION

How wondrous it would be for love, if it is real and meant to be, to stay on course, sweet and pure, requiring little in the way of effort. But no one who has tested the tricky waters of romance holds such innocent beliefs for long. Yet few quests in our lives come close to the power of our wish to find and bond with a special partner regardless of the pitfalls along the way. But how do we recognize and let go of unrealistic expectations? How do we not set ourselves up for heartache and disappointment? How do we profit from our mistakes? Avoid repeating the lessons we learned from watching our parents act out their version of love and relating? How do we move beyond the elixir of drama and excitement and come to trust calmer waters and a steadier pulse? How do we keep hope alive and our belief in ourselves intact when doubts inevitably creep into our thoughts and dampen our confidence?

Be strong within yourself. Be a victor instead of a victim. Never rely on excuses used to avoid actions you know are the right ones to take. Push through passivity, disbelief, and the seductive comfort of the familiar. Becoming more skilled in love is always accomplished by making a stretch. And stretching is usually uncomfortable. Commit to the "stretch" and you'll reconnect with valuable aspects of yourself that may have been lost or ignored.

For love to endure, one must be smart, clear, and balanced. You must be smart enough to use both your head *and* your heart, clear enough to see the landscape of your love without the filters made of wishful fantasy, and balanced enough to nurture and protect yourself as well as your partner. Being smart requires the courage to act strategically even though, at times, these actions may feel counterintuitive or scary. Being clear requires an unwavering personal honesty and a willingness to see men for how they are, not how you want them to be. And balance requires dolling out equal measures of acceptance and protection and knowing when each is appropriate.

Trust your value. Say less, do more. Love is more than an emotional experience; think smart and use your intelligence. Second-guess comfort and ease for they are, more often than not, the friends of habit rather than growth. Take always the way of the woman warrior.

Printed in the United States
By Bookmasters